Paul Gambaccini

Close Encounters

To Tim and Jo Rice, my fellow passengers
on a great ride

Paul Gambaccini

Close Encounters

OMNIBUS PRESS
LONDON · NEW YORK · PARIS · SYDNEY

Cover designed by Pearce Marchbank

ISBN: 0.7119.68403
Order No: OP48040

Exclusive Distributors:
Book Sales Limited,
8/9 Frith Street,
London W1V 5TZ, UK.

Music Sales Corporation,
257 Park Avenue South,
New York, NY 10010, USA.

The Five Mile Press,
22 Summit Road,
Noble Park,
Victoria 3174, Australia.

To the Music Trade only:
Music Sales Limited,
8/9 Frith Street,
London W1V 5TZ, UK.

All uncredited photos from Paul Gambaccini's personal collection.

Every effort has been made to trace the copyright holders of the
photographs in this book but one or two were unreachable. We
would be grateful if the photographers concerned would contact us.

Printed and bound in Great Britain by MPG Books Ltd, Bodmin, Cornwall
Typeset by Galleon Typesetting, Ipswich.

A catalogue record for this book is available from the British Library.

Visit Omnibus Press on the web at www.omnibuspress.com

Contents

1

Sam And Otis And . . .

I recall distinct firsts in my appreciation of popular music. The first song of any kind I can remember is Burl Ives' 'Little White Duck', one of his folk songs for children. Listening to it as an adult, I marvel at the audacity with which he rhymed "water" with "oughta", but I can see how he charmed me, as he delighted millions of British children via repeated plays on *Junior Choice* of his story of 'The Blue Tail Fly'.

The first number one single that made an impression on me was the 1953 smash 'You You You' by The Ames Brothers. I was four years old when this topped the American chart. Its impact may be due to its simplicity. "You, you, you," Ed, Gene, Joe and Vic crooned, "no one else will do, do, do." The lyric was almost like one of those "See Spot run" primers we were to read in kindergarten, in which words were taught through repeated usage. If a pre-school child came out of this Ames Brothers number one without a knowledge of words like "you" and "do", he was probably going to have a tough time in English.

It was not until 1997 that I learned from Joel Whitburn's indispensable *Pop Memories* book that the Ames Brothers had provided the lead vocals on Russ Morgan's 1948 hit 'I'm Look-ing Over A Four-Leaf Clover'. The relevance of this to my life is that it was Russ Morgan who led the list the day I was born in 1949 with 'Cruising Down The River'. This is hardly as earth-shattering as being able to claim that you were born when 'Rock Around The Clock' or 'She Loves You' was number one, and if I could have chosen a list leader from 1949 to be born under it would have been 'Some Enchanted Evening'.

No matter, Morgan provides trivia galore: the B-side of 'Cruising Down The River', 'Sunflower', was legally determined to be the basis of the 1964 number one 'Hello Dolly', and became the state song of Kansas. Russ Morgan had 57 hits in the pre-rock era, including four number ones, and the fact that none of them is played today is a terrible reminder of how almost all our work, no matter how temporarily popular, is destined for the dustbin.

Of course, it lives on in the memory of those it affected as long as they survive. The Ames Brothers are doing pretty well in my mind not just for 'You You You' but for their 1957 million seller 'Melodie d'Amour' and Ed's Sixties solo hits 'My Cup Runneth Over' and the wonderfully weird 'Who Will Answer?'

The first record I heard played on the radio as an oldie was 'The Wayward Wind' by Gogi Grant. I was sitting in the car at Westfair Shopping Center in Westport, Connecticut, waiting for my mother to finish the grocery shopping. Nowadays the airing I caught would be called a recurrent, because the 1956 number one was only a year old at the time. But 1957 was the first year I listened to radio in circumstances under my own control. I had caught the rock'n'roll bug from hearing Elvis Presley sing 'Teddy Bear', and spent several hours a day listening to the music of the great youthquake. In college I developed a reputation for being able to do several seemingly unrelated tasks simultaneously, such as reading, typing, listening to music and conducting a conversation. The origins of this curious behaviour probably lay in doing my elementary school homework while listening to my early DJ heroes.

'At The Hop' by Danny and The Juniors was the first single I was aware was my favourite. It was the first American number one of 1958, and held the top spot for seven weeks. It thrilled me. I understand now that it was as perfect a lifestyle record, summarising a generational attitude, as 'San Francisco (Be Sure to Wear Flowers In Your Hair)', 'Anarchy in the UK' or

'Smells Like Teen Spirit' would be in subsequent decades. At the time I was transfixed by its use of the piano as a rock'n'roll instrument. No matter how many times I have heard this record, and that number must by now exceed one thousand, I have always wondered if the pianist is going to be able to keep up with the group.

I was saddened in 1983 when lead singer Danny Rapp committed suicide. I of course realised that it is probably not best to peak in your work at the age of sixteen, as Danny was when he and the Juniors cut 'At The Hop', but it seemed horribly depressing that he would take the turns in life quite so badly. It was peculiarly unfair that for years after his death I continued to enjoy 'At The Hop' while he was unable to.

Danny's demise was one of two suicides that made me vow never to take an inevitable fall from favour too seriously. When I was a boy, a disc jockey in New York City with a daily show started a short evening programme as a kick under an amusing pseudonym. The new show was a great success, fatally so. The evening romp, during which he assumed an artificially manic personality, became far more popular than his well-mannered daytime slot. Station executives, noting the ratings difference, dropped the show he broadcast under his own name. Thanks to his ability to get into character, this too-talented broadcaster had lost his bread and butter, and the only chance to have his real identity announced to the public. Depressed by this mad turn of events, he took his life.

Alright, I thought when I set out as a broadcaster, that's one thing we're not going to do. If things ever go suddenly sour, let's get a season ticket to the New York Mets and watch a lot of baseball until we feel better.

As much as I loved 'Little White Duck', 'You You You', 'The Wayward Wind' and 'At The Hop,' neither Burl Ives, The Ames Brothers, Gogi Grant nor Danny and The Juniors were my first favourite singer(s). That distinction fell to Sam Cooke, who was number one in the States one month before 'At The

Hop' with his first pop hit, 'You Send Me'. I adored this love ballad, with its heart-rendering simplicity and seemingly effort-less vocal.

What I did not know at the time was that Cooke was a former gospel star who was applying to secular lyrics tech-niques he had learned in church. I also did not know that the word used to describe the thing I craved most about Cooke, "an expressive vocal phrase or passage consisting of several notes sung to one syllable" [Collins English Dictionary], was called "melisma". We would accuse almost any other singer of dragging a word out if he increased the syllable count. With Sam it was like beginning a vacation that could last, as far as we cared, indefinitely.

One of the weeks that 'You Send Me' was number one, television listings warned us that Sam was due to appear on *The Ed Sullivan Show*. Naturally: Ol' Stone Face featured who-ever was hot in any of the arts. Excited little eight-year-old me sat through the entire hour-long show in anticipation of seeing my new hero. Just when it seemed no other act could possibly be accommodated, Sullivan introduced the man with the number one record in America, Sam Cooke.

No other act could be accommodated. Cooke got through less than one minute of 'You Send Me' before his image was replaced on screen by the CBS eye logo. I was disappointed, furious, heart-broken. Somehow the timings on the live Sullivan broadcast had been miscalculated, or some act had overrun.

Years later, when I had my own radio and television pro-grammes, I vowed not to go long, even by one second, if I could avoid it.

The following week, 'You Send Me' was still number one. Sam Cooke was again listed to appear on *The Ed Sullivan Show*. This time he was placed in the middle of the programme, and he got to deliver all of his hit.

So began a delicious seven-year string of successes, includ-ing classic pop songs like 'Wonderful World', 'Cupid' and

'Chain Gang', beauties like 'Only Sixteen', 'Sad Mood' and 'Bring It On Home to Me', and what I thought was something deeply significant at the time, three consecutive number elevens on the *Billboard* Hot 100, 'Little Red Rooster', 'Good News' and 'Good Times'.

All of them sounded so perfect it was difficult to believe they required work to write and perform. The fact that Cooke did both author and sing almost all his hits impressed me enormously. Chuck Berry and Buddy Holly had written their own songs, but most rock'n'roll acts didn't. Not until The Beatles conquered America in 1964 did it become a matter of pride, not to say higher royalties, for most artists to generate their own material.

In 1979 I appeared on an edition of Radio 1's *Roundtable* programme with Kid Jensen and Herb Alpert. The multi-million selling trumpeter and band leader had co-written 'Wonderful World' with Cooke and Lou Adler under a pseudonym.

"Sam had an ability with his lyrics I've never seen in anyone else," Alpert remembered. "He would come in with the words, and you would think they were terrible. 'The cokes are in the ice box/Popcorn's on the table'," he said, quoting 'Having A Party'. "You'd look at them and you'd think, this is awful. And then he would sing them, and they made perfect sense."

It did not make sense when, on the eleventh of December, 1964, Sam Cooke was shot dead by a female motel manager in Los Angeles. If the reader is inclined, he or she can find different accounts of the events of that evening. All I know is that my favourite voice was stilled.

But not yet! In less than a month his new single, already scheduled for release when he was killed, was on the radio. It was his greatest. 'Shake', the A side, was good enough, a powerful dance number soon covered by Otis Redding. The flip, 'A Change Is Gonna Come', is the one that made the hairs on my arms and neck stand up. This was as emotionally powerful and verbally literate as any call for civil rights I had ever heard. It ranks with Bob Dylan's 'Blowin' In The Wind', which is said to have inspired it.

It is a popular recreation to speculate if dead pop stars would be producing good work if they were still alive. In the case of Sam Cooke, there is no doubt in my mind that he would have continued to knock me out for years afterward. He had the combination of talent, business brain and good looks that are rarely found in any area of entertainment.

After the death of Sam Cooke it took me less than a year to adopt a new "favourite singer". Actually, he found me. 'I've Been Loving You Too Long' by Otis Redding jumped at me out of the radio when it was a hit during the summer of 1965. This was a new kind of soul. It wasn't meant to dance to, it wasn't meant to think to. This was made to feel to. The voice was raw as cold red meat, the emotion as sharp as nails. "You were TIIIIIIIIIIIIIIIIred," Redding howled early in the record, sounding like an emotional air raid siren. By the end, the bombs were dropping. "Good God almighty, I love you! I love you!" he verbally ejaculated before the fade. For a sixteen-year-old sexually confused Catholic kid with hormones raging through the bloodstream like floodwater, Otis Redding soul ballads like 'I've Been Loving You Too Long', 'That's How Strong My Love Is' and 'These Arms Of Mine' provided a much-needed emotional catharsis.

'These Arms Of Mine' even provided the punch line of the most bizarre dream of my life. One night while a student at Dartmouth in the late Sixties I dreamt I encountered rhythm and blues legend Wilson Pickett walking alongside the college green. I had loved many of his records, from the obvious thumping classic 'In The Midnight Hour' to the lesser-known soul stirrers 'If You Need Me' and 'I'm In Love'. But I had seen Pickett twice in performance, at the University of Massachusetts and at Murray the K's final package show in New York, and on both occasions the wicked one had teased the

ladies in the audience to invade the stage. When they did, he
fled. End of show. No 'If You Need Me'. Not even 'It's Too
Late'. This really annoyed me. I wanted a concert, not a riot.

In my dream, I asked the singer I will spell Pickitt what he
was doing at Dartmouth. He told me he had some free time in
his schedule and was just looking around. I asked if I could
promote him in concert and he agreed. I was thrilled. When I
asked when he wished to perform, he said "in fifteen minutes".
I was miserable. I couldn't possibly find enough people to fill
Webster Hall in only a quarter of an hour.

Resigned to commercial failure, I wandered in to Webster
and saw, to my utter delight, a full house of paying customers.
Then I looked in the orchestra pit, and my heart sank. There
were a group of students from the Afro-American Society with
jug band instruments. This was going to be the oddest version
of 'Funky Broadway' any of us ever heard.

Then the curtain opened, and my heart soared again. There
was a large orchestra of black musicians with a full rhythm
section. Maybe this was going to be a great gig after all! The
introductory 'Everybody Needs Somebody To Love' sizzled,
and I settled back content that I had successfully staged a show
by one of my favourite stars. Then my dream Pickitt turned
into the man of my nightmares.

"I'm gonna do a song by Otis Redding now," he introduced
the next number, "and I'm gonna sing it like he really wrote it."

"These arms of mine," he began emotionally, like Redding
on the record. "They are lonely, lonely, and fucking blue." My
ears shot up. My heart sank. Once again, the up-and-down
cycle of my emotions was complete. There was no obscenity
on the original single. Just as the real Pickitt had let things
get out of control in concert, the dream Pickitt was making
trouble in my sleep.

"Yes, that's how he wrote it," the singer spoke, interrupting
his vocal. "You can hardly hear it in the mix, but it's there.
Fucking, fucking, FUCKING!"

13

The audience was restive. The show was ruined. I'd have to make hundreds of refunds!

I woke up short of breath. Never was I more pleased not to be at a Wilson Pickett concert. Herein lies the reason that, with the exception of a few obligatory puffs of marijuana, I never did drugs. I dreamt in plots, and figured I was weird enough.

I still enjoyed Pickett's original hits, at least in my waking hours, and I always loved Otis Redding. Many of his records no longer sound current, because recording techniques have changed so drastically. Tracks are recorded separately and layered on top of one another. Otis would just record the whole performance straight through. The result sounds simpler and more primitive than a Madonna record, because it is, but no synthesizer has yet found a replacement for the feeling expressed by an emotive Redding vocal or the excitement communicated when the band, as about one minute into 'Try A Little Tenderness', realises the session is actually cooking and then builds the rest of the way as if one man. When Otis died in a plane crash on 10 December, 1967, I was genuinely sad. So were my roommates, Larry DeVan and Mike Thorman. Our dorm room, 406 Gile Hall, went into mourning the evening we heard the news.

At this point I thought I dare not anoint another personal favourite singer. I had already dispatched Sam Cooke and Otis Redding. But I could not help but complete my trinity. There was one surviving singer whose work meant more to me than any other.

2

Marvin

At two o'clock on 28 September, 1976, I visited my favourite singer Marvin Gaye at the Carlton Tower in Sloane Square. With producer Stuart Grundy minding the machine, I recorded what to my knowledge is the most comprehensive interview Marvin ever gave in Great Britain. Of all the top Tamla artists, Gaye was the least well-interviewed, probably because he made himself available so infrequently, at least during the Seventies. The only decent piece I can recall seeing in print media appeared in *Rolling Stone.*

I am not aware of any other Marvin Gaye interview that went through his repertoire hit by hit, as this one did. We began with his first single and went through his then-current album, *I Want You.* Stuart Grundy was aware of the importance of the talk and made it the basis of two hour-long Radio 1 programmes, rather than the scheduled single show. Miraculously, the BBC, which tossed out or erased so many valuable tapes, retained this one. Excerpts appeared as recently as 1997 on Radio 2. But there has never been a printed transcript of the interview until now. I want to include it in this book, with full acknowledgement to the BBC, because I now realise I will probably never love a popular recording artist's work as passionately and as thoroughly as I have that of Marvin Gaye.

It will become clear rather quickly that the star was in a frisky mood. He may well have been, to use his own expression, flying high in the friendly sky. Resplendent in a full-length robe, he gave the impression of being both out of it and razor sharp at the same time. He frequently came quite close to saying something cutting about a colleague, and then retreated or qualified it as if not to have done so. The effect, of course, had already been made. I believe that as you read this interview you will hear a human voice, a voice that is at least one of the voices, if not the truest voice, of Marvin Gaye.

I believe you started with a group called The Rainbows.

I'm sure Don Covay enjoys that, but I don't think they accepted me as a member of the group. I tried out for the group. Don likes to say I was one of them, but he turned me down! I auditioned for The Rainbows would be a far more accurate statement.

Therefore, The Moonglows would have been your first hit at the big time.

I would say so. We were singing with The Marquees and not doing very well. Harvey [Fuqua] thought our sound was similar and that's why he chose us to fill in for the members of the group who had departed.

Was it Harvey or Anna [Berry Gordy's sister, Marvin's wife] who brought you to Berry?

I imagine it was Harvey and Gwen [Berry's sister, Harvey's wife] and Anna and Providence. I wouldn't go for an audition. I stopped auditioning when I was a very young artist. How dare me not to audition as a young artist! Berry had to hear me at a night club. I think he thought that was rather rash of me, so he might have said, "maybe I ought to go hear the guy who won't audition for us".

Was 'Sandman' the first single?

Probably was. [Thinks.] I think a thing called 'Let Your Conscience Be Your Guide' was the first single. Horrible song and record. Berry wrote it, by the way. He'll probably say I wrote some horrible ones in his next interview, so it's OK.

Your first mentor with the successful records was William Stevenson. What was it like working with him?

'Mentor'. Is that anything like 'tormentor'?

That's up to you to answer.

I don't know that word. Mickey's interesting. Mickey's alright, he's OK. "I'm OK, you're OK." I read that book.

The first two records he did with you, 'Stubborn Kind Of Fellow' and 'Hitch Hike', were very exciting vocals and arrangements. They featured vocal interplay between you and a backing chorus. Was that a style you brought to your sessions or was it presented to you?

I must say with all the humility anyone can have making one of these ego-filled statements, that was all my genius at the time. You don't get a lot of chance to express it, your name doesn't go down, [but] I helped the producers. I was young and raw, but I had a lot of ideas. They used them freely and I didn't mind.

We sometimes hear of people in the Motown family of artists doing back-up work on other people's records. Were any of the backing singers Martha Reeves ['Stubborn Kind of Fellow']?

I think that I can say, with great warmth and feeling, that I am the only Motown artist in the entire stable who has had every act background singing on some occasion, or at least one member of a group singularly. The only act that might be an exception is The Elgins. Every major act has appeared in a background capacity.

In those days we all worked with each other with love. I worked just as hard on the drums and the piano with every other act. I like that distinction, I was thinking about that the other day. The Supremes ['Can I Get A Witness'], The Tempts ['Try It Baby'], Gladys Knight, The Miracles, some part of every group has participated on some record of mine, especially in the early days.

'Pride And Joy' was your first top ten hit. Did it change your life professionally?

'Pride And Joy' didn't change anything. It was still a struggling period. I don't view those days with a lot of happiness because there was a lot of pain. You're young, trying to figure things out. Nobody tells you a lot. Nobody tells you a lot nowadays, it's part of the business.

Did Smokey Robinson bring you out much? He did work with you on two of your big ones, 'Ain't That Peculiar' and 'I'll Be Doggone'.

Smokey saved me during a time when I was non-productive and not even thinking about producing, although I was writing. I didn't have a lot of confidence in my pen at that time, because the giants were around, Holland-Dozier and Whitfield. Smokey was a legend, even in those days, so it was difficult for me to have a lot of confidence in my own pen. Smokey saved me during a period when I needed some records. He saved me.

Does he know you feel this way about him?

Probably not. He doesn't solicit my feelings. We're good friends, and we respect each other a great deal. He knows, he senses.

It was in 1964 you had the double-sided duet hit with Mary Wells. This was the first of the duets you would have through the years. Whose idea was it to team you up like that?

I wasn't very happy with a lot of the decisions that were made about my career during the early years. I should have been, as it has proven out, and I am appreciative now, but I was very rebellious then. Nothing personal at my singing partners. I think they were great decisions now. It was Berry Gordy's idea.

At that time Mary Wells was the only female artist and you were the only male artist who had Greatest Hits *collections on Motown. Perhaps it was strictly a commercial decision.*

I'm sure it was, as most decisions rendered by record companies are, except those that aren't commercially minded. I don't know any of those.

Are you not satisfied with the actual songs like 'What's The Matter With You Baby'?

I was not satisfied with my performances on them. I couldn't sing in those early years. I'm 50% improved as a singer now. I was pure, because I was younger, and you could sense something happening in Marvin Gaye's voice because every now and then a little purity would come through and you'd say, "That wasn't bad, the kid has a chance".

Nothing personal with regard to Mary Wells. She's a great girl and she should be popular even now, maybe singing now, but . . . poor management.

You also had solo hits, 'Can I Get A Witness' and 'Baby Don't You Do It', with Holland-Dozier-Holland themselves. Did you feel you were being shifted from one producer to another?

I not only felt I was being shifted, I felt I was being puppeteered. I got into quite a few arguments. Brian Holland and I got into quite an altercation because I wasn't ready to sing. I should have been, the time was set and all, but I was doing something else. He went and told Berry about it. Berry chewed me out pretty good and I got mad. We all had a vicious argument. It was awful. We nearly had a fight, then Brian and I nearly had a fight.

Do you remember what the song was?

It was 'I'll Take Good Care Of You'. I don't know if you remember it. It was a good song, Eddie [Holland] wrote it.

I wasn't so mad at Brian, but it was a necessary thing. It catapulted me into my own individualness. It caused me to become aware I had some ability to produce. That's when I started thinking seriously about producing myself.

Certainly 'Can I Get A Witness' seems like it has the tight hand of the HDH team. Did you feel comfortable on that song working within the pounding piano framework?

I felt very comfortable with Holland and Dozier because they were serious producers. Me being an Aries, I could understand where they were coming from. I tried very hard to interpret what they were feeling and thinking when they wrote the song. Even today, I feel I'm a good interpreter. My last album [*I Want You*] is strictly an interpretation of Leon Ware, he wrote all the songs. I love to interpret occasionally.

I was trying to interpret what they felt. It was very taxing on my voice, because I was still finding my voice, how to control it, how to sing harsh and not tear my throat out, how to get up on some of the notes. I never quite made it in some cases. Other cases I would.

They cut the songs very high. I would get very angry with them for cutting it very high. They would always say had they not cut them that high they wouldn't have sold. You sing very high, at the point where you are about to gag or about to kill yourself or have a stroke or something.

I used to look at Levi Stubbs of The Four Tops in the studio sometimes. Man, his veins were popping out. His neck muscles! They'd have to stop the tape, spray his throat, and call in the respiratory unit. Hold it, man, hold it! I would do the same thing. "Oh my God, I can't sing this song, man. Please, please do something!" You listen to some of those old records, you'll know what I mean. [Gags.] It was rough.

This brings me to your last big HDH hit, 'How Sweet It Is'. I always wondered if that title was based on the Jackie Gleason [TV] show.

I think so. Expressions have to come from some place. It taught me something. I've learned that lesson ever since. I've been dealing with things that are in the mind, statements, words. It gives you instant communication with the record buyer. He relates to something he's heard over the years and here it is, set to music. It makes the sale easier.

Whereas your teaming up with Mary Wells was a commercial move because she had a Greatest Hits *collection already, Tammi Terrell had at the time of your recording not had a solo hit. Who thought of putting you with this new artist?*

That's not an easy question for me. I wasn't consulted, as I wasn't consulted over any of the girls except Diana Ross. I had finally come to a position with the company whereby Berry felt I should be personally consulted when it came time to record the album with Diana. I had achieved that respect.

With Tammi Terrell and the other girl singers, including Kim

Weston, I was told. I relented in all those cases. With Tammi, I wanted to do it. There was a new team that was brought in, [songwriters] Ashford and Simpson. I liked Tammi. She was pretty, and she was nice ... soft ... warm and sweet. And misunderstood. I enjoyed working with her. That, coupled with Ashford and Simpson, made the project enjoyable.

You were produced in that time by Johnny Bristol and Harvey Fuqua. What was it like with all those people there involved in the creation of those memorable duets?

I had a good rapport with Harvey as a result of having been with him for years as a member of The Moonglows, a mutual friendship and respect. I took direction from him easily. With Johnny Bristol, I don't take direction from people that I don't feel are qualified. Not that I don't feel Johnny was qualified, I just thought I'd make that statement.

With Tammi you had a string of hits. One of the songs you had with her which made the American charts was the first song credited solely to you as a writer, 'If This World Were Mine'. Was that the result of a new-found confidence in your own songwriting ability, or just chance?

It wasn't chance. I'm a good songwriter. I'm probably as prolific a songwriter as any songwriter ever was. I feel I have those kind of songs in my piano bench.

The problem was a political one with Motown. I just don't let my songs go. I still have songs I've written back in the Fifties and Sixties I refuse to record. I feel they're smashes and probably a lot of pop songs and standard songs. My publishing deal with Motown is not flexible enough that I can afford for them to have them.

Does this suggest you're waiting for the day you're with another company?

This suggests, heaven forbid, that I'm waiting for the day they treat me with proper respect.

Which means either more artistic decision-making or higher royalty.

One or the two. [Laughs.] Not especially in that order.

Tammi's unfortunate death really hurt you at the time, from what I understand. Is that why you took a vacation from recording for awhile?

It didn't prompt my decision altogether, but it certainly played a great influence on my decision to not perform publicly for a few years or to record any records, because I understood the bottom line of her death, which I wouldn't like to discuss. [Both men pause.]

It was during the time you were doing your duets with Tammi that you enjoyed your greatest solo hit, 'I Heard It Through The Grapevine'. Gladys Knight and The Pips told me Norman Whitfield cut you on that on a track they had already had for one of their singles.

I don't know why Gladys is labouring under that misapprehension. I think she gets some kind of kick out of that.

I love Gladys very much, she's great. She's always had that little number about this number. It sort of ticks her off, the whole 'Grapevine' situation. There was something unethical involved, and on that score she has a beef, but the reality of the situation is that Norman cut it on me first. Berry canned it because he didn't have a lot of faith in it, or for whatever reason. Maybe because he had the power to can it and I was acting ridiculous at the time. It happened a few times. I'd do the same thing, I must say I've given him some problems.

So as a result of it being in the can, Norman knew he had a good song. He cut it on Gladys and put it out, so she came out with her version first. My song had been in the can for over a year. After she put it out, Motown released it on me, which to Gladys is a bit unethical, because you don't want somebody from your own company covering your own record. There's something not good about that, but it's no fault of mine.

I hope Gladys understands that. I didn't have any control over the situation at all.

With Norman you were involved in a sequence of songs that had already been recorded by other artists. You did 'That's The Way Love Is' and 'The End Of Our Road'. Norman was cutting a number of artists on his material. Was that a bone of contention with you?

No. I'm like O.J. Simpson in the music business, I have no problems with that sort of thing. I feel I'm head and shoulders above . . . [laughs] . . . I just do, I just feel that way. I know what I have and what I am and what I can do if I want to do it. I can be what I want to be. I have that kind of gift, God gave it to me. Nobody can take it away from me. I'm not insecure in this business at all. I have never been insecure.

In 1969 you had a hit in Britain with 'Abraham, Martin And John'. Dion had a hit in the States with the song. As a result of Dion's success your record was never promoted in the States. Did you feel sorry about that?

I wondered about that. Was that the reason? It would've been nice if someone had told me that. You have to go to England to learn these things.

No, I just sing them. That's the business end, which I'm very upset with. I'm just the singer, the artist. I cannot get into the business of it. I can only be upset with the business part of it. As far as running it, not being in control of things, they do pretty much what they jolly well choose to do. They, who are in control, either choose to promote it or not to promote it, and if they choose not to promote it, that's too bad.

Something must have happened in your mind between the release of that record in '69 and '71, when you released What's Going On. *Had 'Abraham, Martin And John' set your mind on to social themes, or did you finally now have either the self-confidence or the power within the company to deliver your own album?*

That's the first time I ever thought about the two songs being rather close together. I do think you're right about that.

While I was recording 'Abraham, Martin And John' it was late at night. There was nobody in the studio but Whitfield and myself and the engineer. The lights were very strangely lit that night. I felt very, very sincere when I recorded that song. It may very well have started me thinking about social problems and the world situation. It may have been responsible for the *What's Going On* album. You could be right.

Before the release of What's Going On, *did you in fact get instructions to prepare material for Sammy Davis Jr.?*

Where do you get this information? I often wonder if Sammy knew I wrote him an album. It's still in my trunk. It's a beautiful album, they're all original songs and they are some of the songs I told you I'm capable of writing.

I had a great deal of respect for Sammy at the time. When Sammy was supposed to sign with Motown, I went to Berry and asked if I might write an album for Sammy Davis. I wrote a song called [hums the song to get to the title line and then sings the words] "thank God for my wonderful life, for my wonderful life". If I could think of the lyrics, I would do it for you now, and I think you would find it really is Sammy. I can't think of the lyric. It's been years. It's still in my suitcase, it's a beautiful song. [Sings: "When I think of my wonderful life, I thank God for my wonderful life . . ."]

So after two years, in which you hadn't really had anything going, because you were doing other things, you came out with What's Going On. *How long was that in the creative process?*

Couple months. I wasn't thinking about time. How ever long it took. I was just relaxing. I was incensed, so I wrote and produced.

Incensed by what?

The war, my brother was in the war at the time, and the world problems and conditions. I wanted to write an album that could be translated into any language and it would still hold its meaning and not be a particularly ethnic statement that other nations and people couldn't get into. It took a little time to think about philosophically. I was much more incensed and I wanted to write stinging things and do music that would really make people all say, "Wow, maybe he's after us", and maybe incense them, also. But something wouldn't let me do that.

It was a very divine project. God guided me all the way. I don't remember a great deal about it. I can't, I was in a sphere or dimension, wrapped in something, and I don't have a great deal of recollection about the project.

Did you project it to Berry before you actually gave it to him? I ask because it was a double album sleeve, though it was only a single record, but a gatefold album in America, you got to write your own liner notes, you had much more of a total authorship of the project than you'd ever had before. What made the company see that this was the time for you to be able to make your statements?

Well . . .

Even at the point when it was released, there was not the total confidence in it most record companies have when they release a project on an artist because it was slightly "different". I use that for sake of being called factitious. I think "innovative". They felt like they were taking a chance, but Berry having an idea that I had something . . .

Everybody always tells me, all my life, "You have something special", and I listen. It doesn't affect me. I think I know what they mean. What they feel is that someday somehow some way I'm supposed to do something that's supposed to affect everybody's lives in some way dramatically. I haven't done it yet, but I suppose I'll do it, God willing. Viewing me in that manner, Berry probably felt that whatever I did, he would take a chance with.

I used to have spiritual battles. I would tell him, "Listen, God will take care of me, trust me". He'd look at me awhile and say, "Well, put it out." We'd have those kinds of conversations.

You mention God and Jesus Christ quite a bit on the sleeve of the album. You do believe He has a hand in guiding your work?

Yes. In my case, most absolutely. Not in the institutionalised religious description most people have in their minds, no, I'm not that kind of person. Institutionalised religion is good for the masses, but I have a special God who looks over me, who is the same God people worship institutionally, but I feel I have a special link. Anyone can have a special link if they will assert themselves.

You . . .

I asserted myself, yes.

Were you thinking of your own children at all when you wrote 'Save The Children'?

No. I had my son, Marvin. I didn't have him, of course, Jan did. I was thinking of children, period. I have great affection for children. I love children. Children are tremendous.

I wrote 'Save The Children' because I was trying to think of how I could say something to get to people, even to a man who has hardened his heart, who refuses to feel any thoughts of goodness, to words of compassion. The only object I could use was children, so, 'Save The Children'. Having been a child himself, that same hardened man would say, "I should save what I have been. Somebody saved me." I was appealing to one's feelings of fairness.

In one of the songs on the album, 'Inner City Blues', you stated they 'Make Me Wanna Holler'. As a result of your success, do you feel a separation from the 'Inner City Blues'?

Being successful has nothing to do with it. I am probably very rich. I'm supposed to be rich. I'm rich because it was prophesied I'd be rich. If I didn't have any money, I'd be rich. I'm rich in many things. I could survive with or without money. People like me, I like people. People respect and love me because I give love, I give respect. I wouldn't have any trouble finding food. If you're ill, I'll come to your aid. I don't care who you are or what you are, I love, because I'm blessed.

God loves me. I love God. I try to do His work as I feel I am supposed to, to the best of my ability. As a result, He blesses me. I could be anything. I could be a monk, I could be a sinner. I'm not a pious person. I don't want to give off that. I enjoy life. I enjoy all the things you guys enjoy. It's only how you enjoy them. If you approach that enjoyment with honesty, some kind of respect for those powers that are greater than thou, you always come out on the winning side. That's the point.

You mentioned O.J. Simpson before, and I can't help but remember reading that you had a couple of Detroit Lions football players on the session of 'What's Going On'. *Is that true?*

Yeah, those guys, yeah. Man, those football players are really far out. [Laughs.]

I love sports, I love football. I know I'm waving my flag a lot in this interview, but Muhammad Ali said, "If you can do it, it's not bragging." They'll tell you, I'm a good athlete. I could have played pro ball. I catch good. I'm a good runner . . . as we all are.

How did you achieve that party atmosphere?

My job was simple. I just directed them. I just got them and Bobby Moore of The Miracles in the studio, and they were just perfect. "What's happenin', man" . . . "Hey" . . . they slapped hands . . . it was just what I wanted. Football players are real good at talking things up, they just had to hold down the profanity. They knew they were gonna be on a record, they held off the cuss words.

What's Going On *was such a big hit people had a lot of expectations for your next work. You either delayed it for two years or did something else no one ever heard of and then came out with* Let's Get It On. *Was it that long in the conception or were you doing something else?*

That was all political. I wasn't motivated. My royalty statement didn't motivate me to do another album.

What's Going On *sold so many. Where did it all go?*

Heaven only knows. I certainly don't. My statement didn't show any tremendous sale. It slowed me down for my next project because I was sitting around incensed and mad and angry. When I get that way, I just don't do anything.

And so you didn't.

I don't have any other way. It's my only weapon.

If Berry has been occasionally as bad to you as you have been suggesting . . .

I never suggested that. Never did I suggest Berry's been bad to me. Where did you get that? Motown did that to me.

There's a difference.

I'm sure there is. There must be.

Let's Get It On *was the first successful album to deal entirely with the pleasures of sex and sensuality . . .*

Really?

Outside of Rusty Warren's comedy album Knockers Up.

Knockers Up! [Laughs.] I didn't hear that. I'd love to hear it.

I had always loved Ed Townsend's record 'For Your Love'.

Yes. Ed was a great singer and great writer, too. Funny guy. He'll tell you the mule joke, he'll kill you.

Was that how you first heard him?

Anybody first hears Ed telling them a joke.

I'm so curious. Ed's big hit was 1957, he worked with Theola Kilgore in the early Sixties, here he is with you in 1973. How did you find him out?

I've known Ed for many years. We've been friends for many years. When Ed came to me with an idea for a song called 'Let's Get It On', I knew immediately and instinctively the phrase alone was a smash. Then he sat and played the melody for me. I knew the melody was beautiful and I just did the lyric. It worked.

Let's Get It On *was a tremendous seller. The single sold at a historic rate as far as Motown was concerned . . .*

Historic rate? Really, I didn't know that either.

Are you being serious?

I'm very serious. These peanuts have got me not talking properly, but I'm very serious.

It sold two million in six weeks.

I didn't know that.

It also is one of the thirty top singles of the rock era, according to Billboard *magazine, which therefore makes me wonder how closely in touch you are with your own, shall we say, business success.*

I just know that my *Let's Get It On* royalty statement didn't reflect that.

OK. Did you feel after that album there was any more exploration to be done along the lines of . . .

Sex? Not particularly. With the *I Want You* album, I didn't know where to take the album on a conceptual basis. After exhausting a couple of possibilities, I found the music leant itself to sex more than any other subject, which is simply my only reason for taking it in a sexual manner.

I Want You was a unified album. I can't help but see that all your work in the Seventies has been individual projects. Gone are the days when you would release unrelated singles. Do you ever think you will get back to doing singles?

Do you think you would like to hear more of that sort of thing? I'm asking you the question in this case because I'm interested. I know you get a pulse from the people, what they like. Because the business isn't going there, you know. The business has sophisticated itself to the point where singles are almost taboo in the industry. Nobody cuts singles anymore. People cut albums, and if they don't have enough singles on the album they probably won't put it out unless one single is strong enough. It's albums. No distributor will order a bunch of singles anymore. Very few.

If you look at your hits in the Sixties, many of them were unrelated to each other in subject matter, even perhaps in musical framework.

I can do that with singles, but I can't do that with albums. If I did, I'd be putting out six or seven albums a year. I could put out four or five singles a year, unrelated, but four albums is an awful chore. You see the difference.

Yes. I was wondering if you miss the singles, but evidently you don't.

No, because you make so much more money off the albums.

Did you seriously think you might have a hit single, as you did, off the Trouble Man *film score?*

The *Trouble Man* film score was one of my loveliest projects and one of the great sleepers of all-time. I'll probably be dead and gone before the acclaim for the *Trouble Man* musical track I feel I should get.

Put to a symphony, it would be quite interesting. I have written a symphony that I have in my bench that I won't give away until people treat me properly, or it'll be there when I'm dead and gone and my children can exploit it for whatever financial gains they might derive from it. I'd rather anyway, which is what I do with most of the music that I won't get published. It's for my children, and their children. In any event, I enjoyed the job immensely. I'd like to do more. I can write a film score. I think that's some of my finer work, *Trouble Man*.

How did you come into contact with Leon Ware for the I Want You *album?*

I've known Leon a little while. Leon was teaming up with Diana Ross's brother T-Boy, who's quite prolific with his writing, both of them are. He did a song a few years ago called 'For The Babies'. I liked them when I heard that song. I liked them ever since.

When I heard the album Berry suggested I do, and he had me up to his place to listen to, I told him I thought this was terrific. "This is some stuff Leon did, do you want to do it, I think you should, you haven't done anything, you know you won't do anything, you're not going to produce anything on yourself, Leon's done the music", so I listened. I thought it was good. Consequently, the *I Want You* album.

Is this an example of what you meant when you were saying your voice has improved? This is almost an entirely different phase of the same man singing.

No, it's just that this is how I wanted to sing this album. Muhammad wants to fight a different fight sometimes, I want to sing differently on an LP. I just refuse to be the old Marvin Gaye everybody knows, right in the pocket.

I'm a lot of people and a lot of things, and I just have to express all of me. A lot of people might get upset, but a lot of people admire me for it. At least there's one thing my fans can look forward to: I'll be different. I don't know what I'll do, but it won't be like the last thing. I can guarantee that.

We had no way of knowing that *I Want You* effectively marked the end of Marvin Gaye's sequence of quality material with Tamla. Five nights later, on Sunday 3 October, he performed at the London Palladium. The live recording of this show, with the addition of the studio track 'Got To Give It Up', provided him with his last top three album. His next release was the bizarre double set *Here My Dear*, the literally-titled LP recorded to pay alimony to Anna, whom he had divorced in 1975.

Marvin's last chart appearance for Motown came in 1979 as one of the star vocalists on *Pops, We Love You*, a tribute to Berry Gordy Sr. By this time he was truly a confused soul. Gaye spent three years in Europe, avoiding the taxman and leading a troubled life. He famously kept an audience that included Princess Margaret waiting into the early hours.

The truly stubborn kind of fellow came in to Radio 1 to attempt another interview when I was sitting in for Kid Jensen, but he was incoherent. When he slept in late for another interview, fellow former Motown star Jimmy Ruffin was sent to his room to wake him. On a pathetic occasion, he was taken to Heathrow Airport to fly to Manchester for an interview. Excusing himself to go to the toilet, he exited the men's room by another door and caught a taxi back to his hotel, leaving his minders waiting for him outside the airport bathroom.

Marvin Gaye shuffled around Ostend in Belgium in what may have been the most odd self-exile in the history of popular music. Footage exists of the soul legend aimlessly walking the streets of the city and dropping into a bar. Director Rod Taylor and I were offered this material when we were preparing *The Motown Story* for Channel 4, but it was of no viewer value except for one soul-stirring scene. Marvin shuffled into a church and sang 'The Lord's Prayer' a capella. It was the most moving performance of sacred music I have ever seen. Gaye was reaching deep down into himself, lost in rapture, employing the great range and dynamics of his voice. Almost completely lost as a human being, he still had his relationship with his God.

The worst start to a birthday I ever had came on the second of April, 1984. TV-am woke me up with a phone call seeking my comments on the shooting of Marvin Gaye by his father in Los Angeles the previous evening, California time. Marvin had nearly but not quite made his 45th birthday. That a minister should shoot dead his own son spoke volumes about how messed up that family was. The career which seemed to be in glorious comeback after the 1982 success of 'Sexual Healing' on Columbia Records was ended forever.

"Marvin had it too easy," Jimmy Ruffin told Rod Taylor and I in trying to explain where a wonderful life had gone off the rails. "He was family, married to Berry's sister, so he had it easy. He got the best songs, the best producers. Artists like myself, who were not on the inside, always struggled. Marvin was always taken care of. When he left Motown, he couldn't cope."

3

I Am Responsible For Watergate

The transmitter of the Dartmouth College radio station WDCR was located in New Hampshire, even though it would have slid into Vermont had the Hanover plain ever tilted westward. It was therefore appropriate that every four years student newsmen covered the New Hampshire Presidential primary. Almost all the candidates who had previously jockeyed for position within their own parties had to turn to the people for a popularity rating.

DCR, as we called the station, had a massive advantage over all other New Hampshire news departments in the size of its talent pool. Unpaid students are far easier to employ than salaried reporters. Our News Director faced a studio full of would-be correspondents when he invited newsmen interested in covering the 1968 primary to an evening meeting.

We could afford to allocate one man per candidate, a luxury that guaranteed thorough coverage of the race. Before making his assignments the executive asked each member of the department which campaigner he would like to follow. As might be expected in a liberal institution of higher learning, the pupils all selected one of the many Democrats fighting to wrest the nomination from incumbent Lyndon Johnson. I thought they were all falling prey to personal prejudice. We were all going to be covering the New Hampshire primary just once. Surely any reporter should want to cover a winner, I reasoned, regardless of whom one favoured oneself.

I had met George Romney, the Governor of Michigan, the previous summer at a select gathering of top New Hampshire politicos. The logic had been that under the leadership of the moderate Republican governor, Walter Peterson, the state machinery might get behind the amiable former auto executive. But Romney disqualified himself with his notorious "brainwashing" remark, in which he attributed his previous support of America's Vietnam effort to having been misled by the military. In pointing out his own lack of judgement he not only lost his place in the opinion polls but eliminated himself from serious contention.

I felt there could be no professional satisfaction in covering a candidate like this, a national novice who might not see through the campaign. Richard Nixon was an old pro, guaranteed not to make suicidal gaffes – at least not in 1968. With the Republican right wing having been humiliated in the Goldwater debacle of 1964, and with the middle-of-the-road Romney suddenly out of the picture, I thought the Grand Old Party was likely to fall back on its old standby. I asked the News Director if I could follow Nixon through the primary. No one else was interested; I got the assignment by default.

In those days Americans were just learning the convenience of shooting dead public figures they didn't like. The traumatic assassination of President Kennedy was still a novelty; the deaths of his brother Robert and Martin Luther King were yet to come and attacks on the likes of George Wallace, Gerald Ford and Ronald Reagan were still unthinkable. Security for Presidential candidates, particularly in the early stages of the race, was far less stringent than today. I recall with bemusement how by flashing a simple press card or ticket we could work our way into almost any political meeting. During that primary I was never searched.

I first met Nixon at a reception in Concord, the state capital. He was officially launching his campaign and had accordingly brought his wife Pat, daughter Julie and Julie's boyfriend, David Eisenhower, grandson of former President Dwight Eisenhower. My lasting impression of this gathering was not so much Nixon, who answered my questions by rote as if he were a jukebox dispensing recorded speeches instead of songs, but Julie. When she asked why we were present, the News Director replied that we were from Dartmouth.

"But Dartmouth's in Massachusetts," protested the girl, who probably knew there was a town of that name in the Bay State because she was attending Smith College in Northampton, Mass.

"No, Dartmouth *College*," my colleague smiled.

"Dartmouth?" Julie queried with an expression that combined dismay with puzzlement. "Where's *that?*"

It is a powerful bolt of lightning that strikes broadcasters dumb, but the News Director and I were silenced by Miss Nixon's lack of knowledge. Almost any student in American higher education would know where the Ivy League schools were. Surely every Smith girl, natural prey to the Dartmouth students who dated their kind every weekend, must know that their lair lay only a hundred miles to the north up Interstate 91? Did not the Athenians at least know the location of Sparta before they were caught unawares? Does not Superman know the colour of Kryptonite?

When the WDCR executive gave the candidate's daughter a geography lesson, she brightened. "Oh yes, I know," she smiled, "a girl in my dorm has a Winter Carnival poster from Dartmouth." Better to be known for something, even a week-end in the snow, than nothing.

David Eisenhower was far more sympathetic, and we felt for him. As the grandson of a former President and national hero he was constantly being asked for his opinions on matters of world consequence, as if in his late adolescence he was already a sage. He made clear his resentment of this interference with his boyhood, and asserted he'd rather be a sports journalist than a politician. This is probably the most intelligent thing I have ever heard at a political meeting.

Nixon proved a convincing speechmaker in his New

Hampshire appearances, winning standing ovations with his reassertion of traditional American values. He never let his audiences know they were small-time, and if the former Vice-President found schlepping through the snow in the boondocks a comedown, he never showed it. He really was a professional.

Late in the campaign Nixon gave a speech in Lebanon, five miles from Hanover on Route 120, a road carved through a hill that inexplicably changed from a two-lane track to a sixty-mile-an-hour highway in its midsection. The candidate could not but help having heard of the rhubarb that had greeted the Alabama Democrat George Wallace on his visit to Dartmouth less than a year before, and five miles was as close as he would come to the spot of the trouble. Indeed, he even prefaced the body of his remarks with a few amusing asides about Dartmouth students, presumably hoping that wit would dilute the antagonism of any that had made the trek. Area residents might also enjoy a few laughs on the subject of the big-brained under-sexed over-boozed boys from Hanover.

He need not have worried. The five mile distance from the campus might as well have been five hundred. Only women and football games would make most Dartmouth men go more than a mile from the Green. Nixon found himself speaking to an audience of New Hampshire voters and only a few curious or supportive students. He was never heckled.

WDCR broadcast the Nixon address live. At the end of the talk he walked over to the small group of assembled press for further questions. I asked him one I had posed in Concord about the role of youth in society and, sure enough, I got the same jukebox recording I had received the first time. But this was not what struck me most. What I could not help but notice was that as Nixon opened his mouth to speak I was hit by a waft of bad breath. I was shocked, and had to consider my response. Should I announce on live radio that Richard Nixon had bad breath? Or, in the interests of manners and considering that he might have had an off night, or had rank game for dinner, make no mention of his odorous calamity?

I chose the latter course, but did phone my father, a Nixon supporter, to tell him the news. I expected him to be vaguely amused, but did not anticipate the events that followed. My father's photo-engraving company, which had long made plates for pharmaceutical journals, had a good working relationship with Warner-Lambert drugs. That firm's chairman, Elmer Bobst, was an intimate friend of the Nixon family. My father informed Bobst's secretary that I had interviewed her employer's pal and that he had nearly blown me into Vermont with his aroma (Dad doubtless phrased it more diplomatically). Instead of chuckling along she reacted with horror.

"Oh no," she cried, "we'll have to send him another case of Listerine!"

Bearing in mind the disagreeable aspects of Nixon's Presidency, I regret having told my father. The amount of people he did not alienate because his hygiene had been improved by the extra shipment of mouthwash could well have swung him the election in his razor-thin triumph over Hubert Humphrey. Ever since I have never joked about anyone's odour problems, for, almost anyway you look at it, I was to blame for Richard Nixon's election, and though I am not a crook, I was responsible for Watergate.

(*"I Am Responsible For Watergate" originally appeared in RADIO BOY by the same author.*)

4

Diana Ross Makes Me Feel Stupid

I first heard the voice of Diana Ross in late 1963. 'When The Lovelight Starts Shining In His Eyes' was a minor hit at just about the time 'Can I Get A Witness' was a major success for Marvin Gaye. Diana sang lead on the former song and, with The Supremes, backing vocals on the latter. In the one-for-all, all-for-one spirit that pervaded Motown at the time, The Four Tops, who had yet to have their first chart single, were offering unbilled support to The Supremes on 'When The Lovelight Starts Shining In His Eyes', a fact I did not learn until over twenty years later when I interviewed two of the song's three writer-producers, Brian and Eddie Holland, in their office in Los Angeles.

The duo's base was then in what looked like an upmarket shopping centre. The brothers could not understand why every member of our television crew collapsed with laughter as he or she approached their office. Finally we had to explain. The legal firm next door to them was called Wank and Wank.

No Briton can believe that two partners would voluntarily name their company Wank and Wank. Holland and Holland, of course, were Americans, and needed to have the salacious significance of Wank and Wank explained to them. At least when you went to these lawyers you weren't going to have your leg pulled.

'When The Lovelight Starts Shining In His Eyes' made a favourable impression on me, but I hardly thought The Supremes had the makings of a major act. Sure, this song, like 'Can I Get A Witness', had been written and produced by the

Holland brothers and Lamont Dozier, but Holland-Dozier-Holland had also cut the massive hit 'Heat Wave' on Martha and The Vandellas. This trio was assembling a string of hits that made them likely to become the second of Berry Gordy's "girl groups", as female vocal ensembles were then called, to top the *Billboard* Hot 100. The Marvelettes had given the company its first number one in 1961 with 'Please Mr. Postman'.

Two years is a long time when you're fourteen, and The Marvelettes already seemed like yesterday's heroes to me. More to the point, that million seller, and their top ten success 'Playboy', made them selective about their material. According to Lamont Dozier, The Marvelettes passed on the opportunity to record a Holland-Dozier-Holland song called 'Where Did Our Love Go'.

"They didn't like it at all," he told me in an interview for our Channel 4 *Motown Story*. "As a matter of fact, they told the same thing to The Supremes. They told them they didn't like it and wouldn't stand for it. 'I wouldn't do that because that's really garbage,' they told The Supremes.

"The Supremes were quite upset about it, but after it came out their whole attitudes changed. When we went to the airport to pick them up a few months later after the song had been number one, the whole attitude was, 'Well, hi, guys.' It was like Star Time. It was fun to see how they grew up fast. It's funny how a hit record can do that. I think it was great."

The Marvelettes' gaffe is the talent equivalent of the famous A&R decision not to sign The Beatles to Decca Records. 'Where Did Our Love Go' began a historic string of hits for The Supremes and Holland-Dozier-Holland. In four years they had twenty hits, including ten number ones. 'Where Did Our Love Go' and its four follow-ups, 'Baby Love', 'Come See About Me', 'Stop! In The Name Of Love', and 'Back In My Arms Again' all scaled the summit.

I first heard 'Where Did Our Love Go' on a Tuesday evening

in the summer of 1964, when Bruce Morrow (a.k.a.Cousin Brucie) was introducing the new WABC Silver Dollar Survey. (I have to this day never figured out why a station attempting to appeal to young people would use such an antiquated image as a silver dollar to describe its chart, but either it helped or at least did no damage: WABC was the most listened-to radio station in America.) I was on my way out of our family laundry room to join my neighbours in an evening softball game.

I loved the sport, and was impatient to play, but I couldn't leave the laundry room. Not yet. Cousin Brucie had just introduced the new number eighteen, 'Where Did Our Love Go' by The Supremes, and that "Baby, baby" business at the beginning was riveting. I was fixed to the spot by the voice, the song, the production. I can't remember anything about the softball game we played that evening, but I vividly recall just standing there with the washer and dryer, thinking this is a number one, this singer, whoever she is, is a star, and these handclaps at the beginning of the record are great. One of Holland-Dozier-Holland's many production innovations was putting ordinarily soft sounds mixed loudly at the beginning of Supremes singles. The results, as on not only the 'Where Did Our Love Go' handclaps but the fade-in of 'Come See About Me', the swell on 'Stop! In the Name of Love', and the bleeps on 'Reflections', were mesmeric.

The Sixties ended with a bang in 1970. The Beatles broke up and that mystery lead singer I had loved so much on 'Where Did Our Love Go', Diana Ross, left The Supremes. (She actually departed in late '69, but the split did not become apparent with separate record releases until '70. The group's collective swan song, 'Someday We'll Be Together', was still a major hit as the new decade began.) Between them The Beatles and Supremes, the leading male and female pop groups of the Sixties, had accumulated 32 number ones. The void they left behind has never been filled. No group has come close to registering their number one totals.

History tells us Diana Ross became a solo superstar and The Supremes drifted through the Seventies with a baffling sequence of personnel changes and diminishing sales success. But at the time, it actually appeared as if the abandoned Mary Wilson, the sole surviving original Supreme, might be having the last laugh. The trio got to the stores and the top ten first with 'Up the Ladder to the Roof', after which Diana stumbled with her initial solo outing, 'Reach Out and Touch (Somebody's Hand)', which limped to number 20. I pushed one of the buttons on my car radio every time that piece of sentimental schlock came on the air. How could one of my heroes record something so banal?

Because she liked it. When I saw her at the Royal Albert Hall a few years later I was amazed to see that she was using this song as a centrepiece of her set, urging members of the audience to touch a nearby stranger's hand, and doing so herself with fervent fans. She went walkabout pressing the flesh. This spectacle was light years away from the intimate desperation of 'Baby, baby, baby never leave me', the first words of 'Where Did Our Love Go'.

Ross regained her touch with her second solo single, producers Ashford and Simpson's re-working of their three-year old hit on Marvin Gaye and Tammi Terrell, 'Ain't No Mountain High Enough'. This sensational piece of work restored her to number one in the United States. Anyone who has not heard the full-length six-minute version of this half-sung, half-spoken marathon has missed a landmark of American pop. It was as if Ashford and Simpson, aware of the great popularity of Isaac Hayes' extended reworkings of recent hits, had decided to create a more refined female equivalent.

'Ain't No Mountain High Enough' was Diana's first American solo number one, and 'I'm Still Waiting', released the following year in the UK, was her first British chart topper. It had been issued after BBC Radio 1 disc jockey Tony Blackburn promised to make the album track his Record of the Week if it were put out as a single. Blackburn had ears, but for his own market only: the UK number one topped out at 63 in the US. Ross did not have another big record in America until 'Touch Me In The Morning' brought her back to the top in 1973.

Of course, she was merely missing in action, filming and winning an Academy Award nomination for Best Actress in her role of Billie Holiday in *Lady Sings The Blues*. Diana had recently been beaten in that category by Liza Minnelli for *Cabaret* when I first met her as a boy reporter for *Rolling Stone*.

It was the autumn of 1973. I was still a student at University College, Oxford, coming up to London three or four times a week for *Stone*, and had just been given a ten-minute weekly slot on Radio 1 offering an American look at the popular music scene. Far from restricting my extracurricular activities, Univ tolerated my travels as long as I kept my academic performance up to scratch. I was pleased that my pals in college could hear me on the radio once a week if they so chose. That was my idea of Star Time.

Phil Symes of the Tamla Motown office in London arranged my interview. I was in the midst of a whirlwind of activity for *Rolling Stone*. In fact, I wound up with more by-lines in the paper that year than any other writer. But I was so lost in love for what I was doing I had no sense that the connections I was making would form the infrastructure for the career that followed.

After a few moments of waiting, during which I mentally worked through the points I wished to cover, She walked in. Yes, She. Maria Callas may have been La Divina of classical music, but Diana Ross was La Ross, a divinity of pop. Part of this stature was a result of her own attitude, some was down to the attitude of her fans, but some of it was beyond the control of both. An artist occupies a space at the intersection of what she has to give and what the crowd wants to get.

Diana Ross did not write her own songs, she did not play an instrument professionally, and, as was often pointed out at the time, she did not sing with the spiritual depth of Aretha Franklin. Yet her voice was unique and seductive, her image glamorous and informed by a love of fashion. As was also often pointed out frequently, Aretha Franklin felt frustrated in this period of her reign as the Queen of Soul that she was rarely asked to pose in designer clothes. It was probably little consolation to her to hear the explanation that the audience did not want her for this. It did not want charisma from her as much as art. From Diana Ross they wanted, and were supplied in spades, glamour and star quality.

She walked into the room wearing nothing more formal than what appeared to be a variation on a tennis uniform, but I almost had to put on sunglasses. I have no interest in beauty pageants, but I was stunned by this vision of female perfection. This twenty-nine-year-old woman appeared to be flawless in both her proportions and her clothes sense. Just as she vocally had set a standard for a new kind of excellence, neither hot with emotion nor cold with high artistry, so she was unique in appearance. Neither buxom nor even erotic, she was nonetheless beautiful.

It seemed odd to ask such a modern monument the hard questions. But I was a boy reporter, and had to pose the obvious points in as pleasant a manner as I could.

Did she mind that Liza had beaten her to that year's Oscar? Well, duh, of course, but the story lies in the phrasing of the answer. Diana was a pro.

"Getting nominated for the Oscar was an honour," she told me sweetly. "I didn't mind losing to Liza. After all, I was running against Liza Minnelli, Lucille Ball, Desi Arnaz, Vincent Minnelli and Judy Garland, and that's pretty stiff competition."

A quarter of a century later, I'm embarrassed to say that the reference to Lucy and Desi went over my head at such a height it risked damaging the ceiling.

Did she care that The Supremes had recently fallen flat in the charts?

"No, I haven't worried too much about The Supremes not having hits lately because I've worried about my not having hits. Before 'Touch Me In The Morning' it had been a long time, and I wasn't satisfied with the last album, *Everything Is Everything*. The movie kept me busy for a year, and so did having a baby."

So far, so good. Did she view as particular competition Roberta Flack, who had scored the number one hit of the year 1972, 'The First Time Ever I Saw Your Face', and the massive number one that would be the big record of 1973, 'Killing Me Softly With His Song'? And what of Roberta's rumoured intention to play Bessie Smith in a feature film after Diana's success in *Lady Sings The Blues*?

"Every female singer is my competition," Ross stated firmly but sweetly. "Not to say we don't get along. Roberta Flack sends me flowers and we talk. If she does a movie about Bessie Smith, fine, I don't mind. Just because we did a film about Billie Holiday doesn't mean I'm going to make movies about everybody's life."

Good, friendly, quotable, moving right along, what about the new duet single with Marvin Gaye, 'You're A Special Part Of Me'? Marvin had previously partnered Mary Wells, Kim Weston and Tammi Terrell. How did Diana feel about replacing Tammi after her tragic early death?

The smiling face of Diana Ross froze. She looked at me as if her gaze were fixed on a point on the other side of my head, staring at and through me at the same time.

"I did not replace Tammi," she emphasised the word "not" coldly.

I felt stupid. I was not a boy reporter anymore. I was a frog reporter, a toad journalist, a gauche . . .

"I've wanted to do something with Marvin for a long time" – wait, she's smiling again – "I've loved Marvin for years and wanted to record with him" – the sun is out once more, she's regained her normal warmth – "We did a great number of songs together during the last year and a half, so many that I didn't know which ones would be selected for the album."

I had survived my most awkward moment. When you are interviewing someone about a career which has involved the death of another person, you have to raise the subject – as tactfully and tastefully as possible, of course. You can't predict how the artist will respond. Richard Carpenter replied with great eloquence and some tears when he related his feelings about the loss of his sister Karen, but Victoria Principal balked at talking about the passing of her friend and recording partner Andy Gibb. In such circumstances I feel like I'm throwing a live grenade into the interview and hoping it doesn't explode.

In the case of Diana Ross, it exploded alright, before it had even left my hand. I have never forgotten her hard emphasis on the word "not" in her reply "I did not replace Tammi".

In 1997, several Diana Ross solo number ones later, I found myself speaking to her again when the two of us joined Dave Clark, Gloria Hunniford and Chris Smith in a photo session, one of those this-group-will-never-be-convened-again shots, when EMI Records launched its 100th birthday exhibition at Canary Wharf. Quite rightly, all the photographers really wanted was La Ross. Her clothes had changed and she was wearing black, not white, but twenty-four years had not diminished her charisma. She had no reason to remember her brief interview with a college student two dozen years ago, and I did not wish to remind her, now that she was making me feel so very fortunate, of the time she made me feel so very stupid.

5

Tim And Andrew And Nato

In early 1974, during my final term at Oxford, I came to London to interview Tim Rice and Andrew Lloyd Webber for the British edition of *Rolling Stone*. The occasion was the release of the film version of their album and theatrical success *Jesus Christ Superstar*. Our meeting was to take place at Tim's home in Northumberland Place.

It was already my practice to take what I call the penultimate train – the train before the last one that would get me to an engagement on time. I had learned that trains don't always run to schedule, and it's better to take one that gets you there early than one that gets you there late. I hopped on to the Bakerloo line from Paddington and got to Charing Cross with plenty of time to spare.

I went to the address I had been given and found to my slight disappointment that some other people were already there sipping drinks. I knew that our interview had been arranged by George Kirvay of the publicists Rogers and Cowan, but had no idea that other members of the press had been invited. It sometimes happens, however, that assignments you think are going to be exclusives turn out to be assembly line interviews, and you just make the most out of the time you are given.

I chatted amiably with some of the other guests for about a quarter of an hour. It struck me as odd that many of them were wearing military uniform, several with medals and badges, but there was no accounting for the vagaries of Fleet Street. Finally, however, I thought the time for my interview

with Rice and Lloyd Webber must be approaching, and I had
to make my presence known.

"Excuse me," I asked someone dressed as a general, "do you
know where Tim Rice is?"

"Who's he?" the soldier asked.

"The author of *Jesus Christ Superstar*," I replied, entertaining
a slight twinkling of doubt that I might have made some sort of
mistake. "Isn't this Northumberland Place?"

"No, this is Northumberland Avenue."

"This isn't Tim Rice's house?"

"No, this is the NATO War College."

I felt like the idiot of all time. I had not yet lived in London
and was unfamiliar with the style of naming roadways that
gives the city five Northumberland Avenues, Northumberland
Close, four Northumberland Gardens, a Grove, two Parks, a
pair of Places, four Roads, a Row, a Street, and a Way. I had
just enough time to leave Northumberland Avenue WC2 and
return on the Bakerloo Line to Paddington to walk to Northumberland Place W2. While on the tube I reflected on how
easy it had been for me to crash the NATO War College.
Security today would be considerably tighter.

Although I was a few minutes late arriving at Tim's house, he
and Andrew had plenty of business to discuss with George Kirvay
and were not upset by my timing. All three were gracious to me.
I was enchanted by Kirvay, the first theatrical press agent I had
met. Over the next few years, his combination of efficiency,
kindness and camp made him my model of a show business
publicist. I was deeply saddened when I learned of his death.

While waiting for the Rice-Lloyd Webber summit meeting to
conclude, I snooped around Tim's recreation room and was
thrilled to find a pinball machine. I had been, if not a wizard,
at least a whiz at pinball at Dartmouth College, and felt that
any man who spent his royalties on a table like this was alright
by me. I was further gripped to discover Tim had a copy of Joel
Whitburn's *Record Research*, the privately printed guide to every

record that had ever made the American Hot 100. I felt it was possible we were the only two people in Britain to have copies of this limited edition book.

Tim, Andrew and I had a good interview about *Superstar* that ran in *Rolling Stone*. Lloyd Webber was kind enough to give me a lift to my next port of call, Knightsbridge tube station, in his car, which was a Mini or some such small model. We were listening to Radio 1, and 'Starman' by David Bowie came on the radio.

"What do you think of this?" he asked. Without waiting for much of an answer, obviously addressing an issue that was troubling him, he said, "I can't stand it. He can't sing. I like people who can sing, like The Everly Brothers. I'm afraid to say I'm losing my interest in pop." And so began our conversation about music which has continued, at intervals, to this day.

The following week I was feeling bored at Oxford. I got an idea, and called Tim Rice. He was at home.

"Tim, I was just wondering. Do you think there's room for a British Joel Whitburn?"

"Yes," he replied without missing a beat, "and I know someone who will publish it."

And so began a book writing partnership that has lasted for two dozen years. It turned out that Tim had been thinking of such a project for some time, but had found neither co-authors nor a publisher. Indeed, the publisher Tim thought would be interested in our project wasn't, but Jo Rice suggested we approach Guinness and we found a favourable response there. (Tim's brother Jo, whose name is short for Jonathan, grew tired after two decades of being asked if he was Tim's wife, and put his full name on our final editions.)

When I visited Tim at home to talk about the book I noticed a piece of paper in his typewriter.

"I'm writing a show about Eva Peron," he replied. He told me he had heard a Radio 4 documentary about the international transportation of the woman's corpse and had found her role in the recent political history of Argentina fascinating.

Tim first approached Paul McCartney about writing the music for *Evita*, but Paul thought writing a musical would not be fab.

"I told him he should write for the theatre," McCartney's father-in-law Lee Eastman once lamented to me. "I told him he could be his generation's Gershwin. He said he didn't want to be his generation's Gershwin."

Tim told Andrew Lloyd Webber about the project and received a more favourable response. The result was show business history, and also the name of Tim's daughter, who was born during work on the musical.

The Rice brothers and I met for lunch at the Concordia restaurant in Craven Street to discuss the possibility of doing a book called *British Hit Singles*. We invited as a potential fourth author James Hamilton, a leading club disc jockey of imposing height and impeccable speech. After lunch James, nicknamed "Dr. Soul", invited me to his North London flat to view his impressive record collection, and told me his proudest accomplishment was to have shared a lover (though not simultaneously) with James Brown, which made him "fuck brothers" with the Godfather of Soul. James declined to participate in *Hit Singles* because he was more interested in playing the records he loved than writing about them. Fair enough, I thought. Tim, Jo and I started our three-and-a-half years of research on *Hit Singles*. In the second year they invited their friend Mike Read to join the team. By a complete fluke Mike also joined the Radio 1 disc jockey squad of which I was a part shortly thereafter.

On 12 August 1997, Eva Rice, Tim's daughter, held the party for her first book at the London Toy and Model Museum, 21–23 Craven Hill, within walking distance of the Concordia restaurant. Tim, Jo and I were all in attendance. I told Eva I had to be there because this was the first book launch by an author I had known since before her birth.

6

Richard Branson Teaches Me

On the 18th of April, 1974, Richard Branson took me to dinner in a pizza restaurant in Notting Hill Gate. I was about to make my live Radio 1 début, filling in for John Peel between 10 pm. and midnight. I had appeared weekly on the network since September, on tape, as part of the Friday night programme *Rockspeak*, but this was the first time I was on my own. Peel was having a two-week holiday; I was doing his Thursday slot and Steve Bradshaw, who went on to become a BBC television newsman, was taking the Tuesdays.

Branson had run a mail order record business in the early Seventies before starting his own label, Virgin, in 1973. I had been writing for *Rolling Stone* while completing my studies at Oxford. Richard and I were part of the central London media counterculture that also included Tony Elliott, publisher of *Time Out*, and, of course, the *Rolling Stone* London editor Andrew Bailey. We were such a small group that everyone either knew, or knew of, each other.

Richard was grateful that I had written a rave review of his company's first release, *Tubular Bells* by Mike Oldfield. It was very rare for *Stone* to place an unknown artist on a new label as prominently as the second page of its album section, but my notice was as gushing as a geyser in its enthusiasm. I had heard the LP while a weekend guest at Peel Acres, and had been transported. 'In the land of should be,' I concluded my rave, 'this is already a gold album.'

Virgin Records in America used my review in advertising *Tubular Bells*, and included quotations on the single sleeve. I was only delighted to help the cause of a work I loved so much. Helped by the use of edited portions of the twenty-five minute long first side in the film *The Exorcist*, the album followed its top three success in the UK by reaching number three in the States. It was indeed certified gold, and Richard's fledgling music empire, which could have had some survival-threatening cash flow problems had *Tubular Bells* not been a hit, was off and running.

Now Richard was thanking me for my small part in his and Oldfield's success by encouraging me on the evening of my UK solo début. I had not made a live broadcast since I had left my college radio station WDCR in 1970. At eight o'clock, he felt obliged to comment.

"I can't believe you're so calm," Branson said in disbelief. "In two hours you're going to be speaking live to the nation. Where do you get the courage?"

Of all the things he said that night, that is the one I remember. I recalled saying that courage had nothing to do with broadcasting. If you loved being on the air, if you loved it so much you had to do it, courage was not a factor. Stage fright, or in my case that evening first night nerves, was an intrinsic part of the process. You lived with it and didn't worry about it, because it was both inevitable and secondary in the act of performing a show.

Nine years later, in late 1983, I had the chance to pass on this philosophy to Holly Johnson, lead singer of Frankie Goes to Hollywood. Holly was visiting Radio 1 the week the band was due to perform 'Relax' for the first time on *Top Of The Pops*, before Mike Read's spontaneous outburst on the breakfast show resulted in the record being banned from daytime play. The new star confided that he was really nervous about appearing on *The Pops*. I assured him there was no need to worry, for fear is an internal event. The viewer or listener cannot tell we are afraid, unless we have a complete collapse. Fear is actually a motivator, prodding us to perform and get on with things. I am pleased to say that Holly's work on *The Pops* was first class, and the single, one of my favourites from the Eighties, rose rapidly to number one.

A few years further down the line and I had reason to contemplate Richard Branson's remark about courage. The Virgin boss, now considerably better established, crossed the Atlantic Ocean in a hot air balloon. You wouldn't catch me crossing the Thames in a balloon for all the royalties of *Tubular Bells* and 'Relax' combined. Where did Richard get the courage for his mission? Don't try to tell me it was good for publicity, even if that is true. Publicity is not useful when you're dead. Recall Oscar Wilde's dictum that, "The only bad publicity is your obituary".

Obviously, courage is a relative thing. The prospect of speaking to hundreds of thousands of people live on the radio for two hours was terrifying to Branson. Crossing the Atlantic in a hot air balloon was not. For me, it was the other way around. Here was a tremendous lesson to remember: courage is relative.

Incidentally, it must have taken a good deal of courage for Teddy Warrick, Executive Producer of Radio 1, to support me on his network, and to produce my first live show. There was no precedent for having a foreigner with no pin-up potential on the station. He trusted my enthusiasm for, and knowledge of, popular music, at a time when Radio 1 was concentrating on star-building. I owe him, if not everything, a great deal.

For the record, my first show consisted of two repeats of John Peel sessions and my choice of current and old records. John Walters, Peel's producer, suggested a couple of discs to keep the programme friendly for Peel regulars. I jumped at the chance to rebroadcast a Top Gear session from Joan Armatrading, my favourite new British artist of the moment, and a 1970 set by Buddy Knox.

His 'Party Doll' had been one of the first two singles I had ever seen. One evening in 1957, when I was eight years old, the big boy on our street, Bobby Shea, said to me, "I have two 45s. Want to see them?" I rushed over to his house to see the latest in recording technology, the other example being 'Gone' by Ferlin Husky. Thirty-nine years later, I sold fifteen thousand 45s at Sotheby's.

The running order of the 18 April 1974 programme was:

'Stay With Me'/THE FACES
'Free Man In Paris'/JONI MITCHELL
'Grand Ole Opry Song'/NITTY GRITTY DIRT BAND
'Party Doll'/BUDDY KNOX
'Come Go With Me'/DEL VIKINGS
'Lonely Lady'/JOAN ARMATRADING
'The Love Of My Man'/THEOLA KILGORE
'A Song For Europe'/ROXY MUSIC
'Uptight'/STEVIE WONDER
'All In Love Is Fair'/STEVIE WONDER
'Rock Your Little Baby To Sleep'/BUDDY KNOX
'You And Me'/SUTHERLAND BROTHERS & QUIVER
'Freedom'/JOAN ARMATRADING
'Tenderness'/PAUL SIMON
'Try A Little Tenderness'/OTIS REDDING
'Sons Of 1984'/TODD RUNDGREN
'The Entertainer'/JOSHUA RIFKIN
'The Entertainer'/TONY CLARKE
'Forever Young'/BOB DYLAN
'Somebody Touched Me'/BUDDY KNOX
'Marionette'/MOTT THE HOOPLE
'I'm Your Puppet'/JAMES & BOBBY PURIFY
'Let Me Roll It'/PAUL McCARTNEY & WINGS
'Some Sort Of Love Song'/JOAN ARMATRADING
'Touch A Hand, Make A Friend'/STAPLE SINGERS
'Hula Love'/BUDDY KNOX
'Where Are They Now?'/KINKS
'Liza'/LOUDON WAINWRIGHT III

'Saturday Nite Special'/SUNDOWN PLAYBOYS
'Take It Easy'/EAGLES
'Midnight Rider'/GREGG ALLMAN

I'm getting nostalgic just looking at this list. I'd happily listen to most of that show tonight.

And I'd happily take Richard Branson out for a pizza.

7

Stevie & Barbra & Paul & Roy

The nicest mutual compliment I ever brokered took eighteen years to exchange. In 1974, I informed Stevie Wonder that Barbra Streisand had just covered his *Innervisions* track 'All In Love Is Fair'.

"She has?" he turned in my direction. "I can't tell you how much that means to me."

In 1992, I had the opportunity to tell Streisand of Wonder's delight.

"He said that?" she asked. "I can't tell you how much that means to me!"

The most bizarre case of a remark I had reported coming back to me occurred with Roy Orbison. In 1974 I had reported in *Rolling Stone* Paul McCartney's remark that 'Please Please Me' had originally been written as a Roy Orbison-type ballad, but had been changed in the studio at the suggestion of producer George Martin.

Years later, before his comeback with 'You Got It', I met Roy Orbison backstage at a British country club after a performance that was virtually a recital of his greatest hits in front of an audience of several hundred adoring middle-aged fans. The Big O was a true gentleman, extremely well-mannered and modest concerning his achievements. When I raised the subject of his early concert tours with The Beatles, he spoke of them with affection.

"And you know, they've been very generous with me ever since. Why, I read that Paul McCartney said that they had originally written 'Please Please Me' in my style."

I didn't dare tell him I was the journalist who had reported Paul's revelation. The quote had crossed the ocean twice to return to my ears, and that example of the miracles of modern media was journey enough for me.

8

John Joins John

During the last week of November, 1974, I sat with Billie Jean King at the Boston Garden watching our pal Elton John captivate his Beantown audience. I knew at the time, and marvel now, that I was in a privileged position: to watch the world go crazy from the inside. Someone else was watching that show, too. John Lennon had come to Boston to see Elton's show, to see if he wanted to join his friend on stage at Madison Square Garden a couple of nights later on the Thanksgiving holiday.

Before the show I found myself a few feet from the former Beatle. I had promised the BBC disc jockey John Peel, also a Liverpudlian, that if I ever encountered Lennon in America I would pass on his regards. I swallowed my awe and introduced myself, explaining that I was a colleague of John Peel and that I would like to convey his old chum's best wishes.

"How is he these days?" Lennon asked.

"He's fine," I replied. "He married Sheila," I added, referring to the woman Peel publicly and affectionately referred to as The Pig.

"Finally made an honest woman of her?" Lennon smiled. The grin was genuine, so the question was not simply rhetorical.

That was the extent of my only conversation with John Lennon. At least I had one.

Elton John had accepted an invitation to play and sing on a track on Lennon's *Walls And Bridges* album, 'Whatever Gets You Through the Night'. There was one condition: that John join John to play the song in concert if it went to number one.

Thinking there was no chance, Lennon agreed. The single did reach number one, and an agonised ex-Beatle agreed to keep his end of the bargain. He and Elton's band would play 'Whatever Gets You Through the Night' and 'Lucy In The Sky With Diamonds'.

There was a strange story behind the second selection, too. In 1974 the Pinner prodigy had wanted to release a single that was a cover version of one of his favourite tunes, and had narrowed the choice down to the *Sgt. Pepper's Lonely Hearts Club Band* classic and the Stylistics' 'Rockin' Roll Baby'. He finally rejected the Thom Bell-Linda Creed song "because of a line about an orthopaedic shoe". 'Lucy In The Sky With Diamonds' was recorded with "the reggae guitars of Dr. Winston O'Boogie", a pseudonym of Lennon's, and entered the American chart en route to number one the week of the November 28th Madison Square Garden concert.

The plane ride from Boston to New York was the bumpiest of my life. We flew through a snow storm on Elton's hired jet, the Starship, with the most frightened group of passengers I had ever seen. It was rather amusing seeing smug music business moguls fearing for their lives. I was strangely calm. I realised there had never been an aviation disaster on the scope of John Lennon and Elton John going down in flames together – the Big Bopper and Richie Valens, bless them, were not of similar stature to Buddy Holly. I felt protected, as if I were travelling with the Pope and the entire College of Cardinals.

"Wait for the third song," Elton advised before the New York show, meaning the last of the three numbers he planned to do with Lennon. When he announced his surprise guest, the hall erupted in a spontaneous affectionate ovation. If sheer emotion could lift the roof off a building, the top of Madison Square Garden would have soared skyward that night. I have never been present in an auditorium for such an outpouring of love as there was for the former Fab, who was making his first stage appearance in two years. After 'Whatever' and 'Lucy' the dynamic duo did 'I Saw Her Standing There', as Lennon introduced it, "a number by an old estranged fiance of mine called Paul".

We had no way of knowing this would be John Lennon's last stage performance. Lennon had no inkling that backstage after the gig he would be reunited with his estranged wife, Yoko Ono. Elton couldn't be sure he was going to retain his composure.

"It was very emotional," he said after the show. "I kept saying to myself, 'Hold on.' " The matches and candles that were lit after the three-song set, when Elton started playing 'Don't Let The Sun Go Down on Me', could have lit a village.

I was subsequently asked to write the liner notes for the live album of this concert and an earlier charity date at the Royal Festival Hall. Referring to the two countries in which the LP was recorded, the disc was titled *Here And There*. The kicker was that, due to contractual reasons, the Lennon tracks could not be included. I had to write acknowledging the hysteria of the evening without referring to its cause, a rather daunting challenge.

"Giants were walking the earth," I penned. "The arena, five floors above ground to begin with, seemed to take off. When the crowd stomped to rockers like 'Bennie And The Jets' and 'Take Me To The Pilot', limousines backstage bounced up and down as if clumsily attempting the bump. When Elton sang ballads like 'Rocket Man' to the light of a thousand matches, an ethereal tranquillity descended on the hall. Elton himself was so moved he cried."

By the time *Here And There* was released on CD two decades later, the question of using the Lennon material had been resolved and all three songs were included. My sleeve notes now seemed even more bizarre than before, avoiding mention of the reason the concert was important. Additional written material by John Tobler explained.

To know Elton in 1974, to meet Lennon, to do a cover story on Paul McCartney, were special opportunities. To be a cub reporter and broadcaster in London in the early Seventies was for a music maniac to be in the right place at the right time, to occupy a spot at the centre of the solar system that would not be available again until some young man happened to be in Compton in Los Angeles during the early Nineties. I know now my experience was special, but what is even better, I knew it then. You may have heard of the 1974 song title 'Rock And Roll (I Gave You The Best Years Of My Life)'. No. Rock and roll gave me the best years of its life. It got me through a lot of hard times. It got me through the night.

9

I Meet Marley

My favourite concerts divide naturally into two groups. The first is the event for which several artists come together, usually for charity. Live Aid, the highlight of all our careers, leads this list, but I have a soft spot for the Nelson Mandela Birthday Concert at Wembley Stadium, Murray the K's last package show in New York in the late Sixties (featuring the unforgettable combination of Wilson Pickett, The Who, Cream, The Blues Project, a Louis Prima and Keely Smith movie, and a fashion show conducted by Murray's wife), the 1979 Song for UNICEF show at the United Nations, and the June 1975 Wembley marathon with Rufus featuring Chaka Khan, Joe Walsh, and The Eagles. The Beach Boys stole this last show, playing their greatest summer hits on a sunny and hot late afternoon tailor-made for their music. What was expected to be an oldies set suddenly became a celebration of the day itself.

Elton John topped the bill and, being the brightest star in the rock firmament at the time, was expected to be its highlight. In fact, by the time he appeared the show had peaked with The Beach Boys. The audience had already enjoyed eight hours of quality music and were exhausted. With the sun setting and temperatures dropping, Elton chose to play through his brand new album, *Captain Fantastic And The Brown Dirt Cowboy*, which he knew well but the baffled audience did not. Thousands of exhausted and music-saturated fans trekked out of the stadium while Elton forged ahead with 'Better Off Dead' and 'We All Fall In Love Sometimes'. It was the only time I have seen people leave one of Elton's shows.

It was Elton who, as described elsewhere, provided my single most memorable pop concert with his Thanksgiving 1974 Madison Square Garden date. As I rounded out my top five single-artist shows I realised each of them was typified by a frisson that could be called The Moment. At Madison Square Garden, it was, of course, the moment that John Lennon, founder of the top popular act of the Sixties, came on stage to join Elton, the leading attraction of the Seventies. Listening now to the three songs they did together then could never capture the excitement of The Moment.

Nor could any recording do justice to the appearance of James Brown at his peak, in a theatre in the round in Connecticut in the summer of 1966, just after the third of his three top ten hits in a year. Someone opened the door, and in entered a whirlwind. 'Papa's Got A Brand New Bag', he announced. 'I Got You (I Feel Good)' he exclaimed, proving that a parenthetical remark can be an exclamation. 'It's a Man's Man's Man's World' he informed us, to the delight of even the soul sisters in the audience. When the cape act was performed at the end of the show, it was not as if it were a ritual he and his troupe had played hundreds of times, but as if this great star, riding atop the American music scene, was genuinely weighed down by the exertions required for his achievements, and that he really was falling to the ground completely spent, receiving consolation, a cape and a pat on the back from his handlers, and recovering sufficiently to break loose and continue the show, time and again. It is the James Brown tape loop, and it plays, forever, in my mind.

There is David Bowie at Wembley Arena on his *Station To Station* tour, which I frequently find myself referring to as the "Black and White" tour. Everything, from lighting to props and costumes, was in black and white. The arena's notorious sound problems had at least for one night been solved. The musicians hit their cues precisely. Bowie himself performed as if his senses had been enhanced, walking a tightrope he never fell off. I neither know nor care if he was on drugs that night, but if he was, it is the only time in my life I have seen an advertisement for their use. I have never seen better timing in music and motion.

Then there is The Moment when Frank Sinatra, playing the Royal Albert Hall in the late Seventies, sat on the stage accompanied only by one musician and sang 'Send In The Clowns'. No, lived 'Send In The Clowns', because when he got to the line "Isn't it rich, isn't it queer/Losing my timing this late in my career", he read it as if he had indeed lost his timing. For a few seconds, until he regained his meter, this great vocalist made art become life.

Although I could not have anticipated precisely how great these Bowie, Brown, John and Sinatra shows would be, I could not have been completely surprised, since the artists each had a record of quality live work. The final of my five favourite shows, last but certainly by no means least, was Bob Marley and The Wailers at the Lyceum in London on Friday, 18 July, 1975.

The Wailers had been favourites of the UK rock cognoscenti for some time. We had thrilled to their early albums *Catch A Fire* and *Burnin'* and watched as Johnny Nash and Eric Clapton went into the charts with Marley's 'Stir It Up' and 'I Shot The Sheriff' respectively, just as mainstream pop acts had successfully covered early Bob Dylan songs. What even Marley's music business mentor and friend Chris Blackwell of Island Records could not have foreseen was that Marley would develop a reputation as a musical poet and humanitarian to rival that of Dylan himself.

Blackwell would have known, but we did not, what to expect from a Wailers' live performance. We went along not daring to anticipate the sample on this earth we were offered of heaven. Black and white concertgoers mingled in a genuine atmosphere of brotherhood. As I wrote in an article for *Harper's and Queen* magazine, "His London Lyceum crowds were composed of almost equal elements of black and white, the whites swaying to the rhythms of The Wailers and some blacks also appreciating the occasional cries of 'Rasta!' coming from the stage. At times the music would stop and a single spotlight shone on the [Haile] Selassie portrait hung on the stage backdrop."

The concert was a revelation. Reggae had not entered the musical mainstream before this moment. There had been isolated crossover hits by artists such as Jimmy Cliff and Desmond Dekker, and there had been reggae-influenced successes such as 'I Can See Clearly Now' by Johnny Nash and 'Mother And Child Reunion' by Paul Simon. The style had been considered too esoteric for general Anglo-American audiences until that night, when Bob Marley and the Wailers made music that raised the spirit, fired the soul and pleased the senses. The audience, which in the Lyceum was a predominantly standing crowd, smiled for the entire show. Halfway through, something previously considered impossible occurred: the roof of the building was opened. My friends and I had not even been aware that the Lyceum had a retractable skylight. Suddenly, on a night as hot as one in their native Jamaica, The Wailers, and we, were under the stars.

When 'No Woman No Cry' began, we were transported. This was The Moment. This was the very time when reggae crossed over. The mood was so loving and tender none of us wished it would end. Some of the magic in the music can be heard on the live recording. The edited concert version became a British hit single within two months, and the live album was in the LP chart for Christmas.

I interviewed Bob Marley at the Hammersmith headquarters of Island Records on Tuesday, 22 July. He was the first man I ever met who chain-smoked marijuana. Despite this, he was completely lucid, and serious about his reverence for the deceased Ethiopian emperor Selassie.

"Haile Selassie is stronger than any," he asserted. "He is Imperial Majesty the Almighty, the Creator. Him can do whatever him want. He is earth's rightful ruler."

Marley recognised the duality of his own appeal. "I think universal," he told me. "I talk Jamaica. To be universal, I still have to talk Jamaica. People might have a hard time understanding what I'm really saying, but some songs I leave Jamaica and deal with universal people." "I think universal, I talk Jamaica" is as cogent a six-word explanation of one's popularity I have ever heard an artist offer.

A purist may have thought a songwriter who had recorded his own work might be miffed when other artists had the hit versions of his songs. Marley was in no such mood. He talked generously about Johnny Nash, and became enthusiastic talking about Eric Clapton's 'I Shot The Sheriff'.

"Someone told me Clapton was doing the recording. I said, great! When I heard it, it sounded good. Eric Clapton did all right to it. I feel we have too much musical break. Eric Clapton just went in, 'I shot the sheriff', wham, right into the verse, wham, 'I shot the sheriff', another verse. Meanwhile, we shot the sheriff, hit some music, then the verse. People can dig it on an LP, but for a 45 it can't work. When you do an original song, someone can listen and try and improve on what you did."

This song was not the only Wailers tune on which Marley raised the possibility of violent social change. The then-current album, *Natty Dread*, included a track titled 'Revolution' which stated that, "It takes a revolution to make a solution." 'Talkin' Blues' famously claimed, "I feel like bombing a church/Now you know that the preacher is lying."

Marley smiled when I recited the latter lyric.

"Some people might not appreciate that, because them love God and feel the church is a holy place. The Man himself isn't in one church. People talk about one church and another church, who preach. That isn't the real thing. Anyone can read dem Bible and get dem education from the Bible."

He also qualified his call for revolution.

"There's a revolution going on, a secret revolution that won't be televised. People want righteousness. The revolution is bringing children back to God. 'So Jah seh/Not one of my seeds/Shall sit in the sidewalk/and beg bread./And verily, verily,/I'm saying unto thee/Inite oneself and love Imanity.' "

The genial artist was soft-spoken, but his message was coming through loudly.

"I don't know if big people can get together, but the youth could. When the youth unite, maybe the big people will follow. Youth have to get a chance to run the earth. Only the youth can do the right thing right now. We need youth, youth have more love inside in this time than the big man, who get lost in the material type of thing. The big man did a great job in getting all these material things, but the youth can rule it."

Bob Marley certainly affected the youth of his time and the young who have come after him. Unlike most pop stars, whose reputations fade after death, his grew. His songs of love and social solidarity took on added poignancy after his death from cancer in 1981. When I interviewed Island Records founder Chris Blackwell in several locations in Jamaica during the filming of Channel 4's *Island 25* anniversary special in the late Eighties, the one time the man had to stop to regain his composure was when he became emotional over the loss of his dear friend. Marley's posthumously released anthology *Legend* had sold nine million copies in the United States by 1998, when it was still ranked third in the Top Pop Catalogue Albums chart of *Billboard* magazine.

On the 4th of February 1997, the charity War Child auctioned original artwork by musical celebrities who had created pieces in honour of their heroes. I was seated at a table with Sinéad O'Connor, whose tribute to Bob Marley, a signed framed photograph with lipstick kisses, fetched £6,500, approximately $10,000. I told Sinéad of the unforgettable Lyceum concert, of my meeting with Marley, of my visit to his family home in Jamaica during the filming of *Island 25*.

"Please stop," Sinéad requested politely. "You're making me jealous."

10

Hero Time One

When I was a boy my three heroes were Carl Barks, Willie Mays and Arthur Rubinstein. Each represented one of my great childhood passions, which evolved to become my adult recreations.

Baseball was my favourite sport, and Willie Mays my favourite player. In my adulthood I had to question if my preference for the Say Hey Kid was not due in some part to his playing for the New York Giants, who played at the Polo Grounds in the city of my birth. No, I answered myself, because the Yankees also played in New York, yet I never favoured Mickey Mantle.

Mays and Mantle were the two teams' respective centre-fielders and were endlessly being contrasted. They both amassed credentials that got them into the baseball Hall of Fame in their first year of eligibility. Yet I always thought the debate over which was the greater required a bit of wishful thinking on the part of Mantle fans. Though every bit the slugger Willie was, and perhaps even slightly more powerful a batter, Mickey was dogged by an injury that kept him from moving as quickly or as gracefully.

Number 24 was consequently a more effective fielder and baserunner than Number 7. The Giant was the most outstanding all-around player I ever saw. More than that, his every move in every game seemed to celebrate his love of the sport, and his gratitude for being alive. Whenever he lost his cap running the bases, whenever he made his patented "basket catch" of a fly ball (pocketing the ball in front of him at waist height, rather than spearing it in the air), we were uplifted.

I say "we" because there were a lot of us. One of us was Bill Clinton, who in the 1990s identified Willie Mays as his favourite player.

You didn't even have to be a particular Mays fan to recognise one of his plays in the 1954 World Series as one of the greatest in the history of the game. As was captured on black-and-white film I frequently saw rebroadcast as a child, Cleveland Indian batter Vic Wertz sent a towering drive to deep centre. Willie turned around and sprinted away from the diamond towards the fence. He caught the ball over his shoulder running at full speed.

It's an incredible sight, which begs the question: how did he time his dash to the fraction of a second required to make the catch? It is, of course, an unanswerable question, because he didn't time it consciously. He just did it. And he "just" whirled and threw the ball accurately back to the infield in one flowing motion, when logic would dictate he could not possibly calculate how to make the toss nor summon his body to gather the required strength. Such are the miracles worked by great athletes in any sport.

I never met Mays, but I saw him play live. I never met Rubinstein, but I saw him play live, too. It was his farewell concert at the Wigmore Hall in London, in May 1976. Once I had been informed it was going to occur by one of my teammates on the Regent's Park Softball Club, there was no way I was going to miss it.

It had been Rubinstein's recording of Grieg's Piano Concerto in A Minor that had most inspired me to press ahead when I was taking piano lessons in the late Fifties and early Sixties. I'm not sure why my father had bought this record, since his LP purchases tended to follow no trend other than the exclusion of rock'n'roll. Indeed, my brothers and I were forbidden to buy 45 r.p.m. singles on the grounds that they were a cheap example of planned obsolescence. Needless to say, the year that I went away to college, 1966, I began loading up with my favourite singles at jukebox dump shops in the Times Square area.

Rubinstein playing Grieg was the part of the family album collection on which I focused. I shudder to think how many times I played this record. It really did conjure up pictures of the fjords, although at that time I had never seen a fjord and had no idea I would one day actually travel to Norway. I thought, in the luxuriously and narcissistically melancholy way adolescents do, or at least I did, that if I had one minute's warning before my death, I would choose to spend those sixty seconds listening to the final moment of Rubinstein's Grieg. This assumed, of course, that a stereo was nearby.

It was when I memorised the first movement of the concerto that I stopped taking lessons. My teacher Mrs. Yi-Kwei Sze, who had succeeded Mrs. Bernard when my earlier instructor was sadly taken ill, was preparing her pupils for a group recital, and I enthusiastically selected the Grieg as my piece. Mrs. Sze took me individually to see one of her former students give a recital at Town Hall in New York. As I watched that poor sucker suffer under the spotlights, in front of the critics, I realised this was what she had in mind for me.

I had no desire to turn professional and, more to the point, insufficient ability. I figured only ten or so pianists in the world made great money and that I would never be in their number. Furthermore, I did not have the "killer instinct" required to become a refined player. I got irritated with practising after about forty-five minutes a day. In addition, my back became stiff. I wanted to play for fun, not for a living, and I stopped studying.

Rubinstein, however, remained one of my heroes. I loved his Chopin playing as well as his Grieg. When he was in his ninetieth year and hanging it up with a farewell appearance at the Wigmore, I got the best seat I could. This was a £20 seat in the circle.

Twenty pounds was a lot of money in 1976, particularly for

someone like myself who was less than two years out of university. I had just experienced the only dark night of the soul in my career, when in 1975 Jann Wenner decided to stop paying retainers to his Contributing Editors of *Rolling Stone*. I would receive income from the fortnightly paper only when I had an article printed.

My modest once-a-week Radio 1 money wasn't going to be enough to sustain me. I sat at my desk one evening in Sinclair Gardens, West London, debating whether this unpredictable profession was really for me. Upon leaving Dartmouth in 1970 I had received an unsolicited offer from an alumnus who was chairman of a New York advertising agency to start with his company at the then-astronomical salary of $20,000 a year. Was my future in a money-making business like advertising? Should I go to Harvard or Yale Law School, both of which had accepted me in 1970, after all? Or should I sweat it out hoping there were better days ahead in London?

I knew I had to be true to my twin passions of radio and music, and decided to tough it out. Thank heavens my financial situation improved, at least enough to afford a £20 seat for Arthur Rubinstein.

This really was a special seat. I could look down on his hands, which for a pianist is the best view of all. It doesn't matter if you're near the stage during a piano recital. If you're on the right side of the hall, your view of the player blocked by the open piano lid, you might as well be at home listening to a record. I thought Rubinstein the best pianist of my time, and here I was with an uninterrupted view of his hands for two hours.

The view was shared by Albert Finney, sitting just in front of me. As might be expected, it was a star-studded gathering. The celebrity who made her presence most known to me was the actress Lauren Bacall, who earlier in the decade had won a Tony Award as Best Actress in a Musical. She was obviously still accustomed to projecting her voice.

"Oh, look," she said in the foyer during the interval, loudly enough for at least me to hear at a short distance. "There's Jacqueline du Pré. How depressing!"

It was indeed the legendary cellist, laid low by her fatal illness, being pushed in her wheelchair by a young man I presumed to be Daniel Barenboim. But I did not consider the sight depressing. Jacqueline was beaming with her enjoyment of the concert, and I thought it inspiring that her love of music was unhindered by the misfortune of her health.

Rubinstein, too, was articulating his enthusiasm for his material and the occasion, even though we knew he was losing his sight. During the first half he declined applause after untypically making a couple of errors in a piece, and insisted on compensating by adding an unprogrammed work. This episode informed us that his vision really was fading, and prepared us for his dramatic leave-taking at the end of the evening. Having played one encore, he politely refused requests for more.

"No more, please," he told us from the stage. "I cannot see the keys."

And with that chilling remark, making us wonder if he had in fact played the last portion of his recital in darkness, Arthur Rubinstein concluded his career.

I don't know how I got backstage, but I had to see my hero. So did a lot of others, including Lauren Bacall, who was standing at the base of the staircase Rubinstein descended to greet his friends and fans.

"Maestro!" she cried, her voice undiminished in volume.

The great man turned and without missing a beat replied, "I am not so blind that I cannot see your beauty."

What a man, I thought, still pulling at ninety!

I have seen many other memorable recitals. Elisabeth Schwarzkopf gave a commanding performance at the Wigmore, looking as if she might discipline ten per cent of the audience if it didn't meet her expectations. Montserrat Caballé held us entranced at Covent Garden with her combination of musicality and mirth. I will never forget the look of thrilled anticipation from my friend Freddie Mercury as he gave the high sign from his box seat just before the show. After seeing his delight, I never questioned his desire to duet with her on 'Barcelona'.

The Royal Opera House was also the venue for an extraordinary charity performance by Jessye Norman. During the interval the actor Anthony Quayle, explaining the nature of the occasion, appeared to ad lib his gratitude that "we are in the presence of this" – he halted to find the word, and then said with emphasis – "queen" – at which point half the audience dissolved in laughter – "of music" – he added. A queen of music Norman was that night and on every other occasion I have seen her.

I have had bad luck with Luciano Pavarotti. During a 1979 recital he consulted his sheet music, a crutch he blamed on nerves from flying. At his prices, the audience had hoped he could remember a few tunes. When I saw him in *Aida* at Covent Garden, he had to stand on stage awkwardly while child acrobats tumbled inexpertly to the catcalls of the crowd. It was extremely odd seeing the most famous tenor of our time standing helpless while the production in which he was performing was being booed. This was not as paradoxical as the moment in an interview during which he told me, "I have to lose weight" while actually eating a cream cake.

I have enjoyed much more the performances of Placido Domingo, who on several occasions has also proved a perceptive and co-operative interview subject. Domingo is that rarity in opera, an actor as well as a singer, and when he told me his favourite role was Otello precisely because it allowed him to do both jobs, I made sure to see him in the Verdi part when he next performed it in London. The special treat was that I went on the eightieth birthday celebration of Sir Georg Solti, who conducted a stellar cast that included Domingo and Dame Kiri Te Kanawa.

I have loved so many artists in recital, from the enthusiastic Dawn Upshaw, who could not help but excitedly share the background of her material with a Wigmore Hall audience, to the formal Dietrich Fischer-Dieskau, from the smiling violinist Isaac Stern to the serious pianist Evgeny Kissin, who looked and played like a Greek god on a bad hair day. It is Kissin who has become my favourite pianist after the death of Arthur Rubinstein, and who has with his fellow young Russian violinist Maxim Vengerov restored my faith in the never-ending cycle of virtuoso music-making.

Yet no matter how much I enjoy a Kissin concert, I doubt it will ever mean as much to me as the night I tapped the bank account to position myself to see my hero's hands and when, for two hours, it was Hero Time.

11

Muhammad Ali Is Upstaged

It is possible to steal the show from the most famous person in the world. I know because I've seen it happen.

I did not know it had happened, however, until the following day. The attention of everyone in the room for Muhammad Ali's 1977 London press conference was focused completely on The Champ. They could not conceive that a photographer could capture a moment they missed entirely.

Here is the best example I know of the difference between written reportage and photo journalism. All those of us who were in the room at the time were concentrating on asking Ali his reflections on the past, his activities in the present, his plans for the future. We allowed him to talk about the raison d'être for his visit, the British opening of his biopic *The Greatest.*

It was a lovefest. There were other people on the podium with him, including his infant daughter, but we paid them no heed. The most famous athlete in the world was in the room.

I was at the press conference to represent Radio 1. Having heard Muhammad Ali was going to make this appearance, I did not want to miss the chance to meet the great man. I had followed his career like virtually every member of my generation, in awe and with respect.

In boyhood I had followed boxing closely, watching all the title fights shown on television, including what seemed to this child to be endless rematches between Sugar Ray Robinson and Carmen Basilio. I lost my interest in the sport when I saw Emile Griffith kill Benny "the Kid" Peret on live television.

Griffith got Peret on the ropes and hammered his head with blows. The head of "The Kid" bobbed back and forth like the top of a Slinky toy. It was obvious to anyone watching – except, evidently, the referee – that something was deeply wrong. Long past the point where we would have stopped the fight, Emile was pounding Benny. By the time the fight was over, so was Peret.

Years later, the author James Ellroy told me that Griffith had been furious because during the run-up to the bout Peret had been taunting him concerning his sexual orientation. Griffith poured out his fury and hurt in the ring, smashing Peret, bashing him, literally destroying him. "The Kid" was carried unconscious from the ring and died later. It was the only time I saw one human being kill another.

So much for boxing for young Gambaccini. But when Cassius Clay emerged and did the impossible, defeating Sonny Liston, and then as Muhammad Ali performed the inconceivable, besting the United States government, and then back in action defeated the superstrong George Foreman using the "rope-a-dope" strategy, I joyfully paid attention. This was not just sport, this was being alive in my time. Ali was as courageous as he was charismatic.

"I have to agree," radio commentator and long-time Ali sceptic Floyd Patterson conceded after the Foreman fight, "Clay is the greatest." I heard him say it – I stayed up to hear the Rumble in the Jungle on the radio – and I agreed.

How could I not attend a press conference with this man? Besides, I reasoned, I had met Richard Nixon and The Beatles. If I encountered Ali, I would have met three of the four most famous human entities of the era, leaving only the recently-deceased Mao Tse-Tung beyond my repertorial grasp.

I entered the room for the press conference and decided this was no time to be shy. I took the seat directly in front of the podium from Ali, while more circumspect colleagues took humbler locations on the sides or back of the room.

The following morning on his breakfast show my Radio 1 colleague Noel Edmonds mentioned my strategic position. How could he have known this, I wondered for a second? Noel pointed out to the nation a picture on page 3 of the *Daily Mail.* Here, it turns out, was a page 3 girl who could really charm the camera.

While Ali was addressing the reporters and I was attentively holding my microphone in front of him, his daughter had turned her back on all of us to smile at a photographer positioned behind the podium. The wily cameraman snapped a classic picture of her grinning innocently, stealing the show from everyone else in the scene.

Now that Ali has justifiably become a living legend, I occasionally look at this remarkable photograph. This is not the champ and his admirers. This is a girl and her father, and daddy is in the background. It is the only occasion I can imagine in which Muhammad Ali would not mind being upstaged.

12

To France For Eurovision

I never heard of the Eurovision Song Contest until I came to England at the age of 21. Imagine: an entire childhood spent without spending several hours around the television once a year, wondering whether Norway was going to get no points or actually win, which country would have the most nonsense syllables in the title of its song, or which contestant would be wearing the boots with the highest heels. Your response as to whether I was deprived or spared will reflect your opinion of Eurovision.

For, as was and still is, the Contest receives zero publicity in the United States. If you introduced an American to Nicole and said the German had won the Eurovision Song Contest, the Yank would probably be as impressed as if you had said Nicole had won the Grafton County, New Hampshire 4-H Beauty Queen competition (a contest of which I was, in fact, a judge when I was a college student in 1967, and which I remember with a sense of trauma because the local congressman's assistant took me to the tent where a woman was doing unusual callisthenics with a cigar).

This is not to say that I had not heard any of the songs which had been in the Eurovision Song Contest. Several of them had become major American hits. But, in an ominous way that seems to say something about the taste of the Contest itself, all the US sales winners had lost the actual competition. The first of these fabulous failures was 'Nel Blue Dipinto Di Blu (Volare)', sung by its author Domenico Modugno in 1958. How on earth could this all-time classic pop song have failed to win any contest? It is such an obvious smash it should even have won the Grafton County, New Hampshire 4-H Beauty Queen competition. Modugno spent five weeks at number one in the American charts and won the trophies for Record of the Year and Song of the Year in the very first Grammy Awards. It was as if the Grammy Awards had been invented as a consolation prize for losers of Eurovision.

Five weeks at number one in the Hot 100 proved doable for Paul Mauriat ten years later when he took Eurovision loser 'L'Amour Est Bleu' all the way under the English language title 'Love Is Blue'. This classic instrumental spent a mighty eleven weeks atop the Easy Listening chart, now known as Adult Contemporary. This was for over a quarter of a century the longest run in history, until Celine Dion started treating the category like her own personal hit list. Other Contest also-rans that proved successful in the States were 'Al Di La' and 'Walk Away (Warum Nur Warum)'.

Even after I first came to Oxford in 1970, the next Eurovision smash in America, Mocedades' 'Eres Tu', had not won the contest. One could see how this haunting tune came to be a Stateside smash: the first three notes of the chorus echo the first three words of Elvis Presley's 'Can't Help Falling In Love'. But given that, the ballad should have swept Eurovision, since the Elvis record had been a worldwide giant. Mocedades remain the only act I have ever interviewed who were slightly nervous of being mistakenly associated with terrorism: they were Spanish Basques at the time the separatist movement was particularly active.

Finally came the 1974 winner, Abba's 'Waterloo', which not only took the title but reached the American top ten. This, perhaps, is because Abba were using Eurovision, as Bjorn Ulvaeus explained to me, not just for its own sake, but to break beyond the confines of Sweden. They deliberately sang in English – "the language of rock-and-roll", Bjorn called it – to score maximum impact in the Anglo-American market. Abba succeeded, of course, beyond even their own wildest dreams.

In 1977, France won the contest at Wembley. The following year, *Radio Times* sent me to Paris to write about the French music scene in preparation for the 1978 competition. Fortunately, I had been at an event in 1977 that put the subject in perspective, and gave me my lead for the piece.

"Marie Myriam looked frightened and alone," I wrote. "Less than one week earlier hundreds of millions of viewers had seen her win the 1977 Eurovision Song Contest at Wembley. This night 200 guests at her record company's party for Neil Sedaka were paying her little attention. Almost everyone who came to her table stopped not to congratulate her but to exchange pleasantries with a more important guest sitting across from her. Noel Edmonds would be an important influence in the British music business for the foreseeable future. Marie Myriam was already yesterday's hero. Even more damning in the eyes of the gladhanders and backslappers, Marie Myriam was French."

Score me a full twelve points for the Noel Edmonds prediction, although a spectacular "nul points" for the man himself when it came to foreseeing his own future. On the Radio 1 team bus after a charity match in Scotland one afternoon in the late Seventies, I sat next to Noel when no one else dared. He had blown them all away in the pre-game applause sweepstakes. The amount of clapping we got when we individually came onto the pitch was the only real way we had of knowing our popularity relative to our peers. That day, for the first time, Noel's reception had been wildly more frantic than that given to the previous favourites, Tony Blackburn and David Hamilton.

"You heard it," I said. "Where do you want to take it from here?"

"I'd like to be my generation's Frost, interviewing world leaders," Noel answered, little realising that his generation's David Frost would be, in fact, David Frost himself, making room for no young upstart, and that Noel Edmonds would become – Noel Edmonds, every bit as popular but wildly different in image.

As for Marie Myriam, interest in her fate is confined to the other side of the Channel, with the exception of enthusiasts who meet regularly to watch videos of exotica such as the 1974 Swedish qualifying round. Knowledge of French stars abroad is shockingly slight. When the American rock group Mink de Ville arrived in France in late 1977, lead singer Willy asked if he could be taken to the grave of Françoise Hardy. He had to be informed that she was alive and well and living in Paris.

Hardy was one of the artists I interviewed on my *Radio Times* trip to Paris. The Sixties poster girl was lively and self-effacing.

"Either French music is not good or it is a copy," she told me. "I did achieve some popularity in England, but what was popular was my image rather than my songs. In France my physique was not fashionable. Brigitte Bardot was the big thing. I was half-boy, half-girl. I didn't like my physique. I thought I was ugly. But this was fashionable in England, where people like Sandie Shaw were popular. When I came to London, it was the first time I ever felt my physical aspect was liked."

Someone who achieved only one minor chart entry in the UK ("Tears On The Telephone") but huge royalties from Paul Anka's English language translation of his French hit 'Comme D'Habitude' was Claude François. I had been due to visit him at his village home, but a light snowfall paralysed Paris, causing power cuts and making travel dangerous. I phoned him instead, and asked if the snow was a problem for him.

"Not at all," he said. "I am here in the dark listening to the radio, and I am the new number one." He had no problem with French records doing poorly in Britain, since he thought that, comparatively, they were poor.

"English music is much better quality," he explained. "Until 20 years ago we had accordions in our pop songs. The waltz was our rhythm music. The blacks gave America jazz. Britain had big bands. We had accordions. We are only now beginning to understand rhythm.

"Johnny Hallyday was impersonating, I forget his name, Elvis Presley. But that's all right for Johnny, because he never tries to go abroad. If he did, it would be like some Englishman coming over here trying to be like Maurice Chevalier. It would be strange."

There was for François one exception to his rule of quality: he preferred his 'Comme D'Habitude' to Frank Sinatra's 'My Way'.

"I like the original better, because in French it is about the end of a love affair. In English, it is about the end of life."

So spoke a romantic, a pop idol in his homeland for 16 years until he attempted to change a lightbulb while standing in the bath, a fatal error.

I may not have met Claude François, but I was determined to meet the great Charles Aznavour. This living legend had scored a number one in the UK in 1974 with 'She'.

"It is the first French record to get to number one in England," label head Eddie Barclay boasted proudly to me at a celebration ceremony. "This is a real achievement, yes?" Well, yes.

I had been told that the *Radio Times* office in London had scheduled my interview with Aznavour in Lyons. I was to fly from Orly Airport to Lyons, where I would be met by his representative. While waiting for my flight at Orly, I thought I should just check with my contact number to make sure someone would be waiting for me at the other end.

It was a good thing I called. Aznavour's people had not been told of my project and were not anticipating my arrival. As a matter of fact, they had no idea who I was.

I had two choices. One was to return to my Paris hotel and have another Perrier. The other was to be a real adventurer, to be like big game hunter and author Frank Buck of *Bring Them*

Back Alive fame. I decided I had nothing to lose. I was in a country in which I did not speak the language and knew nobody. What did it matter if I was in Lyons, Paris, or St. Tropez? I would fly to Lyons and, somehow, bring Charles Aznavour back alive – or, at least, his comments.

I flew to Lyons and went to my hotel. I figured the concierge would have a Lyonnaise equivalent of *Time Out*. He did; I found where Aznavour was playing, and asked for directions in sign language. I walked the mile or so to the venue and decided I would wait in the foyer until I saw someone who looked like his manager. After ten minutes or so I did see someone who looked like his manager, and it was. I explained my predicament – thank heaven he did speak English – and waited while he went backstage to ask Charles if he would see me. He returned to tell me that Aznavour had agreed to be interviewed during the interval. This huge star then earned his place in my all-time top ten of gratitude, for he gave me the entire interval, talking about the differences from his unique experience of entertaining French, English and American audiences.

Speaking from the perspective of someone who for years played to sold out houses in the UK and US as well as at home, he was convinced that it was the desire of French artists to adapt to English-language rock that had predestined their failure overseas.

"Chevalier was Chevalier, Piaf was Piaf," he said. "They were popular abroad because they were themselves, not because they were French. Now the emphasis is on groups and the sound of the record, not the songs. People are still imitating The Beatles. Why abandon a way of expression to jump on a bandwagon it will take a generation to assimilate?"

He excused himself for the second half of the show and, after receiving my profuse thanks, proceeded to knock out his audience, including myself, with first class versions of his hits including 'The Old Fashioned Way' and 'What Makes A Man'.

When I told my parents of what a gentleman this star had been, they told my father's three business partners, for they, like Aznavour, were all of Armenian descent. My stock suddenly went up in their eyes, because, I was told, whenever Charles visited New York, he was treated as a hero by the Armenian community, among which, I was also told, he had a reputation that was not explained for being a swordsman.

Aznavour was the artist who most impressed me during my survey of the French scene, but the record of the moment that grabbed me was 'Ça Plane Pour Moi' by Plastic Bertrand. My report on this fantastic plastic was its first English-language press.

"Originally a rock singer-songwriter," I wrote, "Patrick Bertrand was chosen to be the visual symbol for a record made by an ugly Belgium-based group. He changed his first name from Patrick to Plastic and posed for publicity photos eating McDonald's hamburgers, an act which may be declassé on the Right Bank but is hardly a punky gesture. Bertrand's top ten hit 'Ça Plane Pour Moi' comes complete with Beach Boys harmonies that would not befit a Sex Pistol."

I took the first opportunity I could to interview Plastic when he came to London. Told to go to a certain hotel room, I knocked on the door and was greeted by Bertrand himself wearing only a towel. He was obviously not ready for the interview.

I went back to the lobby and was met by his representative, who apologised for the delay and then said, for no apparent reason and in direct contravention of every known public relations convention, "Plastic is, how you say it, be sexual, you know."

I did know what it was to be "be sexual", but hadn't the foggiest notion why I had been told this. Perhaps bisexuality was considered a Belgian form of rebellion. Maybe I hadn't arrived too early at Plastic's room after all. At any rate, I thought it best not to pursue the topic. I was more interested in asking my new punk hero what his ambitions were.

"My ambition," Plastic Bertrand told me, "is to be my generation's Sinatra."

Of course, as Noel Edmonds' generation's Frost turned out to be Frost, Plastic Bertrand's Sinatra turned out to be Sinatra, and Plastic himself, a few years later, wound up . . . singing in the Eurovision Song Contest, and losing. It was a comedown from the glory days of 'Ça Plane Pour Moi', but it increased his chances of one day making it in the States.

13

But I Was In *Star Wars*

During the summer of 1976 Mike Stern, the outstanding pitcher on our Regent's Park Softball Club, asked me if he could invite one of his American friends to meet us at my apartment after a Sunday afternoon game. My Hyde Park Square flat would make a convenient rendezvous point. I agreed.

Mike explained to me that his friend Mark was an actor in a television western back in the States, but he really was a film buff who went to the movies all the time. After the game we returned to my place, where we were greeted by Mark. His friendly smile was infectious as he took a seat on my sofa and explained what he was doing in London.

"I'm here making a science-fiction movie," he said. And that was the last he said about the job, as he and Mike Stern began catching up on lost time.

I have never forgotten this episode because it seems to be the classic case of understatement in my life. Mark was Mark Hamill, "a science-fiction movie" turned out to be *Star Wars*, and his character was Luke Skywalker.

Director George Lucas's film opened the following year in the United States and, to Hollywood's surprise, was a success of historic dimensions. It took little brain power to realise it would duplicate its performance in Britain, so I managed to convince the powers-that-be at Radio 4's *Kaleidoscope* to allow me to prepare a special full-length edition about the phenomenon to tie in with its London premiere. Mark and Alec Guinness were among those who contributed generously to the programme.

Hamill spoke amusingly about the *Star Wars* dialogue.

"From Harrison's classic, 'It'll take a few moments for the navicomputer to calculate the co-ordinates' to Carrie's, 'I should have recognised your foul stench when you boarded the starship' right down to my, 'Gee, it's lucky you had these compartments' right after the compartments save our lives, I could almost feel the vegetables flying towards the screen. We were nervous because we couldn't see the vision as totally as George did.

" 'Who talks like this? Is it a joke, camp or what? Give us a break, guys!' And George wouldn't. George never sat down and said, here's the style of the film. He just wanted to see what you did."

Sir Alec was delighted with the company, but confessed to receiving some unusual mail.

"It's funny how people identify. Some of the letters seem to think that I personally am a Jedi knight, rather than a Knight of the British Empire, and they seem to think I have some sort of wisdom. I've even had a letter, a perfectly sane letter, saying, 'I wish to be a Jedi knight and I wish to come to outer space with you'.

"These give you pause. What do you write back? I write back and say I earn my living as an actor. I am at the present in the Queens Theatre."

Two years later, in 1979, I was queuing outside the Dominion Theatre in Tottenham Court Road for the press screening of *Alien*. Kenny Everett had already warned me that something horrible and unexpected was going to happen to the John Hurt character, so I was somewhat prepared for the shock that rocked the house. If you can imagine a cinema full of people watching *Alien* but unaware that the creature would make its first appearance by exploding out of Hurt's chest, you can understand how, at that moment in the movie, the Dominion was filled by screams and howls from critics and celebrities who had thought they had seen everything.

All the audience knew going in was that this picture had great word-of-mouth from the States. The invited crowd was pushing its way forward at the doors of the Dominion, anxious to get good seats.

Out of the corner of my eye I saw someone trying to get in via the door next to the one I was approaching. He was a dissolute young man, apparently a gatecrasher, who was being restrained by a bouncer. I thought, "That looks like Mark if he went to seed". The unlucky fellow then spoke in an out-of-it whine.

"But I was in *Star Wars*", he whinged. My God, it was Mark!

"That's alright," I said to the bouncer. "He's with me."

"If he's with you, it's OK," the bouncer said. I escorted Mark into the lobby. It turned out he was waiting for his girl friend, Marilou. She arrived and with one knowing glance took in the situation.

"Thank you, Paul," she said, and took Mark into the cinema.

There are four reasons this episode left a deep impression on me. One is that it demonstrated more clearly than any event in my life the fleetingness of fame. In a period of only three years, Hamill had gone from, "I'm here making a science-fiction movie" to being the lead character of the most successful film in box office history to whining, "But I was in *Star Wars*".

Not only was fame fleeting, it was relative. To the doorman who admitted us, I was the celebrity, not Mark. If he had known he was denying access to Luke Skywalker, he would have been horrified, but because this young man in everyday dress looked dishevelled, he did not recognise him. On the other hand, my appearance never varied wildly, and he did identify me.

There was a lesson for my own life. I should be grateful for a relatively low-key broadcasting career in which you enjoy a fulfilling life with career continuity but never make so much money that you can retire or indulge in excess.

And, not that I needed it, here was vivid evidence of the dangers of substance abuse. I am not saying I know what Mark had been ingesting earlier that day, but I am pretty sure it wasn't bacon and eggs.

Drugs have taken their toll amongst my friends ever since college. I have known too many dead people or walking wounded to think that most drugs are harmless pleasures. But although several recreational users of my acquaintance have fallen foul of drugs and drink, some have managed to rejoin the land of the living, and herein lies the happy ending of this story and, indeed, the purpose in its telling.

In 1997 the *Star Wars* trilogy was re-issued with spectacular box office results. Mark Hamill came to London and once again met the press in a series of interviews, this time not the fresh-faced actor but a living legend. Almost all the articles noted that he had enjoyed a successful long-time marriage to his wife Marilou and that they had raised three children. The excesses of youth, and the days of filming the two *Star Wars* sequels, were long behind him.

Although he had not done any further comparable work in movies, he had spent his time doing several things I quite admired, including starring in a Sam Fuller war film, acting on Broadway, and becoming an important voice-over artist. Close to my heart, he was writing his own comic book series, *Black Pearl*, which he intended to turn into a screenplay, and had on one never-to-be-repeated occasion been photographed with three founding fathers of the comic book superhero, Jerry Siegel [*Superman*], Bob Kane [*Batman*] and Jack Kirby [*Captain America* and most of the famous Marvel characters].

The public often assumes that a celebrity is unhappy if he is no longer as popular as he once was. In fact, it is precisely after the whirlwind that a man can gather his wits and settle down to a balanced and productive life. This Mark Hamill did. Thinking about the ambitious boy on my sofa and the accomplished man on a settee in a Park Lane hotel, I always smile.

Then I reach for my light sabre.

14

I Dance With Dame Edna

I danced with Dame Edna at Studio 54. Match that, disco wannabes, or even disco survivors. And there's more. Dame Edna didn't just honour me with a dance. She talked in the voice of Barry Humphries.

Studio 54 really was the ultimate Seventies disco. I would call it the Mecca of discos, except that a company called Mecca did have a chain of dance halls in Britain. Everyone who considered themselves a serious disco bunny made a pilgrimage to Steve Rubell's place in midtown Manhattan.

I always thought of being there as a visit to an intergalactic car wash. At certain carefully chosen moments, metal tubes would descend from the ceiling, lights would flash, and smoke would fill the floor. All that was missing was spraying water to give the full effect of a good polish and wax job.

My few visits to Studio 54 were all work-related. This meant my admission was guaranteed. I would not have to endure the ritual humiliation of being rejected at the door while far more famous and attractive people were invited to walk by, past and over me. Some New Yorkers didn't mind this treatment, thinking with some sort of demented logic that at least if they were forced to stand at the door for a couple of hours they would see a lot of stars walk by.

On the 4th of April, 1979, I went to Studio 54 in the company of *Kaleidoscope* producer John Boundy. We met and interviewed Steve Rubell himself for a programme about New York discos. Although self-confident, perhaps with reason, Rubell was gracious and polite. I warmed to him more than I did to the discotheque hostess Regine, who kept John and I waiting half an hour getting her hair done under the mistaken impression that the interview was for television, not radio.

The transfixing moment of this visit came when the disc jockey began a set with the title track of the new album by Sister Sledge, *We Are Family*. I had not yet heard this song; the single Sister Sledge had led with, 'He's The Greatest Dancer', was still in the charts. I was transfixed. The floor filled as rapidly as if free money had been thrown into the middle of it. On the loud Studio 54 sound system, the track sounded great. It sounded greater than great. It was anthemic. I couldn't wait to return to London to introduce *We Are Family* to the Radio 1 audience.

Memorable though that moment was, it was shared by the others in the club. My Dame Edna moment is far more personal. Elton John was hosting a party at Studio 54. I could write a book on Elton's generosity as a host and gift-giver through the years. Indeed, every year or two some publisher does ask me to write a book about Elton. But I am content to await his autobiography, and leave the subject of his life to him.

Barry Humphries had come to New York to do some promotion of his Dame Edna character. Housewife Superstar she may have been in Britain, but her campaign to conquer America was still in the strategy stage. She was being looked after by Nancy Lewis, the American representative of *Monty Python* and a friend of mine since she had worked as the press officer at Neil Bogart's Buddah Records.

What everyone who encounters Barry or Edna professionally learns immediately is that they are two separate people. Neither will use the first person in talking about the other, nor speak in the other's voice. To address one of them as if they do in fact inhabit the same body is to be intolerably rude.

Nancy, Dame Edna and I were in conversation with a New York-based gentleman when the Studio 54 disc jockey started his music set. Our speech was immediately drowned out. There was only one thing to do, dance. Our New York companion gestured to Dame Edna and I and shouted, "Why don't you have a dance?"

The suggestion probably struck the Australian celebrity as the height of folly. Dancing with Gambaccini at Studio 54 was probably not in the top 1000 on the list of things she had hoped to do in the city. Nonetheless, Dame Edna lifted her head and threw her shoulders back with a look of carefree resignation as we boogied to something. Whatever it was, it wasn't 'We Are Family'.

When the song was over, so was the joke. Edna wanted out. A hard day lay ahead.

"What time should I call in the morning, Nancy?" she asked in her soprano voice.

Soprano is not a range to use if one wants to be heard over loud pumping disco music. The question did not transmit beyond my ears, and to Nancy Lewis it must have appeared that Dame Edna was making an unsuccessful attempt to mime to the music.

Soprano was out. Barry Humphries' voice was in.

"What time should I call in the morning, Nancy?" Dame Edna asked in Barry's deep voice.

Neither Nancy nor I was prepared for this. Linda Blair speaking in Mercedes McCambridge's demonic tones had nothing on this shocker. Nancy kept calm and made arrangements with Dame Edna, who then disappeared into the midnight madness of midtown Manhattan.

"Have you ever heard that before?" I asked Nancy.

"No. No one has that I know of," Nancy shook her head. "That was strange. Very strange."

Over the course of the two decades that followed, I laughed on many occasions at the wit and spontaneity of Dame Edna, one of the great comic creations of our time. But I never again danced with her, nor heard her speak in a man's voice.

The original Studio 54 is gone, though it is soon to be reopened. Steve Rubell is gone, never to return. Edna and I dance on only in my dreams.

15

I Nearly Poison Elton

When, after four years of preparation, *The Guinness Book Of British Hit Singles* was published in 1977, its quartet of co-authors promptly forgot about it. We had it to refer to, which is the reason we had written it.

Ten months later, I happened to spot the Top Ten book chart in *The Sunday Times*. To my astonishment, we were number six in non-fiction. No one from the publisher had told us the book was selling, nor that it had been reprinted. Because the initial run had been a modest ten thousand, we had no sense the project was a commercial one.

The following week we were number four. Suddenly *Hit Singles* was Big News. Guinness asked if we would prepare a second edition. So began a sequence that teamed me with the Rice brothers for thirty-one volumes, many of them with Mike Read, both widening the wallet and keeping me from producing several other tomes that went unwritten. You can't have it both ways.

The new edition would include two new years of chart material, an updated statistical section, and fresh photos. It also needed a different cover. One of us thought it would be great to get a photo of chart stars through the years assembled as in a family reunion. Since no such picture existed, we had to organise it.

We planned a lunch at a function house in Belgrave Square. Each of us invited a few artists of our acquaintance. Looking back I'm amused to see that most of my invitees were the youngest artists present – Kate Bush, Bob Geldof, Billy Idol,

Elton John and Tom Robinson. Though I never realised it at the time, I was once on the cutting edge. That sharpness has now dulled.

What made the event work as a social event was not that it had several artists from the same generation, but that it cut across the age barriers that usually separate pop stars. I was thrilled to see older and younger artists meeting each other for the first time, and with mutual respect.

"If my mother knew Johnnie Ray was here and I didn't get his autograph, she'd never forgive me," fan and dutiful son Elton John remarked as he headed off to get a signature. Bob Geldof asked for and received an introduction to Vera Lynn, and the two got on famously.

So did old pals Johnny and Vera. "How are you, Johnnie?" the Sweetheart of the Forces asked the Prince of Wails with affection.

"I'd go anywhere to see Dame Vera," Ray said in explaining his attendance.

New friendships were made, too. Elton and Tom met outside the building, John in a limousine and Robinson on a motorbike, became friends and subsequently wrote a couple of songs together. (One of the compositions, 'Sartorial Eloquence', required a name change to '[Sartorial Eloquence] Don't Ya Wanna Play This Game No More?' when released as a single by Elton's record company in the United States, on their assumption that American radio listeners were such mental midgets they would understand the meaning of neither "sartorial" nor "eloquence".)

In between making introductions and facilitating conversations, the Rice brothers, Mike Read and I exchanged glances that said volumes. "It's working" and "Thank God" were the two phrases our eyes spoke most eloquently. Champagne flowed, seafood pancakes were consumed, and all the artists stayed at least long enough to be in John Timbers' photograph.

The final line-up shows Jonathan King in his multi-coloured

fright wig standing in the top row next to Kate Bush, Danny Williams, Elton John and Cliff Richard. At the time I wished Jonathan would remove his rainbow afro, but I now realise that if he had the result might have been even more terrifying. Standing in the second row were Paul Jones, Billy Idol, Tom Robinson, Mike d'Abo, Russ Conway, Hank Marvin, and Johnny Moore and two of his Drifters. Seated below them were Craig Douglas, the triple threat line-up of Bob Geldof, Vera Lynn and Johnnie Ray, another Drifter and Errol Brown. The unassigned seating positions made it appear as if the Hot Chocolate leader had become the latest of the many members of the Drifters. Sitting at ground level were Carl Wayne, David Whitfield, Dave Dee and Joe Brown. Looking facially flushed in the photographs, the legendary 'Cara Mia' singer Whitfield passed away within eighteen months.

Like the overgrown schoolboys we were, Jo, Mike, Tim and I were thrilled we had managed to convene a unique group of stars for the cover of our second edition. One day later, that pleasure turned to horror.

I was walking out of Broadcasting House when I saw the front page of an early edition of the *Evening Standard*. Elton John had been taken to a Harley Street hospital with a mystery malady! The photo on the front page made him look really rough.

I was of course upset that my chum was poorly. But I had an even greater dread. What if his illness were food poisoning? What if he had been felled by the seafood pancakes we had served the previous day? What if those seemingly delightful salmon-whatever concoctions were actually loaded with salmonella?

I had pictures of Britain's leading pop stars passing out all over the country. There goes Vera Lynn, brought down to earth not by Nazis but by Gambaccini, Rice, Rice and Read. Look out below, Cliff and Hank, the latest Cliff-and-a-Shadow reunion ruined by gruesome grub. Bombs away, Geldof, Idol and Robinson, the New Wave crashing on the beach with some dodgy fish.

What was the penalty for the mass murder of a nation's most beloved musical legends? At the very least, this was a bad career move.

There has never been another day on which I have purchased more than one edition of the *Evening Standard*, but I was among the first to buy the next print of the paper. In the updated story it was reported that Elton had collapsed from overwork, stress and too much tennis, having played for hours with Billy Jean King. There was no mention of food poisoning. Hooray! So much for exercise being good for you and pancakes bad. Elton was recovering and would be fine, and I could exhale for the first time in hours.

To launch *Hits Of The Seventies* the following year the GRRR team held a pop star party sponsored by the Rt. Hon. Norman St. John Stevas in the Members Dining Room of the House of Commons, and for *Number One Hits* we convened a mighty crew at Abbey Road Studios. Both events were extremely memorable, yet for the life of me I can't remember what we ate. I do know that we didn't serve seafood pancakes.

16

Tony Blackburn Shows Me

When I came to England as an Oxford University student in 1970 I was denied an audition at BBC Radio Oxford on the grounds that I was an American who, if employed, would take the job of a Briton. I was devastated. While at Dartmouth College in rural Hanover, New Hampshire, I had been General Manager of WDCR and the top-rated DJ in the tiny Tri-Town area of Hanover, the strangely-named Lebanon, New Hampshire, and the even more strangely-named White River Junction, Vermont.

I couldn't appreciate why I wasn't even allowed to test for a show at Radio Oxford. I concentrated on writing for *Rolling Stone* while at Univ. In 1973 Radio 1 producer John Walters asked me to do a ten-minute talk, an American look at the scene, on a new programme he was starting, *Rockspeak*. Soon I was supplementing my weekly feature with interviews. I was the youngest regular Radio 1 ever had until Keith Chegwin took the title in the Eighties as co-presenter of *Junior Choice*.

In 1975, I was offered my own American hits show. I was tremendously grateful to Walters for my initial opportunity, to producer Stuart Grundy, who had supported me during the interim, and Radio 1 Executive Producer Teddy Warrick, who backed me for my own big break. Oddly, my predominant reaction was not one of glee, but of relief. Although I loved writing for *Rolling Stone* and enjoyed *Rockspeak*, which after one year changed name to *Rock Week*, my primary ambition was to host a chart show as I had done on WDCR. To me, the American hits on Radio 1 was the Tri-Town Top 25 writ large. I had no idea of the social role Radio 1 played in the country, nor how to almost all other presenters a job on the station represented, not a return to normal service, but an ascent to the pinnacle of the profession.

Tony Blackburn put it all into perspective for me. We were at one of the Radio 1 Race Days at Brand's Hatch. I had absolutely no interest in motor sport. To me it was another of those activities, like boxing, in which the primary objective was not to win but to survive. I could never understand why enthusiasts seemed shocked when a driver bought the farm, since by getting into the car in the first place he had surely made his down payment.

Nonetheless, there were racing enthusiasts in the Radio 1 management and, perhaps crucially, two of my famous colleagues, Noel Edmonds and the Emperor Rosko, were supporters. So every year the whole gang trudged out to Brand's Hatch and waited in the Grovewood hospitality suite for the Radio 1 event.

One year, as we stood around morosely awaiting our turn, Kid Jensen surveyed the scene.

"I have come to the realisation," he announced, "that the Grovewood suite is the only reality in life. The remaining 364 days of the year are a fantasy."

He had it exactly right. No matter what we had done since the last race day, whatever the developments in our individual careers, it all came back to the same spot every year. All things changed save the Grovewood suite, which remained the same.

When it came time for our vehicular performance, we paired off and went to assigned points on the race course. Each twosome was to travel to the next point on the course riding some unusual form of transport. A gold disc, rather than a baton, was passed among team members.

The first year in which I participated, I was placed on the most remote part of the course with Anne Nightingale. This was fine by me. We were to race each other on children's

97

scooters. If I had to be seen to be an idiot, at least I would be so tiny to the audience that I could not be identified.

It was the following year that I learned the significance of the team I had joined. The race began with Tony Blackburn and I drawn on donkeys by Dave Lee Travis and Noel Edmonds. Dave and Noel would proceed with the second portion of the race while Tony and I walked back to the last leg of the course, which we would complete on bouncing beach balls.

Everything began as to plan. Noel was an excellent donkey puller, and our side got off to a quick lead. We maintained it until the very end. I got handed my gold disc before Tony, and started bouncing away.

It hurt. I wasn't prepared for this. My previous experience with beach balls had reasonably enough been limited to the beach. No one had warned me that when you are sitting on one bouncing down tarmac it is you, not the ball, that gives. Each bounce hurt where it counts. Still, duty called, and I hopped away. The race, the pain, the embarrassment, would be over soon.

Sooner than I thought. Blackburn decided to do something it had not occurred to me to do. He played to the crowd. It was a crowd, too, in its many thousands. Radio 1 events in the Seventies regularly drew huge throngs; on a day when we played a charity football match at Roker Park in Sunderland, we outdrew over half the Second Division.

After a few bounces on his large ball, which were obviously as unpleasant to him as my hops were to me, Tony realised he was never going to catch up. The race had effectively been decided before it even got to the last leg. Therefore, to spice it up, to lessen the anguish of every agonising thud on the tarmac, and to play to his image, he would cheat. Tony Blackburn got off his ball, picked it up and ran with it.

For a few foolish seconds I thought the audience would hoot such unsportsmanlike behaviour. On the contrary. They cheered. I looked to my left and saw a sight I had never imagined and would always remember. Thousands of people were going wild at the sight of me bouncing on an inflatable rubber ball, with a grown man running past me holding his own giant sphere. My film hero James Cagney had starred as a racing driver in Howard Hawks' 1932 film *The Crowd Roars*. Now I was on the racetrack and the crowd was roaring for real.

Blackburn crossed the finish line first, on foot. The audience went mad for another ninety seconds or so. We all went back to the Grovewood suite and within a few minutes forgot which sides we had raced on.

But I remembered Tony and his brazen behaviour. That such a large group of presumably representative British citizens, not inmates of an institution on day release, could care so passionately about something so inherently inane informed me better than any listening figures what an intimate part of UK life the Radio 1 DJs had become. Blackburn had played the occasion precisely correctly. He knew his fans were not there to see a conventional race played by the book. They could come to Brand's Hatch any day of the sporting year to see that. These paying customers – they had paid, they had not been forced to march to the course at gunpoint! – wanted to have some Fun, with a capital F, and Tony had provided it. I had been his straight man, the Wise to his Morecambe, but I was no less part of the act for it.

And so I came to realise the social importance of the radio station I had joined. None of us knew or could possibly have known that we were there at its peak, that within twenty years its listenership would dwindle to about one third its mid-Seventies size. We were just doing our jobs, going along for the ride.

On the final Brand's Hatch occasion it was a terrifying ride. The last leg of the relay was to be contested by Noel and Rosko, the two genuine enthusiasts amongst us, not on gimmicky vehicles but in real race cars. What was more, all of the

DJ competitors were to be human batons. We were each to be picked up along our points on the course by our speed-loving captains.

What was perhaps an amusing fancy on paper turned out to be an exercise in horror for the less confident amongst us. What no executive had planned was that Edmonds and the Emperor were going to take this one seriously. Given racing cars, they actually went fast, not as fast as the cars could go, but quickly enough to cause some dreadful damage had there been a collision.

By the time Rosko picked me up at the last leg of the course, he and Noel were in furious competition. I just piled in the car on top of Anne Nightingale. There were no social niceties nor seatbelts here. This was the closest encounter I ever had with another Radio 1 DJ. Rosko and Noel were racing to the finish line, and the rest of the station's presenters were so much human cargo, a twisted mass of flesh without form. There is something unpleasant about going at speed rolled into a ball on top of another person. The thousands of screaming spectators loved it, of course. To them, Noel Edmonds and the Emperor Rosko were daredevil heroes.

A few of us protested afterwards that this time things had gotten out of hand, that the race day had actually turned into a race, and that we were lucky to have all gotten off the track without incident. We might not have put a down payment on the farm, but we had certainly glanced at the prospectus.

The Radio 1 executives had to face a thought that had never occurred to them. They had almost wiped out the DJs. If things didn't turn out so well next time, they might have to find a presenter tree from which to pluck a dozen new announcers.

That was it. There were no more Brand's Hatch race days. The other 364 days of the year became our reality, and the Grovewood suite Kid Jensen's nightmare.

But amongst the blue plaques of my career, one is placed,

like a speed bump, on the last leg of the Brand's Hatch course. It is where Tony Blackburn made me realise that what we were doing was not just personally satisfying. It played a part in the social network of the nation. I have tried to behave responsibly ever since.

Tony, of course, is still running with the inflatable oversized beach ball.

17

To Israel For Eurovision

After my trip to Paris to preview the Eurovision Song Contest in 1978, *Radio Times* suggested I follow it the next year by going to the 1979 host country, Israel. They did not have to ask twice. Paris was a mere channel-hop away, the type of trip I could undertake from London both at a moment's notice and on a shoestring budget. Israel was not the type of place visited on either whim or an empty wallet. And so, in January 1979, I joined photographer Kim Sayer in journeying to Jerusalem.

Israel is not a country in which you can write an article, whatever the subject, in ignorance of the greater story around you. The first paragraph of my finished piece put my profession in perspective:

> It is 10 a.m. My *Radio Times* colleague and I are trying to
> get to the Tel Aviv headquarters of the Israeli Broadcasting
> Authority. It isn't that we can't find the building; we have,
> but the entire premises are surrounded by a seven-foot
> fence topped by two feet of barbed wire. We walk around
> the fence until we reach a guard with a machine gun. This
> is the entrance. Our contact meets us and takes us to the
> IBA canteen. Twenty yards away from the machine gun
> and the barbed wire, this radio staff, like any radio staff, is
> taking tea, discussing internal political intrigues, and
> complaining about being underpaid.

By the end of our brief visit, we were not just observers but participants in the never-ending struggle for security and sanity in Israel.

It is 10 p.m. and my *Radio Times* colleague and I are
taking a short cut from the old city to our hotel. What
looked on the map like residential streets are in fact
shabby stretches of deserted garages and derelict
warehouses. My colleague remarks in the near total
darkness that taking this route in hostile times would be
asking for trouble.

These are hostile times. A spotlight shines on us, and as
we walk forward we realise the spotlight is moving with us.
Without saying a word to each other we agree to keep
walking the deathly quiet street as if we were still on a
casual stroll. The sound that breaks the silence is a sharp
exclamatory *phhhetoo*. In the moment it takes me to learn
whether it is the sound of gunfire or a practical joker, I do
not care whether Izhar Cohen deserves to be a pop star. It
seems unimportant whether Matti Caspi ever has
international success.

When no impact followed the *phhhetoo*, Kim Sayer and I
heard a soldier laughing on top of one of the deserted
garages. He had found his own way to combat the curious
combination of stress and boredom that comes from having to
always be prepared to shoot somebody but never be allowed to
shoot anybody. He pretended to kill strangers, in the middle
of the night, deriving amusement and release from their fear.

A seasoned surveyor of the scene might wonder what on
earth we were doing walking at night down a deserted drive in
Jerusalem. The answer, quite literally, is that we were walking at night. In London I had become accustomed to being
able to go anywhere on foot without fear. This was a marvellous freedom, a great joy to someone from New York City
indoctrinated not to venture into Central Park after sunset,
and it did not occur to me to give it up on a mere junket to
Jerusalem.

In fact, Sayer and I strolled around the entire city. Everything that had ever happened here to help shape three of the world's great religions had occurred long before the invention of the motor car. If you wanted to get a feel of what it was like to walk in Christ's footsteps, you had to do just that, walk the streets on which He had trod. And so, on a moonlit January night, we did just that.

Reporter and photographer walked the streets of the old city. With the exception of a few juvenile Hasidim we encountered as we began our tour, we saw no one else out of doors. It was about ten o'clock. I figured that, although the eight degrees Centigrade temperature was balmy for a January night in London, it was cold for Jerusalem, and everyone was staying warm indoors. It did not enter my mind that perhaps some people had no desire to risk violent death for the sake of a moonlight stroll.

Sayer and I walked the cobbled stones of the Via Dolorosa. This was the very route travelled by Christ as he carried his cross to his own Crucifixion. Despite the cool temperature, I reached the verge of sweating as we navigated the slightly uphill slope.

"I can understand how difficult this must have been," I said. "I'm not carrying anything, and I'm finding it a challenge."

"I know," agreed my struggling colleague. "Jesus!"

We stopped on the spot. Kim was appalled by what he had just inadvertently said, and he looked to the sky.

"I didn't mean it!" he cried. "I didn't mean it!"

I could not believe it: a man had taken the name of Jesus Christ in vain on the very route He had taken to his death. On a one-to-ten scale of sacrilege, this had to be at least a nine. I can report that He is very forgiving, for Kim Sayer was not struck by lightning, nor was I hit by an errant bolt.

We continued our journey, sobered by the deep significance of the road we were on. We reached the Church of the Holy Sepulchre, the site of Christ's entombment and Resurrection. As we stood silently for a few moments, I felt smaller than I have ever felt in my whole life, and not only because we are all humbled when contrasted with a religious figure. What did or did not happen on this spot had affected the future course of human civilisation as few events had approached doing. The fate of billions of lives and scores of nations had hinged on what was said to have taken place here, and yet, at this moment, Kim Sayer and I were the only two people present. We were alive, yet minuscule, dwarfed by the past of this place. It had been five minutes since my photographer had not been struck by a lightning bolt; this was the moment of my life when I most feared I might be smote for audacity, just for daring to stand there.

Two very sober foreigners returned to their hotel. We played cards before retiring. Sayer drew a bad hand and cursed.

"Jerusalem!" he exclaimed.

This really was unbelievable: he had done it twice in one night! At the horror of invoking the name of the very city in which he sat, he again asserted aloud that it was all coincidental.

Here was proof that Jerusalem was the geographical equivalent of *Hamlet*. Shakespeare's play now reads like a collection of familiar quotations, so many lines have entered the language, and the people and places of Jerusalem have done the same. For example, the BBC wall at which record promotion men looked at posted running orders to see if their songs had been played on Radio 1 was known in the trade as The Wailing Wall. Social clubs around the world have had their Last Suppers. Celebrities who get a rough deal in the press are said to have been crucified.

No disrespect to any religion is meant by the familiar use of these terms. And, in Jerusalem, no ill will is meant by the unavoidable mixture of the sacred and profane, because here the sacred is the everyday of long ago. I was being given a tour of the town by the top Israeli disc jockey, Avi Etgar. He had his station, Radio C, on the car radio.

"Oh, and there's the grave of the Virgin Mary," he pointed out nonchalantly. 'Hit Me With Your Rhythm Stick' by Ian Dury and the Blockheads was playing. The juxtaposition was jarring, but Etgar was utterly unphased. This was his home, and these absurdities occurred every day.

Avi Etgar was a great Kenny Everett fan. He had a chance to hear British radio for a year when recuperating in Putney from a serious road accident. His fast-paced programme was considered the country's best. In another surreal mix of past and present, Radio C operated in the late Haile Selassie's Jerusalem retreat. The estate of the former Emperor of Ethiopia was kept in top condition in case the Israeli Broadcasting Authority should ever have to return it, although to whom was debatable.

Etgar was a generous host who typified the Israeli radio and record people I encountered. They knew enough of their profession to realise they were unlikely to reach the international audience their more conveniently situated peers took for granted.

"I was the top producer in Israel. So?" shrugged Zvika Kagan backstage at the Hall of the Nation, where the Israeli Song Festival to select the country's Eurovision entry was about to occur. "When you make it in Hebrew, there's nowhere else to go. I had dreamt for nine years of breaking out of the Israeli market, and Sherry was my chance."

Sherry was a disco singer whom Kagan and songwriter Rony Weiss had perform in English.

"Hebrew does not fit disco at all," Weiss explained. "It sounds ridiculous, more middle-of-the-road. With a Hebrew lyric, you are more conscious of the meaning of words. The song is more personal."

Kagan and Weiss hoped that with an English lyric and disco beat listeners abroad might not notice Sherry's foreign accent. They invested their personal savings in their project.

"We gave Sherry a really huge production compared to the usual Israeli production," Kagan remembered. "We thought 5,000 LPs sold would be very nice. We wound up selling 15,000 and made the disco charts with 'Let's Go Wild' in Brazil, Britain and Spain."

Bless them. A sale of 15,000 would drive British stars to despair, but in Israel it was an achievement. In 1979 a gold disc was awarded for 20,000 sales. With so little profit available for promotion and reinvestment compared to the receipts obtained by multi-million selling British and American stars, it is no wonder that the Israeli stars whose work I encountered in Jerusalem in 1979 toiled without recognition in the UK and US. You will not have posted pin-ups of teen idol Svika Pick, you will not have been moved by the ballads of Hebrew singer Matti Caspi, and you will not have rebelled to the anthem 'Get Off My Television' by punk rocker Rami Fortis.

All of this makes the achievement of Izhar Cohen, the first Israeli to win the Eurovision Song Contest, more remarkable. Izhar was upset that in England he didn't get much airplay, especially on Capital Radio, that he wasn't allowed on *Top Of The Pops,* and that Terry Wogan made fun of his Contest winner "A-Ba-Ni-Bi" on air. But his countrymen realised the magnitude of what he had done. He had achieved what was impossible.

Until the following year. After I had returned from a trip to Tel Aviv, giving a lift in my taxi to none other than Izhar Cohen, whom I had encountered by chance in his manager's office, I went back to the rehearsals at the Hall of the Nation. I entered the auditorium and was dumbstruck.

"This is the winner," I thought. No, knew. Whoever was singing whatever it was they were singing had distilled the quintessential Eurovision ballad.

I went over to Hanoch Hassan, Israeli television's Head of Variety. I recognised him from my original *Radio Times* description:

Of moderate height and build, he is slightly balding but
old enough to have gone completely hairless if it ever was
going to come to that. He paces the stage like a nervous
coach on the sidelines of an American football game. He
claps his hands, he clasps his hands, he points and rotates
to speak as if his feet were wheels.

Hassan, who was more courteous and helpful to me than a
man with the nation's most important entertainment broadcast of the year to worry about had any cause to be, saw my
shock.

"Milk and Honey," he said. " 'Hallelujah'. It's good."

Good enough to win both the Israeli Song Festival and the
Eurovision Song Contest. Good enough to reach the top five
of the British charts.

Not good enough to do the same in America, where Steve
Lawrence and Eydie Gorme released a cover version of 'Hallelujah' under the pseudonyms Parker and Penny, and got to
number 49 in the Adult Contemporary chart. Like the Eurovision Song Contest itself, Milk and Honey went unheralded in
the United States. Such is the difference between being a big
fish in a small pond and a piece of plankton in the ocean.

Any British or American star suffering from a loss of career
perspective should spend a few days in Israel studying the fate
of his fellows. There a major artist's complete career sales
would equal those of one successful album by an international
hitmaker. And in Israel bullets are not symbols of upward
chart movement in *Billboard* magazine. They are projectiles to
be dodged by civilians or imagined by bored soldiers shining
spotlights, not on a stage, but on lost pedestrians late at night.

18

I Keep Liz And Burton Together

Unlike many of my disc jockey colleagues at Radio 1, I did not appear professionally at occasions like village fetes and birthday parties. There was a reason they would that went beyond the merely financial. Because there were so few radio outlets in Britain on which DJs could get on-air experience, would-be broadcasters made do in alternative situations.

Foremost of these was the discotheque. Several men, and the performers were all male at this time, excelled in spinning records for dancers in nightclubs. In the Nineties, it would be a mortal offence in most clubs for disc jockeys to abandon the segue and start talking, but in the Seventies, before mixing and scratching became commonplace, it was expected the music man would speak between every record or pair of records. Some DJs, like Emperor Rosko, became as famous for their live work as for their radio programmes, playing a scorching soul selection too torrid for the airwaves, while performers like Dave Lee Travis were noted for the entertainment value of their act.

Whenever the Radio 1 team made an ensemble charity appearance, I watched my colleagues with a great sense of distance. Why combine the introduction of records with competitions like seeing which of three contestants could drink a pint of lager quickest, or seeing which blindfolded young man could identify his girl friend from three mystery kissers? I had grown up with no reference point for this combination of duties. My DJ heroes Dan Ingram and B. Mitchell Reid were on the radio, not the dancefloor, and Dick Clark confined his platter patter to television.

Yet, in Britain, on-stage stunts were de rigueur for disc jockeys. One colleague who became one of television's highest-paid stars brought the house down by bringing three couples on stage and asking the women to remove pairs of shorts worn over the trousers of their boy friends, using only their teeth. This style of stunt was phenomenally popular in the discos of the land, and Radio 1 DJs earned many hundreds of pounds for an hour of playing records and conducting competitions. Our most famous workmate electrified us with his claim that he wouldn't get out of bed for less than £1000.

We didn't even spin the discs ourselves, letting the house jockey play in the songs of our choice. This was not considered a menial task by the local announcer. The culture decreed it was an honour for would-be national figures to serve as Robins to our Batmen.

Seven hundred and fifty pounds an hour plus a boost to the ego! Too bad that era passed away. Pass it did, of course, done in by the growth of local radio, which demystified the disc jockey, sophisticated turntable technology, which made live DJing an art rather than a sideline, and extended dance mixes, which made frequent chatter intrusive.

I never felt motivated to develop an in person act. I even dreaded so-called "outside broadcasts", shows done on location, because in these situations acknowledgement had to be made of the physical surroundings and the people in attendance. It was impossible to retain the tightness of a studio show.

On only one occasion did I agree to be the DJ at a birthday party. I cannot think of any member of my profession who would have passed up this opportunity. I was asked if I would play records at Elizabeth Taylor's fiftieth birthday party.

I received this invitation because the event was going to be held at Legend's nightclub in London, where I was a frequent early evening visitor. Campbell Palmer, owner of the club, treated it like his front room, acting as a perfect host to his show business friends. His generosity was legendary. On one occasion, the disc jockey Mike Read informed him that he would no longer be able to visit weeknights. He was about to begin a stint on the Radio 1 breakfast show which would require him to leave his Surrey home early in the morning.

"That's no problem," London property magnate Palmer replied. "I'll give you a flat."

Mike's expression evolved from incredulity to regret to conviction before he stated, "Thank you, Campbell, but I can't accept that." You'll get no more selflessness from a Pope.

Elizabeth Taylor had by the time of her fiftieth birthday transcended celebrity and become an icon. For most of us who work in show business and the media, it is necessary to have a current project to stay in the public eye. A few great artists compile a body of work so impressive they need never work again to remain popular. Then there is a very small group of individuals who become famous for being themselves. It may even be difficult for younger persons to determine how these people, who range from Quentin Crisp to Zsa Zsa Gabor, became well known in the first place. But well known they are, and cruise through their later years without any evidence of effort in extending their limitless shelf life.

How many people are known around the world by only three letters, one less than Cher and two fewer than Sting? Liz is internationally renowned strictly for being Liz. The days of being recognised as a child actress in *Jane Eyre* or *Lassie Come Home* or as an Oscar-winning adult have long passed. Now she is the eternal beauty who has survived multiple marriages, life-threatening illnesses and fluctuations in weight. Elizabeth Taylor is 'I Will Survive' on two legs, an inspiration to all women that they can outlive bad relationships and bad health and become a philanthropist in the process.

The only two instructions I was given for her birthday music concerned two of her marriages. I was told she would enjoy hearing the theme of *Around The World In 80 Days*, the film produced by much-loved husband Mike Todd, who was killed in a plane crash. The only record I was forbidden to play was 'Tammy' by Debbie Reynolds, whose husband Eddie Fisher briefly became Taylor's spouse.

I was to play easy listening music for dinner and then disco music for dancing. This was no hardship for me, as I rarely got a chance to play my favourites in either category on my American chart show on Radio 1. I loaded the discs into the promotional shoulder bags provided by various record companies – they had a use after all! – and drove down to Old Burlington Street, parking near Legends before guests or press arrived.

Ah yes, the press. This was not just Elizabeth Taylor's fiftieth birthday, this was the occasion of one of her public reunions with Richard Burton. They were the marital equivalent of Simon and Garfunkel or the Everly Brothers. Lovers, partners, siblings, whatever the relationship, these people could neither live apart nor together. Their lives were a never-ending approach-avoidance conflict. The media treated each of their reunions as an event of earth-shattering importance.

I did not have to be told that Taylor and Burton had arrived. I could tell from the flashbulbs of the assembled paparazzi. The level of light outside Legends rose not just dramatically but hysterically. This was not the mere taking of photographs. This was the explosion of the sun. I wondered how celebrities like this couple, periodically subjected to such unnatural brightness, avoided damage to their vision.

The party was tasteful. The guests actually appeared to be friends of the host, and good food was served in generous proportions. I was touched by the amusing option of bangers and mash, one of Elizabeth's favourites.

I kept to my brief and played middle of the road classics during dinner. Sure enough, the guest of honour appeared pleased when 'Around the World' was played. I was amused to notice a middle-aged actor lip synching the words to Perry Como's 'Magic Moments' while his younger companion looked completely baffled. I did not spin 'Tammy'.

The dancing selection began with what was at that time an appropriate opener for an up-tempo section, 'Start Me Up' by The Rolling Stones. The next one I put on was 'Boogie Wonderland' by Earth Wind and Fire. I carry in my mind a mental snapshot of Tony Bennett momentarily looking disconcerted at the prospect of disco dancing. Like a good sport, he shrugged his shoulders and gave it a go.

All was proceeding happily, guests smiling and records not skipping, when word was sent to me in my control booth that Richard Burton thought the music was too loud and I was to turn it down. I obliged, feeling that any instruction of his must also represent the wishes of Elizabeth Taylor.

I was wrong. A few moments later, I received a message from another emissary that the hostess wanted the volume turned back up.

This I did. Ten minutes on, I was told to come downstairs and see Mr. Burton.

He was furious. He hated disco.

"If you don't turn this down now," he roared, "I'm leaving."

That's the only thing he ever said to me.

I've often marvelled at the tangential intersection of two otherwise completely separate lives. I have touched for five seconds the life of a woman in New York, who bumped into me at the intersection of 57th Street and 2nd Avenue and yelled, "You big fucking horse!". I met a Frenchwoman in the middle of a Paris crossing for one second, during which she burped. That was all the two of us shared in our entire lives, a burp. I once bumped head-on into a woman in the busy lobby of a building on Park Avenue. We both backed off, she smiled, and we moved in our different directions, ending my three-second acquaintance with Jacqueline Onassis.

And the only intersection my life had with Richard Burton's was his shouting, "If you don't turn the music down now, I'm leaving."

I dare say that would have made the sun of flashbulbs explode again. I had a terrific responsibility now – to adjust the music to a level that would please both the party girl and her erstwhile husband. I did not want to bear the onus for causing yet another break-up between the world's most famous living couple. What did Gambaccini do with his life? Oh yeah, he was the guy who broke up Elizabeth Taylor and Richard Burton by blasting him out of her birthday party.

I rose, or sank, to the occasion, and found a suitable volume that pleased them both. They left the club together, though they never again remarried. And I got a classy thank you letter personally signed by the hostess, remarkable evidence of her thoughtfulness to those even outside her inner circle.

I would have further reason to be an Elizabeth Taylor fan when she became a tireless fundraiser in the fight against AIDS, but I became an admirer as of the evening of her birthday party. Behind the icon was a human being with class. I'm glad I kept Liz and Burton together, if only for that night.

19

Sting Makes Me Feel Fat

I first met Sting one autumn afternoon in 1978. I had been having lunch with my friend Alan McGee of the promotions department of A&M Records and had returned to the company offices in New King's Road to play table tennis with him. I thought that by consulting my 1978 diary I could find the precise date of the encounter, but I find to my considerable embarrassment that I had lunch with Alan at Pomegranates on 10 October, lunch in the Broadcasting House area on the 26th and dinner at the Greenhouse on the 30th. We followed this with another lunch on the 9th of November and a Thanksgiving meal at Joe Allen's on the afternoon of the 23rd. We were joined by Mike Read on the first day of December and had a Christmas lunch for two on the 20th.

The above reconstruction of My Dinners With Alan only goes to show that 1) McGee and I were great pals 2) The A&M expense account runneth over, or at least did in 1978, and 3) People in the music business used to eat lunch. I can't imagine now how I could possibly find the time to go to the West End for a lunch of ninety minutes' duration and then journey to near Putney Bridge to play ping pong in the middle of a working day. Maybe because I was still under thirty and building my career contacts, or maybe because the social interaction between the record and broadcasting fields was highly developed, the boundaries between work and play merged. I certainly felt no guilt about playing ping pong with Alan McGee.

If I had to pick one of those dates for my introduction to

Sting it would be 9 November, because by that time the second single by Police, the group of which he was lead singer and bass player, had failed to crack the top 40. 'Can't Stand Losing You' had entered the chart the week of 7 October and peaked at 42. This was a better showing than that of the trio's first single, the complete flop 'Roxanne', but it was hardly anything to either write home about or, more to the point, justify A&M's considerable promotional expenditure.

As Alan and I walked down the corridor to the table tennis room we passed a crisis meeting between the Police (Sting, Andy Summers and Stewart Copeland) and the label's managing director, Derek Green. They were having a post mortem on the flopola of 'Can't Stand Losing You'. I will always remember Green's admonition to the Police concerning A&M's top American duo: "I never want to hear you criticise the Carpenters, because it's the money we've earned from them that we're spending on you."

I had never thought about the ways of the music-making world this way before, but it made perfect sense. A record company makes profits from the sales of its hit groups and spends part of them launching new acts. In this show business equivalent of *The Lion King*'s 'Circle of Life', the established artists nourish the newcomers. A slight irony is that it is the veterans whom the rookies will criticise in the press to acquire a rebellious image. Heaven, and A&M's accountants, know how many young performers were launched in the Eighties using money made from the Police.

This was all in the future when Sting, Andy and Stewart huddled with Derek Green on, shall we say, 9 November, 1978. (A check of their individual diaries might provide an exact date, as well as a listing of how many times Derek had lunch with Alan McGee.) It turned out, of course, that the career salvation for the Police would not come from Great Britain at all, but from the United States. It was on their tour there in the spring of 1979 that 'Roxanne' made a slow climb to number 32 on the *Billboard* Hot 100, moving the début album *Outlandos D'Amour* to 23 and finally jump-starting both single and LP in the UK charts.

During this tour I saw the group play the Bottom Line in New York. Backstage after the show, Sting gave me a big hug.

"My mother heard 'Roxanne' on your show," he referred to my Radio 1 programme of American hits, "so she knows we're doing well." I was pleased to be the unknowing bearer of good news between separated family members, a role I unwittingly played in the cases of several British parents who I later learned listened to the show to hear how their boys were faring in the United States.

I was also pleased for Sting, whom I liked immediately. He struck me as one of those rare artists who, not just satisfied with exploiting his talent, was determined to learn things he did not already know. He could go far, I thought, but first he would have to get a better bathrobe. The one he was wearing did not befit a star.

You knew Sting would expand his area of achievement because he was always expanding his area of experience. It was not for nothing that both his first and second wives came from the theatre. His wife today, Trudie Styler, has joined him in doing substantial and effective charity work that does credit to both of them. His first wife, Frances Tomelty, continues her acting career; I saw her in late 1997 at the National Theatre. I could not help but cast my mind back over a decade to the first night party after the triumphant Royal Court UK premiere of Larry Kramer's *The Normal Heart*. After congratulating her on her outstanding performance, I sympathised that the persistent radio play of 'Every Breath You Take', which Sting had revealed had been written about her, must be haunting her.

"I only wish he would stop talking about it in the press," she said with resignation. Neither of us, nor Sting himself, could have foreseen that the song would return to number one

117

fourteen years after it originally topped the charts as the basis of Puff Daddy's 'I'll Be Missing You'.

I saw several more Police performances during the following few years, and Sting went through a few more dressing gowns. Actually, the latter is an assumption, but he certainly could have afforded them.

Here was a group where each of the three individuals was a formidable musician. Together the Police outstripped all other bands of the late Seventies and early Eighties. Their charismatic image as what might be called the Bleach Boys, three young men who dyed their hair blonde for a TV commercial and kept it that way, and the aggressive dedicated management provided by Stewart's brother Miles Copeland, buttressed their talent. They had musical novelty (the incorporation of reggae-like rhythms in rock), quality songs (all singles were written by Sting) and charisma. For a moment, the Police were in that happy position in popular music where they were turning out better and better material just when the public was more and more interested in their work.

During their ascendancy Sting occasionally appeared on my programmes. On the 6 July, 1979 edition of *Roundtable* on Radio 1 his fellow guest critic was A&M labelmate Joe Jackson. Knowing them both to be fans of vintage comics, I presented each with a fresh copy of *Justice League Of America 21*, dated August 1963. In the historic story "Crisis on Earth-One", the Justice League met the Forties hero group the Justice Society of America for the first time. This was such an important event in the history of DC Comics that I had bought several copies. For the first time, I now shared them.

In the early autumn of 1982, I began a regular series of live celebrity interviews on the BBC1 programme *Pebble Mill At One*. The name of the show betrayed its studio origins in Pebble Mill, Birmingham. The artists and I would have to trek up from London, unless they were on tour and already in the Midlands. I managed to assemble a season of guests that included Kate Bush, Judi Dench, and Elton John. John Cleese did not make the trip to Birmingham, but was interviewed in Broadcasting House, the only time I made a TV tape in the building in which I did my radio shows.

My boyhood musical heroes were represented on *Pebble Mill At One* by Gene Pitney and the songwriter team of Jerry Lieber and Mike Stoller. I got Lieber and Stoller, whose songs were subsequently gathered in the Broadway musical *Smokey Joe's Cafe*, to perform their rock anthem 'Kansas City' in the style in which they originally wrote it, a blues. As they were singing and playing I could not help but have the rather self-satisfying thought that I, an American, had hijacked the BBC's highest-rated television frequency to present Lieber and Stoller in live performance.

They were great storytellers. When I told them how, in Kansas City during the spring of 1970 while on the Dartmouth College Bicentennial Glee Club tour, I had made a personal pilgrimage to the intersection of 12th Street and Vine they had immortalised in song, only to find it a dump, they confessed they were only looking for a rhyme for "wine" and had looked at a map. When I speculated it was strange they should have written their classic song 'Only In America' for Jay and The Americans, not normally their kind of act, they revealed they had written it for The Drifters but decided not to release their version because black people in the United States had not yet reached the level of opportunity expressed in the song.

Stoller related how he had survived the sinking of the Italian liner the *Andrea Doria* and was greeted at the pier in New York by Lieber, not with expressions of gratitude for his saved life, but with shouts of "Elvis Presley's recorded 'Hound Dog'! Elvis Presley's recorded 'Hound Dog'!" The Lieber-Stoller song had already been a number one rhythm and blues hit for Big Mama Thornton, and Mike, who had been out of the country, had no idea how huge Presley had become in his absence.

Until Lieber explained, Stoller thought he had lost all sense of priorities and was merely informing him of another cover version.

Sting began this series of memorable *Pebble Mill* interviews, and in a manner which I will never forget. We had a twelve-minute slot, including clips from his current film *Brimstone And Treacle*. Two or three minutes into the interview, I saw a trapped look in his eye. It wasn't panic; he was too much of a professional to get upset by live work. It was an oh-my-God-this-is-live-television-and-I-can't-move-for-the-next-ten-minutes expression. I was accustomed to this feeling. You can't scratch your nose or get out of your seat on television, as you can on radio.

On the train back to London, he confided, "Paul, you know I wouldn't have done this if it wasn't for you," and I expressed my gratitude. My feelings were of the "What a pal!" variety. Sting had become in four brief years too big a star to be schlepping up and down the country on a train to do a television programme. He had not needed to put himself through the stress of a live twelve-minute interview. I, on the other hand, had needed a major name for the beginning of the series. He had delivered.

In 1986 he delivered again. I was compiling an album to benefit Amnesty International, and assembled appropriate material like Dire Straits' 'Brothers In Arms', Paul McCartney's 'Pipes Of Peace' and Elton John's 'Passengers'. On this occasion Sting not only donated a track, he recorded a new one. He performed his own version of Billie Holiday's 'Strange Fruit', accompanying himself on double bass and vibraphone. Any Sting completist will have to find a copy of this album, *Conspiracy Of Hope*, which in America was rather gauchely retitled *Rock For Amnesty*.

In late 1983 and early '84, director Rod Taylor and our *Other Side Of The Tracks* crew made two trips to the States to do interviews for our second Channel 4 series. On one of these occasions we began the day in New York doing a feature on the new television sensation, MTV. One of the VJs, Alan Hunter, was from Alabama, and I asked him where we should dine that night in Birmingham, the southern city that took its name from the very place where *Pebble Mill At One* originated. We were flying down in the afternoon to see the Police in concert that evening. The trio was now the biggest British group in the States. Its current album *Synchronicity* was in the middle of a chart run that would include seventeen weeks at number one.

"It should be more," Sting told me seriously, "but we've found out they've kept *Thriller* there even though some weeks we've outsold it." I personally had no information to confirm or reject this suggestion, but I had enough knowledge of some spectacular examples of chart manipulation in the recent past to know that few outrages would have surprised me.

I had intentionally never visited Alabama, one of the states I had considered to be beyond the pale in its resistance to racial integration in the early Sixties. During my boyhood the images of police racists turning on civil rights demonstrators had been seared on my memory, and I could never forget the church bombing that killed four Negro schoolgirls. Birmingham, the site of the outrage, was notorious for its treatment of protesters. With the moral certainty of a child, I hated the Birmingham police. Now I was going to Birmingham to see The Police. Such are the tricks played by time and show business.

We flew to the city and went directly to dinner at the recommended restaurant. It had good cole slaw. Rod and I then went to the arena where the Police were appearing. We walked in backstage and there was Sting, hanging upside down as he used to do before concerts.

It was a wonderful sight, seeing an artist so centred on his performance and fitness that he would go to an extreme of preparation. It was also a poignant sight. I often found myself in the position of seeing a British performer I had known for some time being approached by Americans who had only met them at the height of their career. While some of his old British record company acquaintances would attempt to hold on to some degree of personal familiarity by calling the star by an antiquated nickname, some Yanks would attempt to appeal with near-comic sycophancy. Where did I fit in to this picture? I never bothered to think. I merely considered myself The Watcher, the Marvel Comics character who could see all and affect nothing.

After the Birmingham show, we flew on the chartered Police plane to New Orleans. It was, I have to say, a step up from the Starship. Rock-and-roll aviation had improved in a decade.

The next day our *Other Side Of The Tracks* team filmed the introduction to the Police piece even before we did the group interview, which was to take place the following morning. This was not to presume the content of the talk itself, but instead to summarise the band's career to date. Rod and I walked up and down Bourbon Street and had breakfast at Antoine's, where we were intrigued to find bananas and ice cream was considered a morning dish.

That evening I went to the film *The Right Stuff* with Sting. We were both tremendously impressed by director Philip Kaufman's great achievement in bringing Tom Wolfe's book about test pilots and astronauts to the screen. At the end of the decade I cited *The Right Stuff* on TV-am as one of my top ten films of the Eighties.

As we rose from our seats I was intrigued that the few autograph seekers who did ask Sting for his signature did so in a very polite and calm manner. Seeing as the Police had just spent eight weeks at number one on the singles chart and a longer spell at the top of the album list, this was a remarkably restrained performance by American fans. I attributed the calm to the fact that these individuals were a subset of cinema fans willing to see a three-hour film without a major Hollywood star about a passé subject. They were, by definition, patient people.

I also felt this strange serenity had something to do with Sting himself. I have learned that you really do get back what you give out. The feedback a performer receives from fans is a reaction to the image he or she projects. Being a bright and positive man, Sting was bound to be treated with intelligence and optimism.

We then went to have dinner. After the 193-minute movie, it was more like a late supper.

"I wrote a song today," Sting mentioned in an exchange of how-was-your-day pleasantries. "I think you'll like it."

Great. I had bananas and ice cream for breakfast and he wrote 'Moon Over Bourbon Street'. As if that didn't make me feel overfed, I asked what he would like for dessert as we surveyed the menus again after the main course.

"Oh, I don't eat desserts anymore."

Those half dozen words made me feel like the biggest pig in the world. Here I was, with perhaps the fittest pop star in the business, who exercised regularly and hung upside down before concerts, and I was talking about sweets. I wasn't obesely overweight, and I have never been particularly paranoid about my figure, but those six thrown away words made me feel like Tubby.

During his years as a celebrated solo artist I have had fewer opportunities to see Sting than I did in our younger days. This is what happens when people grow up and develop their circles of family and closest friends. Most of the times I meet him we are doing our respective duties at benefit shows, or I am hosting the Ivor Novello Awards where he is receiving trophies for writing wonderful songs like 'They Dance Alone'. He is always in shape. Each time we exchange friendly words, and each time, though he does not know this, Sting makes me feel fat.

20

Tina Turner Returns

One of the greatest pleasures of making the series *The Other Side Of The Tracks* was interviewing Tina Turner just as her comeback was gaining momentum. She was thrilled that 'Let's Stay Together' had returned her to the top ten for the first time in a decade. The life-changing American number one 'What's Love Got To Do With It' was less than half a year away.

Here was a great artist, thankful for what she had and motivated for more. Before *Private Dancer*, before *Mad Max*, before *I, Tina*, we spoke in a London studio. No matter how familiar some of the episodes in Turner's life have become through her written and filmed biographies, these excerpts from our interview offer fresh perspective. Some artists come alive through their transcribed words. Tina Turner is one of them. You will hear her voice, and like her as much as I do.

In three different versions of your life, I've read three different years of birth and two different original names. In fact, the only thing they agree on is that you were born in November. Why should you be such a mysterious person?

You know how the gossip goes that if you put a pillow outside on a windy day and you break it, the feathers go and you can never pull the gossip in, so it's just wrong words that's got out? I read today that my name was Annie May Braddock. And I went, oh God, a new one now. I mean, even now it's still coming in. I don't know what it is. Maybe it's just a strange sound, the name of Anna Mae Bullock. It's very simple to me. *That was your name.*

Yeah.

And did you become Tina before or after you met Ike?

After. It was decided because Anna Mae doesn't sound very good. To say, "Right now, ladies and gentlemen, Anna May!"

We felt Tina had more of a ring to it and you could remember it easier. Ike and Tina sounded better. I didn't accept it readily – how can you accept somebody giving you a name – it took about seven years to adjust to it and to answer to it, except for stage reasons. Then I accepted it.

You were still a young teenager when you went to see Ike's show. You wanted to sing with him, but he didn't want you to at first, did he?

I think he thought that I couldn't sing. Afterwards he did tell me that he really thought that I couldn't. Because I was a very thin little girl, and to have a voice like this inside of this body! He probably thought I had this little tiny voice. The night I finally got the chance to, after asking him for months, the drummer set the microphone down teasing with my sister, and I took the mike and started singing. And he was really excited and surprised. He came running down and said, 'I had no idea you could sing.'

He asked what songs I knew and I started naming a lot of blues things, and he was real surprised. Actually, for the second show that night I got on stage and I did about three or four numbers, and he was very impressed. So I started doing demos and a little bit of work on weekends with him before the career actually started.

Is it true that the actual first record, 'A Fool In Love', was meant to be someone else singing?

Yes. Art Lassiter. I don't know what he feels about that. He and Ike were having problems, and the day of the recording session, he didn't arrive. So Ike says, well . . .

At the time I was Little Anne. It went from Anna May to Little Anne. He says, why don't you just do a demo on it, because I had been working with him at home as he was writing and arranging it. So I did just basically a demo, and when he decided to go to New York with it, the companies said that he should keep the girl's vocal. I was the girl. So that was when he decided, we'll make a new name.

And 'A Fool In Love' became a million seller for Ike and Tina Turner.

Yes.

Now a million seller with your first record! Did you think, "Well, this is it, this is over now, I've made it"?

No. I didn't like the record. I was very disappointed with travelling. I thought there would be a big star on the door, I would be announced, and I would arrive with chiffon. [Laughs.] It wasn't like that at all.

As a matter of fact, it was a theatre, a very old theatre in Philadelphia, and the dressing room was basically a storage room. And it was like, "Oh, no." But the show went great. We were with Jackie Wilson, and the hall was full of people, and to me it was like, oh, so this is what it's like.

But I never felt that star rush. I just didn't get it. It was just different.

Perhaps one reason was that Sue Records, the label you were on at the time, was an independent, run by a fellow called Juggy Murray.

Juggy Murray. Isn't that a name, huh? Juggy. Yeah.

We were with Juggy for about seven years. It was like a continuous fight between him and Ike. Ike was very much in control of his career. It wasn't that he was the kind of artist who would just sit back and be told by a company what to do. And Juggy being on his own and an independent company, it was just very hard. The communication was just not really good.

You said Ike was a good businessman. He does have a reputation for being a keen taskmaster with his band and the girls. Was he?

Yes. I must give respect to Ike as a businessman, for being totally in control of his life and how it was run. He controlled everything. He was like a king in his own world. All the steps he made for himself as he wanted. You have to respect that if someone is successful at it. Sometimes it's done where you can make enemies, but then business is that way.

You had a record called 'It's Gonna Work Out Fine'. Not unlike Mickey and Sylvia [the 'Love Is Strange' duo who sang back-up on this single] in the sense that both of you were singing. Did you prefer records on which you both sang, or did you want to sing on your own?

All the time I wanted to sing rock-and-roll. I never wanted to sing those type of songs I was doing in the early days. I never wanted to. I hated them all.

A lot of times people ask me, are you going to do your act. And I say, no, I'm not going to do those old records. I wanted to sing rock-and-roll, and that's why, when the first time I walked into a record shop and I heard The Rolling Stones' 'Honky Tonk Women', I went, that's it, that's what I want to do.

The Stones reached back to get black music and make it over, and I could feel what they were doing, so I wanted the energy and the style of rock-and-roll but to sing it with my own emotions. So for all those years, I was able to sing whatever I was told, and I did it well, and I gained a great amount of discipline from it, but there's very few that I really, really like. You can try on a shirt and say well, this is not really me, but I can wear it. That's how my early career was.

You did do a record produced by Ray Charles. We all know he is a great artist. What was he like as a producer?

With Ray it was very much like being in church. It wasn't like being produced produce. We worked together. He was there. He was in control with what he was doing, but we basically sat there and just had communication. It was just as if we were all as one.

Shortly thereafter, Phil Spector heard you singing and asked you in. You did a couple of songs with him, the most famous of which is 'River Deep Mountain High'.

Yeah.

Now in a sense you said you wanted to sing rock-and-roll and that was rock-and-roll written by New York rock-and-roll songwriters.

Yeah.

Jeff Barry, Ellie Greenwich and of course Phil Spector himself. On that song, Ike is not even evident. I have to ask, was he even around?

No.

First of all, just to set the record straight, our first contact with Phil was when he saw our show in a small club on Sunset called Gazzaras. He wanted us to participate in a television show. After we did his television special, he wanted to produce me, and he asked that Ike not attend the rehearsals or be involved at all. That was the agreement. And Ike said, well, OK. Because he respected the man's total control, and he didn't want to have any influence with what we did.

The song was strange for me. I had never actually just sung a melody. It had always been delivery, and getting involved in delivering the story and ad libbing. But with Phil he only wanted the range, the quality of the voice, and the melody.

Ike was not allowed in until the tracks were actually cut and I went in and put my vocal on. We went back in for a few other minor arrangements. That was when Ike was allowed, so to speak, and we were both blown away. It was like, "Oh, God, listen to this." Amazing. Just amazing.

And certainly with the hardest shriek in the history of recorded music, that high note you hit there. Did you do many takes of that?

That and the very beginning of the song. I stood for seemingly an hour getting "when I was a little". I didn't know what he wanted. I said, how can you say it? That should be the simple line, just to say "when I was a little girl", but that wasn't it.

He wanted total enunciation, he wanted a certain amount of vibrato. He wanted total control of the way he heard that line.

And that shrill. I had to do that shrill. There was no way of getting out of it. Oh, my goodness. I think my voice left for about two days after that.

Those were the hardest parts. The verses and all were fine, but those parts were very difficult.

G with some of the 15,000 singles he sold at Sotheby's.

A teenage PG with early mentor Scott McQueen (foreground) at Dartmouth College radio station WDCR and, right, Richard Nixon whose halitosis PG helped cure. (right: Rex)

Muhammad Ali is upstaged by his own daughter while PG grabs pole position during the press conference – see Chapter 11.

G with Bob Geldof, Kate Bush, Tom Robinson, Paula Yates and Elton John at the party to unch the second edition of *The Guinness Book of British Hit Singles*. The next day Elton was ushed to hospital – see Chapter 15.

he Radio 1 DJ's football team at Roker Park in the mid-Seventies, outdrawing most of the econd division. Back row: Dave Lee Travis, Teddy Warrick (Radio 1 producer), Kid Jensen, PG, like Read, Steve Wright, Richard Skinner, Jeff Griffin, Andy Peebles; front: Dave Most, John eel, Paul Burnett, Peter Powell, Noel Edmonds and Alan James.

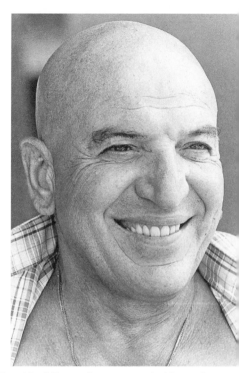

Left: Liz Taylor and Richard Burton, whose relationship PG may have extended by at least tv
hours – see Chapter 18 (Rex); right: Telly Savalas – see Chapter 23 (Rex).

PG with Mary Wilson of The Supremes and Anna Ford.

ft: Mark Hamill as Luke Skywalker – see Chapter 13 (Rex); right: PG with Freddie Mercury
the House of Commons launch for the *Hits of The Seventies* book.

evie Wonder, Smokey Robinson and Diana Ross - all of them interviewed by PG - pictured
gether during an early Motown Revue. (Rex)

Top: PG with Paul McCartney in the late Seventies, and, below, with his prized collection Carl Barks comics.

Rod Argent, Andrew Lloyd Webber, Bob Harris and PG, and below: PG with lyricist and *Singles* co-author Tim Rice.

The author at work. (Rex)

I notice in performance you called the song 'Rivers Deep Mountains High', with "s"es. Whereas in the original recording it's singular. Did you feel there should be an "s"?

There are all kinds of things that happen on the stage when you're singing the story. It becomes a reality when you really start singing it and sing a song as many times as I have over the years. It's something that happens subconsciously and comes from a part in which you feel, that is an actuality. It became that from actually performing it.

It was a monstrous success in Britain, but not so in the United States. Phil Spector was very upset. Were you?

No. You see, in the beginning of my career I wasn't all that involved in the business end of it. I heard. I was surprised it didn't get any response in America, and then there began to be a lot of controversy about it, and then I sort of learned from Ike and the business end of it that it was all a big mess. Mess meaning that it was a little bit more than just not being allowed to be played in America.

Ike and Phil were both very upset about it. They pulled all kinds of strings, but I guess they didn't have enough power.

Did you ever find out the whole story, or didn't you care to know?

It's like politics and running the world. In the business of music in America, if you are a black artist, no matter what type of song you do, you have to go black on the radio first before you can make the crossover.

Ike and my history was basically R&B and so it was like, no matter that the song was basically a pop song, it had to be done going through the black radio stations. And there was no way that black radio could play it because it was just not accepted. It was a sort of racial thing at the time, which was kept hush hush, of course, because most of those things are. With your back against the wall there was nothing you could really do.

Do you feel that racial situation is changed now [early 1983]?

It's changed a bit, but it is still a problem. I came into this problem with a producer, Richard Perry. I was about to sign with this company and I wanted to record rock-and-roll. This is my comeback, this is what I want to do. And he said that was too much of a chance for him to take because I would have to be programmed R&B first.

I said, well, I'm rock-and-roll. I haven't done any records, but I've laid the foundation, it's there.

Producers are in the business. They know it more than the artists. That's when I realised that it still exists.

You did another single with Phil, 'A Love Like Yours'. Kim Weston had the original. Did you enjoy making that one?

Yeah. That one was easier. Maybe it was because I had already worked with Phil and I knew the style and what he wanted. But I didn't. I never felt that it was as good as 'Rivers Deep'.

Were you surprised or disappointed that it ended so quickly with Phil Spector?

No. I hadn't anticipated it would be something lasting. I felt within my own self it would be just a two album deal or something. I didn't anticipate any long term relationship there.

By the mid-Sixties you had established a reputation as a tremendously physical performer on stage, a very sexy one. There's a very amusing account by the writer Nik Cohn, who went on to write the article on which Saturday Night Fever *was based. He saw you in a London club, and you leaned over, shall we say backwards, into the audience. Three rows fell backwards just in shock and surprise. You were a cannonball, he said. Was being a physical performer something that came naturally, or something that you worked at?*

Always nature for me. I've always been just like I am now. From the time that I can remember myself always dancing to music, always singing for my parents after movies. I always watched and took things that I wanted from professional people and from street people and sort of made it my own.

And I always made things my own. I took it and turned it

130

around. I still do it. It's something that is a gift for me.

Undoubtedly the high point of the physicality of your performance for many years was 'I've Been Loving You Too Long', which you had recorded on the Blue Thumb label and turned into a very erotic duet with Ike on stage.

I think I'll drink a bit of tea here.

That's right. We won't let our microphone get too near you at this point because of the things I remember you used to do. When you look back on that are you amused or embarrassed or . . .

Embarrassed, and I don't do the song anymore. It became a nightmare. It was one of those times on stage when creativity just took over me and I decided to be naughty. I started piddling around and making love to the microphone.

Ike thought it was fantastic. He thought, oh great, people love it. Keep doing it. And then he started. He wasn't hugging the mike, he was just making all these awful sounds. God, I was so embarrassed so many times.

And I had to live with that for such a long time. Each time I did the song, it was like having to take a deep breath and say, oh, God. It was very hard to even look at the audience afterwards. It was no longer fun. I like to leave a little bit to be imagined, and all of a sudden it was totally out there for everybody.

Now I know people want to hear it, but I just can't sing it, because I still have that gut feeling of embarrassment. I am just not as bold as that. I do things in my sexuality, as hopefully my audience see me, as fun, not to make it look nasty. It's for everybody to feel and enjoy, but not to be offended.

I tried to do the song the first year I was on my own, and I didn't do all of that. And I figured, well, forget it, I cannot do it. I'm sorry to my public, it became a nightmare.

You said that in the late Sixties you'd discovered The Rolling Stones, and they discovered you, they had you open for them on their tour of America.

Well, you know, 'Rivers Deep' was number one here, and at

131

that time, the Stones, when they would go on tour, would bring whoever was at the top of the charts as their guests. It was like an introduction and a promotion from a business standpoint.

Our first trip here was because we were guests to perform with them, and also to promote our record as well. And what more promotion can you have than if you're going to work with The Rolling Stones? You've got all the kids there to announce it to. You don't have to go through television. It was the very beginning of meeting the guys and seeing what they did and watching them grow.

Looking back on it, Mick was just a pale skinny kid beating the tambourine, but he was always in the wings watching, you know, and he used to come in the dressing room and say, I like to watch you girls dance, and we used to teach him Pony steps and try to get him to move. It was fun.

We had fun in the dressing rooms then, eating strange foods. And he would say, oh, this tastes good, this tastes good. And it was again like the Ray Charles situation. We all became like one. It was like in and out of dressing rooms, sitting and eating and laughing and dancing, onto the stage, and it was wonderful.

The girls who sang with you were called The Ikettes.

Yeah.

The Ikettes even made records on their own. Did you think, hey, wait a minute, this is getting out of control?

You know, I still don't have that attitude towards being a star. I think that everybody is. All talent put together makes it better.

Actually, I sang with The Ikettes. I was on the bottoms of their recordings, you know. And I loved it when they would go on stage and sing their songs. It was great.

When the Sixties became the Seventies, you had a new record deal with United Artists, and you were singing versions of rock songs that had been hits. This was what you wanted to do, wasn't it?

132

Yes. I remember this very well because it was important to me.

Seattle, Washington was one of those towns where I went into the record shops with Ike for our repertoire. We always took from the top ten, the top twenty, and mixed our show, our recordings with songs people were familiar with. Because we were never that much of a record act. We might have had one [hit] one time or another, but it was always performance, taking other songs, doing them over and then adding our songs.

It was 'Come Together' when we walked in and I went OH! Really and truly, it was almost like hypnotising me. Then after that they played the new Rolling Stones album and I thought, this is what I want to do. This is just what I want. I was so excited. I was just running all over the shop, "I want to do this song, and I want to do this," and he agreed. He felt the same.

And you had a smash in the States with 'Proud Mary'. Was the tantalising introduction worked out or was it fairly spontaneous?

That was another 'I've Been Loving You Too Long' situation. It was in Oakland, California, when Ike had been badgering me to start talking to the audience. I don't like to talk to the audience, because sometimes they don't want to talk. They're shy. You have to depend on an audience talking to you. I don't like to depend. I like to perform for them. Let them watch, let them speak if they want to speak. And I didn't think that was a good idea for me, because I'm not a joker, you know, I'm a dancer and a singer.

It was one of those hypnotising nights where the place was packed, the lights were very misty and blue, and we brought the music down, because we had been doing 'Proud Mary' without that opening. And I just started talking. The words just came right out of my mouth that night. After the show we thought, great, that was a great opening. It was almost like something you had created was fantastic.

It gave you a top five record in the States. Not so much a hit in

Britain, but then again that situation was reversed a couple of years later with 'Nutbush City Limits'. You had a hand in writing this, didn't you?

I was born in Nutbush. That was a track Ike had around the studio for it seems ages. He just cut track after track. I'm sitting at home and this track drove me nuts. It was just dah-dah-dah-dah-dah and I just felt as if I was going spare. I hated it.

Finally one night, I was sitting there and I was really upset, I mean frustrated. I thought, I can't think of anything to write to this song except Nutbush City Limits. So I just wrote about Nutbush – the highway, the stores, the gin.

I went in the studio the next day and I said, OK, I wrote six songs last night. He goes, great. I sang them all to him, sitting there in the control room, and when I gave him Nutbush, he went, I like that one. And so I went in and, ha, one take – unusual, you got to record with Ike for six months on a vocal track. I thought, great, I don't even have to sing it forever.

I didn't care about it. I didn't care at all. And it was a monster. Three times a hit in Australia. Three times.

You got a chance to sing 'The Acid Queen' in the film Tommy. *Was this something you had direct experiences of?*

I had no experience at all. I was so naïve at the time of my life when it was put to me. 'Acid Queen', I said, oh, no. I'm not going to do a hooker part. I don't want to do that.

In the front part of my career, I was always embarrassed by those horribly ugly pictures. I wasn't as big as I'm photographed. Now I hear they're asking me to be a hooker? It was totally against all I ever wanted to be. The only thing I ever wanted to be was a pretty singer. So here he is asking me to be a hooker.

The guy who was in charge of our booking at the time says you must do this, it's a major film. It'll be great exposure for you, just read the script. So I read it, I found I had a chance to act, it wasn't just being a hooker. I felt, OK, fine.

I was still with the attitude of not really liking it because I wanted to really do the other side. I just wanted to be in dialogue. So I went and grabbed my red lipstick and took all stockings with lace and stockings torn – when you see hookers, they're always torn – and I had a Yves St. Laurent black jersey skirt, because I thought I had to wear black.

I said, here it is, and Ken Russell said, well, we'll need a black skirt and so I said, have my Yves St. Laurent skirt. And he said no, no, no. And he bought me this little skirt, and, oh God, these platform shoes, and it was horrible. So I said, well, I might as well become this person, and I put a mole here and I got a cigarette in a holder, when I don't really smoke, and the lips went red, and the nails went red, and I became the Acid Queen. I started enjoying it, and so did he.

It was one of the highlights of the film for the viewer. Did you enjoy it?

I hated it! It was fantastic, but I had no idea what he was doing with the fish eye lens or whatever that is. I expected to go in and see this great masterpiece. Well, it was a masterpiece, but it wasn't what I thought. I was dragging this kid up the stairway, and I looked like this horrible mad woman and it was like aargh, is that what I was doing?

When you get involved with your acting, you're not totally aware, because you become something else, and I had actually become mad for that moment. I wasn't really mad so they had to tie me down afterward, after every cut I was sane again, but I was actually the Acid Queen.

Do you wish you could do more films?

Yes, that's my dream. My dream is to become an actress, not just of musicals, but to speak.

Separating from someone personally is one thing, but professionally is another. What was it like to be Ike-less as the solo artist Tina Turner.

It was a relief. I felt I had done my duty with him in 16 years, in every respect. I had done as I was told. He had gotten practically everything out of me that I could have given so far as him producing me, and so then I felt it was time for me to go and get out there and do what I wanted to do. It was something that was finished, so I had no regrets.

Were you an artist who had won financially from her success, or were you one of those who, through bad deals or whatever, had not profited?

We gained a lot from our career together, but I gave it all away for my peace of mind. Divorces can be awful. Mine was becoming a war because of property and things that weren't important, things that could be gotten again. And that's why, when it became a war, I said, this is it, no more wars, forget it. I walked out and I left everything. What was important to me was me, not to own anything.

In your stage show, as a solo artist, you have concentrated on the rock material that you love.

The first year was basically what people knew me for when I was with Ike. Then I got with new management and told them what I wanted. They said, well, if you want that, this is what you're going to have to do. You've going to have to select rock-and-roll tunes. You're going to look more rock-and-roll. You've got to become what you want. That's when the hair went punk, the dresses went shorter, and the music went wilder, and I had fun. And I started laughing. I started smiling. That's when I started waking up and feeling that I feel good today, not waking up going, "I'm depressed again".

'Let's Stay Together' has been your first top ten record in a decade. Your feelings?

Last night on stage was the first time I had a real rush. I almost wanted to say ten years ago there was 'Rivers Deep, Mountains High', ten years later, 'Let's Stay Together'. That's what I felt, but the kids don't really know, so it wasn't important.

When artists from groups go on their own, sometimes it takes a long time, and sometimes it's immediate. For me it took a decade, on my own, as a single.

So after two dozen years you're not tired?

No. I'm still having a real good time. I have my moments, but overall I'm having a good time.

21

Chrissie Hynde Slouches

I learned from my Channel 4 TV series *The Other Side Of The Tracks* the final evidence I needed to conclude that parents and children will never approach life from precisely the same perspectives. The experiences on which they base their judgements are different. During our second season in 1984, my parents came to London for a ten-day vacation, during which they were able to see two programmes of *Tracks*. We planned to meet for dinner after each of the Saturday broadcasts.

The main item in the first programme was an interview with Chrissie Hynde and Martin Chambers of The Pretenders, shot in the Sydney Botanical Gardens. If this sounds like one of the jammy assignments of all-time, it was. It was delightful being in beautiful surroundings with two old friends who were at the peak of their careers. 'Back On The Chain Gang' had recently reached the American top five, and *Learning To Crawl* was en route to being their greatest US album success.

My history with The Pretenders had gone back to their very formation. My good friend Dave Hill, a record company promotion man, loved music as much as any of us. He was responsible for pushing Freddy Fender's American hits 'Before the Next Teardrop Falls' and 'Wasted Days and Wasted Nights', but exulted even more about the album track 'I Love My Rancho Grande'. (Typographical errors have given us all delight – my all-time favourite is the *Guardian*'s listing of Simon Gray's play *Otherwise Engaged* as "Best Lay of the Year" – and I owe Polygram Films a good chuckle for mislisting Fender's US number one as 'Before the Next Eardrop Falls' in its promotional material for the film *Resurrection Man*. If you know the Fender lyric, and substitute 'Eardrop' for 'Teardrop' throughout, you wind up on the floor in hysterics.)

It was Dave Hill who invited me over to his King's Road apartment in the summer of 1975 to hear his import copy of Bruce Springsteen's *Born To Run*. Within a minute of the needle hitting the record, I was on the floor, not in hysterics, but in awe. And it was Dave Hill who introduced me to Steve Jones of the Sex Pistols before the group had even released its first single. Shortly afterwards, on a late November afternoon in 1976 after a premature one-inch fall of wet snow, I met Jones on Wardour Street, and he excitedly gave me one of the new Sex Pistols badges he was distributing. The band was one month away from the release of 'Anarchy in the U.K.', and Steve had no idea of the explosion the Pistols were about to detonate.

In the late 1970s Warner Brothers gave Hill his own custom label, Real Records. He asked me to provide the voice-over for his first description of the label's plans to a Warner Brothers sales meeting. After I had done so he introduced me to a young American woman around whom he was going to assemble a group. It was Chrissie Hynde.

I liked Chrissie at once. Not only were we both expatriate Americans, we both loved good records. When she and Dave had finished putting together The Pretenders, we had a meal together at Joe Allen's, at which I presented Chrissie and bassist Pete Farndon with the first promotional computer game I had been sent. They seemed delighted; I should have been warned that this was a harbinger that computer games were one part of the information technology revolution that would completely pass me by.

The Pretenders were an outstanding group who, curiously enough, were first class from their very first single, 'Stop Your Sobbing'. Usually a group, like Harry Truman, grows in office. The Pretenders were of stature from the start. Chrissie completely bypassed all the 'women in rock' nonsense that was written whenever a female succeeded in the field and simply got down to business, turning out astonishing lyrics like 'Tattooed Love Boys' and 'Brass In Pocket'. Things were looking great for the group when I attended guitarist James Honeyman-Scott's wedding reception, not so great when this gentle and warm man died unexpectedly in 1982. It was less of a surprise but equally tragic when Pete Farndon died the following year.

Chrissie's song 'Back On The Chain Gang' was perhaps the finest pop song I had ever heard about recovering from tragedy. There have been several deeply moving records made about loss, not just the all-time number one 'Candle In The Wind 1997' but songs ranging from 'Missing You' by Diana Ross to 'Jesus To A Child' by George Michael. 'Back On The Chain Gang' was about getting up and starting all over again, and to me typified the courage Chrissie Hynde exhibited as both artist and activist.

It was against this background that she and Martin Chambers joined me in the Sydney Botanical Gardens on a beautiful Australian summer day. The discussion was good, the pictures were pretty, the group was hot. I was pleased with the piece. During the course of dinner that night my father offered his evaluation of the show.

"You know that woman you had on TV tonight?" he asked.

"Yes," I replied. "Chrissie Hynde."

"She was slouching."

No congratulations on having a TV series, no comment on the content – just "she was slouching". The following Saturday evening, the last of my parents' stay in London, I waited for dear dad's rating of my scoop interview with entertainment mogul David Geffen. In this rare TV appearance Geffen touched on all aspects of his empire. I was proud that *The Other Side Of The Tracks* enabled me to present viewers with leading figures in show business that they would not see on the usual music show.

"You know that man you had on TV tonight?" Dad inquired over dinner.

"Yes," I said, with more trepidation than I had the week before.

"You didn't say 'thank you'."

I had to explain that in real life I had of course said "thank you", but that this unrevelatory remark had wound up on the cutting room floor.

Father's comments on the two TV shows still did not prepare me for his evaluation of the new home I had bought in North London. This was my first detached property, and I showed it off, perhaps with pride, but certainly with relief that my housing problems had been solved for the foreseeable future. As I gave my folks the grand tour my mother asked questions while my father took it all in with hardly a remark.

He finally commented as we were walking out of the front door.

"You left the butter out."

That was it! Not "Congratulations on affording a house" or "Why did you choose this neighbourhood?" but "You left the butter out."

I first had to explain that it wasn't my butter, since I didn't use the stuff, but that it belonged to my short-term lodger, the model Ali Espley, who appeared in the 'Too Shy' video and subsequently married the American comedian Dennis Miller. I then had to reach a conclusion for myself. There was no point in hoping that my father was going to comment on how I earned and spent my income in any way that was meaningful to me. He was coming from another place in another time, where remarks like "She was slouching", "You didn't say 'thank you' " and "You left the butter out" really did mean more than "Good timing on getting Chrissie Hynde", "David Geffen was an exclusive", or "What's the house worth?"

If our parents spoke a foreign language, we would know at once why we don't understand what they're saying, and vice

140

versa. Since we all talk in English, we assume there's some-thing wrong with our relationships when we don't connect in conversation. But although we are using the same words, we are using them to communicate different viewpoints. "She was slouching" and "You left the butter out" were such extreme departures from anything I thought my father might be about to say that it was glaringly obvious he was visiting Gambo World from another universe. Far from coming down on me, he was merely coming from another place. I could now stop worrying about whatever evaluation he might have of my current work and circumstances.

After that acceptance my relationship with dear old dad was free from anxiety. I recommend every son take this stress-free approach to his relationship with his folks.

22

I Get Up Early

I met Anna Ford in the late Seventies at a Motown Records reception. Anna on ITV and Angela Rippon on the BBC were pioneering the presentation of news by women and in so doing were attracting enormous media attention. This particular moment was captured by a photographer who caught Anna addressing Mary Wilson of The Supremes with the same precision she might use addressing Mary Wilson of Harold Wilson.

Years later Anna and I lunched at the Ivy, a favourite restaurant of mine where the eating area is in an inner chamber beyond the cloakroom. Upon arrival, before entering the dining room, Anna queued to check her coat. She stood behind a man who was retrieving his after finishing his meal.

"Do you know who that was in the restaurant?" the man told his female companion excitedly. "Anna Ford!"

"No it wasn't," Anna interrupted in her familiar here-is-the-news voice. "I'm Anna Ford."

The man turned around, looked as horrified as if he had seen his own demise enacted before him, accepted his coat and fled the premises wordlessly, his woman behind him.

"What was that about?" I asked.

"We'll never know," Anna replied.

She was wrong. The moment we walked through the door into the restaurant, we were greeted enthusiastically by Angela. The star-spotting diner had mistaken one pioneering newswoman for another. It wasn't the first time. Anna and Angela became associated for all time in the minds of a generation of media watchers when they left their newsdesks and became part of the Famous Five founding TV-am, ITV's first breakfast television service.

The programme was to be launched in 1983. The preceding year, newspapers were full of debate as to whether breakfast television was a Good Thing for the nation or another step on the stairway to brain rot American style. The matter was even to be debated at the Oxford Union.

I was a frequent guest in that hallowed chamber, being both a fairly recent graduate of University College and a Radio 1 DJ. If at any space in any time I was ever considered hip, it was in the Oxford Union from the mid-Seventies to early Eighties. I was even invited to speak at the Farewell Debate of President Benazir Bhutto, whom I had known in my final year. Pinkie, as she was known to friends, envied me because I had met David Cassidy in the Radio 1 lift. Benazir is the only person I have ever known to become Prime Minister of her country and be placed under house arrest.

On one occasion in the run-up to the opening of TV-am the debate was not about the future of Pakistan. The great and the good minds of young Britain were debating the wisdom of having breakfast television at all. Arguing in favour of the motion was Peter Jay, who was to be the programming head of TV-am. I was asked to oppose the motion.

I accepted the assignment, even though I favoured the introduction of breakfast television. It wasn't that I intended to spend my mornings watching the box. But it seemed obvious to me that increasing the amount of time in which people could watch television was an inevitable and desirable development. Only a Nanny State would want to limit the hours viewers could use the medium, and only a country obsessed with what was proper would assume that everyone went to bed at eleven, got up at seven and then went off to work or school. In the modern economy, everyone from shift workers to the sick could quite reasonably watch television during the daytime without being accused of being morally lax.

At the Oxford Union, however, what mattered was not the side for which you debated but rather how you played the game. Style, wit and the art of the insult were the skills to be refined. I soon learned that debaters scored quickly with the audience if they could put down the members of the opposing team. Ego was currency at the Union. If you could prick the balloon of someone's self-importance, you had verbally thrown them to the mat. I came to enjoy walking down the ranks of my foes, trying to come up with novel ways of embarrassing them.

Part of the challenge, of course, was that this had to be done with deference and without rancour. No matter what the issue, it was assumed that everyone invited to speak was of sufficient note to deserve respect. The put-downs could not be personal.

On one occasion, I flattered the entire opposition bench, then got to the scheduled closing speaker. A recent graduate, still a habitué of the Union, he had been imported to shore up the side. I welcomed him, said he was "known for . . .", thumbed through a prop copy of *Who's Who*, silently closed the book with a shrug and put it down. The audience howled.

Another time I was arguing on the same side as the noted sexologist Sheri Hite. When I came to her I claimed, "I accepted the invitation to be here tonight because I've always wanted to meet Cher". This one sailed over the nervous author's head, but the students got it.

Peter Jay was an easy target for Oxford Union ridicule. A noted economist, he had been Britain's ambassador to Washington and was now starting a breakfast television service! How déclassé! But Peter went to the heart of the matter, fighting precisely this prejudice, and spoke in favour of both viewer choice and business opportunity. He talked as if he had absorbed lessons from the nation in which he had just spent several years.

He spoke for me, in other words, while I dutifully trotted out the old warhorses about the United States becoming a nation of airheads due to spending too much time in front of the box and how breakfast television would inevitably accelerate the stupefying of Britain.

I don't even remember the outcome of the debate. The great irony for me was that Peter Jay, eloquent champion of TV-am, was forced to leave the company when it received the rudest of receptions not long after its introduction. I, on the other hand, having trashed the channel completely before it even began broadcasting, enjoyed a thirteen-year stint on air, the longest stretch of any performer.

Years later I reminded Peter of this oddity. He recalled the debate with bemusement, but was glad the entire matter was behind him. By this time he was making televised economics reports of a high intellectual standard. If he was affecting the nation's IQ in any way, he was increasing it.

At the time of our Oxford Union debate, of course, I had no idea his tenure with TV-am would be a short one or that I would have any role at all. Then one day at lunch, Anna Ford stated, "I'm going to be on this new programme, TV-am. You should do something for us."

Anna and I were having lunch together occasionally at the time. It was both a friendly and convenient thing to do, as our workplaces were only a few hundred yards apart. I would say "offices", but I never had an office at Radio 1. Producers had offices, and you worked out of their rooms.

Anna Ford was a true television star in the early Eighties. She found it odd that a journalist or newsreader could command such attention, but she was certainly not going to fight it. The clout could be useful, particularly behind the scenes. Anna was the centre of attention wherever we went for lunch. I usually considered this amusing, except in the case of our visit to Ken Lo's Memories of China. I had been there the previous week, on which occasion I had engaged the famous proprietor in conversation, and thus was in a position to recommend it to Anna. This time, only days later, Mr. Lo completely stiffed me and talked only to Ms. Ford, as if I did not exist. Rarely had I seen such a blatant case of, shall we say, starfeeding. A slight can work both ways, and I never returned to his restaurant.

At Anna's invitation, I journeyed one day to the new TV-am building on Hawley Crescent in Camden Town. The offices were still taking shape, but then so was the programme schedule. The first day of transmission was approaching, but much of the content of the show had yet to be decided. Anna accompanied me into the office of Michael Deakin, one of the executives.

"What would you like to do, Paul?" Michael asked.

"Well, since I do the American charts on Radio 1, something to do with pop music seems sensible," I replied.

A pained look came over his face.

"I can't offer you that," he said. "I ran into Tim Rice last night and offered him that area, so that's gone. What else do you like?"

"Well, I go to the theatre at least once a week, and I see a lot of movies."

"Good!" he smiled. "You can be our theatre critic!"

"Will that be of interest to viewers outside London?" I asked.

"Sure, it's in all their morning papers, we might as well scoop the papers. Well, that's fine. Now, Paul, are you willing to write for other people?"

Huh? What was he talking about?

"I don't understand what you mean," I said. "I've never written for anyone other than myself."

"Ahh," he sighed. "It's just that everyone who works for us has got to write for the presenters."

A frisson of dread passed through the room. Deakin obviously thought I was applying for a job.

"Michael, I think there's been a mistake," Anna spoke up. "Paul hasn't asked to work for us. I asked him to come here. I should have made that clearer."

With that little burst of professionalism, she both defended my status as a broadcaster and allowed the executive to backtrack from the mess into which he had trod.

"Oh," he said. "Well, that explains things. So, you'll be our theatre critic. Arrange a meeting with Kevin Sim. He's in charge of our features. Do a sample review, and everything should be ready for the start."

It sounded simple, but I had never before tried to arrange a meeting with Kevin Sim. After an introductory hello and how-do-you-do as I left the building, I spoke to his secretary on the phone and booked lunch with Kevin at the Gaylord Indian restaurant in Mortimer Street, where my plan of action would be discussed. After waiting a few minutes I ordered a Perrier and some poppadoms to keep me happy. This was a fatal mistake, as it committed me to eating a meal without guaranteeing that my host would show. After a quarter of an hour, I called Kevin's office to find out if he was en route to the restaurant.

"Let me look in his diary," his secretary said. "Oh, I see the problem. He's double booked himself. He's also supposed to be having lunch with someone else. But that doesn't matter, because he's out of the country today."

Was this a bad sign or what? If this was typical of TV-am organisation, no wonder the ship sailed straight into an iceberg. I consoled myself with the Gaylord's Special Dal, then and now my favourite lentil dish in London, finished off with their kulfi, and walked home to Hyde Park Square. I never reviewed a single stage show for TV-am. Nor, for that matter, did Tim Rice ever discuss pop music on the channel. I wonder if his prospective employment even got to the lunch planning stage.

Kevin Sim's inability to arrange a meal in a restaurant saved my television career. The weekday and weekend programming regimes at TV-am were different, and I was asked by Michael Parkinson's team if I would appear on his Saturday show reviewing pop videos. I would not be competing with my friend Tim Rice's weekday pop news.

Although London-based bands had pioneered the form, Queen virtually inventing it with their 'Bohemian Rhapsody' promotional clip and the Boomtown Rats galvanising the nation with 'I Don't Like Mondays', the video did not take off in America until Michael Jackson hoofed his way through 'Billie Jean'. MTV was just taking off in the States in 1983. It had not yet appeared in Britain, and my weekly video review could present a summary of the finest new releases. Ironically, it was to be MTV that would take over the TV-am building when the company lost the breakfast television franchise ten years later.

History records that the weekday TV-am programme drowned as it floundered in the water trying to find a format. It turned out, and this is a lesson worth remembering by anyone entering the media or show business, that just because the personalities were effective at certain things did not mean they would be accepted doing other things.

It was anguish watching these beloved individuals struggle from the comfort of a settee at home. Imagine how agonising it was seeing them suffer from the perspective of their very own sofa on the weekend programme. Michael Parkinson was a pro, and with his wife Mary he carefully crafted a show with a team of young professionals that may not have been a BAFTA Award winner but was gradually building an audience. As the rest of the famous folk went down in flames, members of our weekend squad were brought in to fill empty spaces on the couch. Nick Owen and Mike Morris, ultimately long-time breakfast television hosts, started as sports reporters on Parkinson's Saturday show.

In the second year of TV-am I was asked by Show Business

Editor Jason Pollock if I would be interested in being the channel's film reviewer. It seemed that whenever he went to a press screening, I was there, using my free Radio 1 tickets. I began what I thought would be the complement to my Saturday pop spot, but trends overtook me. Music videos became so ubiquitous on television it was no longer necessary to have a special slot, but by the time I stopped doing the Saturday show I was established as the weekday programme's film critic.

I reviewed movies for a dozen years. Guests sitting on the sofa while I was doing my piece to camera would always notice that I did not appear to be using autocue, that I was ad libbing. In Eighties television, this was inconceivable. Everyone had their set pieces scripted and printed on the large camera face. Viewers may think that presenters are looking at an empty glass camera lens as they talk, but they are actually reading their remarks printed on the face of the camera and rolling along, turned by a studio assistant.

When I was addressing the camera on TV-am, the screen was blank. It would amuse me to see out of the corner of my eye how long it would take visiting celebrities to notice that I had no autocue. Some, particularly actors or actresses accustomed to having their lines written for them and dreading the prospect of verbal spontaneity, did a visible double take when the realisation hit. A few scanned the studio to see where the hidden script was located.

When I went to the film clip during a 1985 review of a version of *King Solomon's Mines* starring Richard Chamberlain and Sharon Stone, the recent Presidential candidate Jesse Jackson asked me, "How did you do that?" I had to chuckle: the Great Orator, for so he was, wanted to learn more about ad libbing. His great campaign speeches were mainly memorised.

So, in truth, were my reviews. It was just easy for me to memorise them. My style had developed out of necessity. Unlike a news story, where the top of the story was at the beginning, the punch line of my film review was always at the end, when I summed up my reaction and gave a points-out-of-10 rating. But in the early days of TV-am, the timing of items by the directors was a shambles. There was no telling when you would get the rolling hand signal to wrap it up, or the moving-finger-across-the-neck signal to stop now. I realised that I could not deliver a film review and have my conclusion trapped deep in the autocue machine when I got a wrap-up signal. Therefore, it all had to be in my head.

This was easier to achieve with breakfast television than it would have been with a service broadcasting later in the afternoon or evening. My mind then would have been cluttered with the business of the day. Each night before a broadcast, the last thing I would do would be to select a start line for each review and then proceed mentally until I reached a point I didn't like. I would rewind the tape in my head and start again from that spot. When I had finished my two or three reviews, I would lie in bed and go through the whole thing once as my last mental exercise before going to sleep. When I woke in the morning, I would go through it in my mind as the first intellectual exercise of the day. The first-thing-in-the-morning, last-thing-at-night regime was enough to settle the script in my head long enough for me to deliver it two hours later in the studio.

I did not find addressing the camera without notes stressful. I was reminded of the Wimbledon tennis champion Bjorn Borg, of whom it was said that his pulse rate actually went down when he was on Centre Court. In that admittedly unusual setting, he had found his milieu, and was at peace. So it was for me on breakfast television. But this is not to say that I never suffered an anxious moment.

My absolute worst attack of nerves came the morning that the famously large Cyril Smith, M.P. came onto the show and occupied the wing of the sofa on which I normally sat. I mean, the entire wing. Ordinarily three of us could set ourselves there comfortably. As we were going into the break before my review segment, the director realised there was no way I nor anyone else could squeeze onto the sofa wing with Cyril Smith. Alternative accommodation had to be found at once.

I was banished to the far end of the studio, assigned to a deep armchair. A wave of panic came over me. You didn't just settle into this armchair, you were swallowed by it, and I felt that I was going to be struggling to project from this devouring piece of upholstery. I feared I might freak on air, so I had to take a preventive measure. I asked weather woman Wincey Willis if she would stand behind the camera for me. In effect, I would be addressing her, and her familiar countenance would compensate for the unfriendly last-minute surroundings. I have no idea what would have happened on air had Wincey not been generous enough to humour me.

Other than this episode, nothing was more anxiety-provoking than reviewing a film starring a person who happened to be sitting next to me on the sofa, promoting the film. There was such a severe possibility of unintentionally insulting the guest that I made it my policy not to review a film I had genuinely negative feelings about if the artist was going to be present. I would not compromise my critical integrity by pretending to like a movie I did not, nor would I subject a visiting actor to a negative review.

It was no problem reviewing *Out Of Africa* in the presence of Klaus Maria Brandauer, who co-starred with Meryl Streep and Robert Redford. He gave the best performance in the film, and he agreed with my 9 out of 10 rating. I recall giving *Sirens* with Hugh Grant, Tara Fitzgerald and Sam Neill an 8 out of 10. Supermodel Elle MacPherson was making her début in this film. She was so pleased with my comments that she embraced and kissed me on the screen, which briefly made me the most envied man in Britain. I was a little less taken with one of the Muppet movies, and gave it a 7, but Kermit the Frog didn't seem too upset. At least I had given him a personally favourable review.

The odd part was having Kermit sitting next to me and hearing his voice coming from behind the sofa. Well, of course, dumbkopf, I hear readers chorus, what did I expect, to hear the frog actually speak, but when you see the Muppets on television the voices are not coming from any particular point. It is unsettling to be on television and to have your neighbour's voice coming from somewhere else.

The appearance of Kermit was not the only reminder that persons on the set have different sensory experiences than viewers at home. On one occasion a young man who was a Mr. Mind of the Olympics came on the programme. He was sitting between me and his interviewer, Mike Morris. Since I am fairly confident this mastermind has bathed in the years since, I can say without fear of contradiction that he was the smelliest guest we ever had on the show. Eye contact between Mike and I confirmed that we were both not only in shock but distress, but we could not indicate on camera that we were undergoing an olfactory ordeal.

It was unpleasant for me, but all I had to do was sit there. Mike had to keep a straight face while conducting an interview, pretending that he was actually interested in who had won a certain dash in 1948 when all he really cared about was getting the item over with before he keeled over.

I have always thought that Mike Morris never received the credit he deserved for hosting TV-am during its most settled years of success. In respects that the general public and tabloid television reviewers don't even realise exist, he was a complete professional. One of these was that he successfully feigned interest in every item. There cannot be an individual in the world who is genuinely intrigued by the full range of subject material that appears on breakfast television. Morris appeared to be.

He also managed to look personally concerned about every young guest who appeared in what we called amongst ourselves the Sick Child slot. The programme planners loved to schedule ill or dying children after the 8 o'clock news.

Presumably tugs at the heartstrings enticed viewers to keep watching when the urgent items were over. We marvelled at how Mike managed to appear absorbed by every youngster's dilemma. No matter how cynical he may have thought some of the programming strategy, he never revealed it in the company of a guest.

Towards the end of the run, Morris set himself an additional challenge. Knowing that no one would be thrown off the show in its last weeks before GMTV took over, he accepted the dare from the technical staff to work their choice of word of the day into the show. He always pulled it off, even when they informed him early one morning the word of the day was "testicle". During an interview with agony aunt Claire Rayner, who was advising on the wisdom of giving children hugs and other forms of tactile encouragement, Mike asked if she would demonstrate by giving him a "test tickle".

I was always amused by the media commentators who spoke of the success of TV-am as if it were merely the product of executive decisions. The formidable and praiseworthy Greg Dyke has often been given credit for saving the channel with the introduction of Roland Rat, yet I don't recall any kind words for the person who actually was Roland Rat. Can any of the analysts who praise Greg Dyke even name the character's creator and operator?

I know that I would say this, because I was on the sofa myself, but I personally credit the talent that clicked. From my perspective, TV-am was saved because Anne Diamond and Nick Owen worked together. For a couple of years, the chemistry was palpable. It was neither the critics nor executives who deserve the credit for this. Anne and Nick deserve the credit. They were thrown together in breakfast television's hour of deepest despair, when we literally did not know if there would be a show the next day because the company had been unable to pay the electricity bill and we were all at the tender mercy of LEB.

No matter how skilled the salesmen or imaginative the decision makers behind the scenes, the relationship the viewer has is with the talent on camera. Charisma cannot be invented. It is rare, and when it is encountered it is thrilling. One of the most exciting feelings in the profession comes when you are sitting on the set and realising that a new contributor is happening, at that moment. This assistant Ulrika is presenting the weather, but she is doing more than presenting the weather, she is registering as a charismatic personality. The personal trainer Derrick Evans is leading the exercise sessions this week, but he is doing more than minding the spot, he is creating a character, Mr. Motivator. Hilary Jones is giving the medical advice, but he is projecting not just the counsel but a character, Dr. Hilary, sexy young physician. He and we might laugh about it off camera, but what matters is what happens on, and on camera Hilary, and Ulrika, and Motivator worked. Anne and Nick clicked. Tim Mallett, who in 1976 was a spritely disc jockey on Radio Oxford, was a phenomenon as children's presenter Timmy Mallett. These individuals, and talents like them, are the people who made breakfast television a success during my thirteen years with the two franchises, TV-am and GMTV, and I salute them.

Of course, not all the personal memories come from moments on screen. After make-up and before appearing on screen, we would gather in the Green Room, and there meet the world of celebrities and its mother. Breakfast television eats guests, and the most bizarre collection of public personalities this side of *Time*'s party for people who had appeared on the magazine's cover would assemble every morning in the green room. I met Alan Shepard, America's first man in space. (In the *Kaleidoscope* studio I shook hands with Buzz Aldrin, who was promoting a novel, and realised that I had just shaken a hand that had been on the moon.) I held the America's Cup, which was being displayed by its Australian winners en route home. I talked with evangelist

Billy Graham about secular matters for half an hour, which must be some sort of record.

I met virtually all the stars of soap operas, which was handy since I had neither the time nor the inclination to watch any of them. By speaking to them in the Green Room I could have a sense of what was happening on *EastEnders* or *Emmerdale* without actually watching the shows.

Long after I stopped playing their records on radio, I continued to meet the latest teen screams. Almost every boy band on the planet seemed to appear on GMTV. They were almost uniformly kind and respectful to me, an unusual combination of attitudes that reminded me that, whereas I had been a peer of the Elton Johns and Rod Stewarts, I could have been an uncle of Boyzone and Upside Down, and if the last two groups had different levels of success, it was not because one of them was less personally charming than the other.

In January of 1990 the lead singer of a pop group suddenly and massively popular with teenage girls appeared on the show. He had been looking for his big break for several years, during which time we had met and become friendly acquaintances. While waiting to go on he came over and spoke to me as casually as he would have a couple of years previously. The difference now, of course, was that others present were interested in what he might be saying to me. A year or two before, no one would have cared, nor would anyone a year or two hence, I feared. The shelf life of teen idols is a short one. After a pleasant conversation he returned to his group.

"I hope he enjoys his month," I whispered to one of the woman presenters. It sounds terribly catty, putting some sort of hex on his chart career, but in fact I literally meant it. Since this hit single had come in the progress of rather than the beginning of his work, it was more than likely to be the exception to the rule of his struggles as a singer. The female teen audience is the most fickle of record buying markets, and moves on to new pin-ups as bees go from flower to flower.

Once the girls have gone, they've left forever, and it takes perseverance and imagination to re-emerge as an adult artist.

It was easy for me to know this. I had seen it happen many times as a student of pop history. But I had also learned that every young artist lives the star experience for the first time. There is no sense trying to tell him what others have been through. For him it is all new, and what happened to those who have gone before will not necessarily happen to him. In saying, "I hope he enjoys his month," I wished that my friend would literally do that, enjoy the few weeks in the spotlight given him by the public. They were unlikely to come again.

They did not. Within a month his hit record had left the top ten. Within half a year his group were gone from the charts for good. Five years later, despondent over his stalled career and romantic disappointment, he attempted hari-kiri. Fortunately, he failed. He had not realised that the Japanese ritual of seppuku is not imitated lightly. It requires knowledge of how to cause fatal injury. Otherwise, as my friend learns, the self-assailant merely sticks the blade into his belly and rattles it around, causing messy damage to internal organs but nothing deadly.

A month after his mutilation, my friend called me in a newly distressed state. His suicidal phase had passed, but had left him with a scar on his stomach which he was afraid would affect his ability to pull potential lovers. I assured him that one scar was sexy, it was only several that constituted a trend. More than that, his attack on his abdomen had affected his deep breathing and limited his ability to sustain long notes as a vocalist. I hoped his wounds would fully heal and that in time he would regain his complete singing strength, but I was left with the reminder that when someone is so lost in subjectivity they consider suicide they fail to think of the consequences should they survive their self-inflicted injury.

TV-am died not from self-inflicted injury but because Prime Minister Margaret Thatcher killed it. Her system allocated television franchises to the highest bidder, subject to a panel's estimate of the ability to deliver quality programming. This process produced laughable results at both ends of the financial spectrum. One brilliant executive fronting the bid for Central Television inquired of financial institutions in the catchment area if any had made large loans for the purpose of broadcast investment. None had, and his £2,000 bid took home the infinitely more valuable franchise.

"Do you realise," I asked a full house at a theatre in the Strand during a Labour Party benefit, "if we each paid £2 we could have bought Central Television?"

Our exalted leader Bruce Gyngell was not so lucky with the breakfast franchise. He made what he thought from his experience was a financially responsible bid, not realising that two consortia would shoot the moon and more than double his offer, and that his track record of running a healthy station and his friendly acquaintance with the Prime Minister would count for nought. When we read the estimate of the competing bids in Raymond Snoddy's remarkably well-researched columns in the *Financial Times*, we knew we were doomed, but Bruce honestly seemed to think he would be renewed. He laid on a gala party for the morning of the allotments, and appeared before us in tears to express his shock and regret when the bad news was faxed through. We had worked the sadness out of our system eighteen months before, and had a good party.

GMTV took over and insulted the public by dropping all the presenters except Dr. Hilary, who at the time was too hot to discontinue. The new management made a cardinal error in broadcasting, which is repeated over and over again by new managerial brooms who want to sweep clean. The fundamental relationship in television is between the viewer and the presenter, not the viewer and the executive. No longer waking up to the Queen of the Morning, Lorraine Kelly, and watching talented individuals flounder trying to do what other persons had done better before them, not what they could best do themselves, viewers tuned out in droves. Three months later, several of us were begged back.

I do not flatter myself by saying this. It was the only time in my television career I was ever the subject of any pleading to perform. But GMTV was heading for a financial disaster, and needed some of the familiar faces back. Research carried out in the final two years of TV-am, but completely ignored by the original GMTV planners, had showed that Jimmy Greaves and I were the two feature presenters from whom the public wanted more. Of course: our subjects were football and films. Along with Lorraine, Jimmy and I were brought back to breakfast television. With the addition of Eamonn Holmes, the station's fortunes quickly improved.

But with Eamonn, the nature of the show changed. This was inevitable. Every host has a different dynamic with his colleagues. Anne Diamond was boss, but bright enough to realise she needed other talents to make the show work. Owen and Morris were gentlemen who willingly shared the sofa with anyone. One short-lived male host raised the anxiety level in the studio through his own nervousness.

Just as Nick and Mike were grateful to have been promoted from sports, Lorraine was in seventh heaven having been elevated from regional news, and transmitted her delight to others sitting on the sofa with her. Not only did she know the joyride could end at any time, she knew it would end. She had come on board in the latter days of the franchise and counted every day in the spotlight as a blessing.

Eamonn could not do the programme without treating himself as the central figure. This is not at all unusual in television, which usually emphasises one host per show. But heretofore breakfast TV had been a team effort. Eamonn did not seem comfortable with that approach. He turned many items into reflections of his own experience.

On one occasion, he interrupted a film review of mine by

relating that he had seen the movie in Texas in the middle of the afternoon, the only person in the cinema. A fascinating anecdote perhaps, but other presenters in the studio sympathised with me for the interruption of my unscripted flow. What if I had been unable to resume my concentration or my train of thought?

The classic example of Eamonn's turning an item around to reflect his own personality came with Victoria Wood. He got off on the wrong foot by noting that she succeeded in finding material in mundanities, and then proceeded to talk about how he would go to Heathrow after Friday shows to get the shuttle to Belfast, at which point airport procedures would sometimes go infuriatingly wrong. Wood sat there during this mini-monologue, her precious screen time being eroded. He then asked what it was like being part of a show business marriage, and named her magician husband – or, to be precise, misnamed him.

Victoria corrected the error and then icily said, "I never talk about him in interviews." The fight was lost with minutes still left to go. Eamonn was on the ropes, and the witty woman kept delivering body blows. Lorraine and I, both off-camera, made eye contact indicating we knew we were present for a rare moment.

When the interview was over, Lorraine introduced my film spot. I had to decide quickly whether to acknowledge the fracas or not. Ordinarily in television one does not draw attention to a mistake, in the hope that the viewer will not notice something has gone wrong if attention is not drawn to it. But this episode had been of several minutes duration, and anyone watching would expect some sort of comment.

"I didn't realise that was the cookery spot," I said, "and that Eamonn would be fried." I then proceeded normally. The entire episode, including my remark, became the basis of the TV column in *The Independent* the next day.

On GMTV I quickly felt like part of the past. Not only

did I regret the passing of what might be called The Team approach to presentation, I bemoaned the growing degree to which breakfast television programmed itself in response to tabloid newspapers. With so much money at stake, contributors were urged to follow the lead of the daily scandal sheets, rather than encouraged to suggest topics of their own. Nor did I feel comfortable with the tone of the show: what a new generation of programmers considered informal I thought sloppy. Finally, I was for the first time in my tenure told what films I should and should not be reviewing, rather than being trusted to make my own judgements.

In March 1996, I was told that I could not review my choice of film of the week, *Get Shorty*. When I asked why, I was told by someone who had not seen the film that the editors, who had also not viewed it, had been told that a character was shot during the course of the movie. In the aftermath of the Dunblane tragedy, this could not be mentioned. I explained that I wasn't intending to mention the incident, since it did not involve a major character, that the film was a comedy, rather than a disturbing drama, and that John Travolta and Gene Hackman, firm family favourites, were the stars. No, I was told. We are informed there is a shooting.

I felt compromised, but did not long have to worry about how to deal with this editorial interference. My spot was dropped entirely in favour of a report in which Lorraine Kelly, sent north because she was Scottish, traipsed around the Dunblane graveyard.

The next month, I was astonished when, having informed the features department at the beginning of the week of which films I was covering, I was told in a message at mid-week not only that I would be reviewing different movies, but that I would be doing so from Legoland near Windsor. Completely befuddled, I called the station to learn that a decision had been made to make my slot that week a guide to good children's films.

My editorial independence had been not only challenged but removed. I had not worked thirteen years to build a reputation as an adult critic only to be sent to Legoland to become a children's presenter, even if only for one week. I resigned.

I was persuaded to return by an executive who cancelled the Legoland plan and allowed me to review my original choice of films, but I had made a decision which I realised would soon be reciprocated on the management side. I was clearly out of sympathy with the direction in which the programme was travelling.

In the summer of 1996 I was taken to lunch by the boss, who told me my slot was being rested for the autumn with a 50% chance of return in the winter. He promised to get in touch soon, but did not. In November I unexpectedly encountered the same manager in the reception of Broadcasting House. He asked what I was working on. My recitation of activities concluded with the suggestion that I was thinking of calling another TV programme to see if they needed a film reviewer.

"Oh, don't do that," he pleaded. "There's still a 50% chance we'll want you back. I'll be in touch by the end of the year."

He never phoned again.

23

I Scare Telly Savalas

Some things you see on television jump out of the box. They are too passionate, too real, to be contained by a small appliance.

Telly Savalas, the film actor who in middle age became a television star as the detective Kojak, appeared on Michael Parkinson's BBC chat show. Parkinson was the King of Talk on the Beeb.

In the course of the interview Savalas told a tale so frightening it imprinted itself on my mind. He had been driving into what was for him a new town and decided he needed a drink before he settled in. He saw a man hitchhiking out of the city and asked him if he could recommend a bar. The stranger told him of a suitable hostelry and added, "Tell them all Joe [to use a neutral name] sent you."

Savalas went to the bar, enjoyed a drink, and then said, "Oh, by the way, Joe says hello."

Happy faces turned sullen. You could hear an ice cube melt.

"You bastard," one of the revellers finally spoke. "You know he died yesterday."

Telly told of how he had met Joe on the outskirts of town. He matched his physical description of the man with the account of the deceased's old friends.

Then he knew. Telly Savalas knew he had met the spirit of a man leaving his home town forever.

Parkinson's studio audience oohed and ahhed a bit, and then Michael proceeded to ask more questions about television and film. I just sat there going, ahem, we have just heard something a little more extraordinary than the details of another episode of *Kojak*.

A couple of years later a friend of mine named Simon Turner had a Saturday morning children's television series called *Kim*. It was, apparently, big news in Germany, but not big enough to find me sitting in front of my TV on Saturdays. When the last broadcast was only a few days away, I told Turner's best friend, the magician Simon Drake, that I was embarrassed I had not yet seen any of the shows. Drake admitted that he hadn't either, and was unlikely to since he did not have a television.

I invited Simon over to watch Simon. The magic man slept in my spare bedroom the night before the broadcast; the start time was too early for him to contemplate commuting to my TV.

Just before my alarm went off, I had a dream starring Simon Drake. He was an aquaboy on the deck of a naval ship, standing next to a mermaid, accepting the thanks of the crew. He and his female companion gave a final salute and jumped into the water, swimming into the watery sunset. They each turned back once to give a last wave.

My alarm went off. I walked next door and woke up Simon, telling him in detail of his starring role in my dream. Noting only three minutes remained until the final episode of Turner's series, I suggested we go into the living room and turn on the television.

Kim was preceded by a Japanese cartoon. We tuned in just in time to see the conclusion. An aquaboy was on the deck of a naval ship, standing next to a mermaid, accepting the thanks of the crew. He and his female companion gave a final salute and jumped into the water, swimming into the watery sunset. They each turned back once to give a last wave.

Simon Drake and I stared at each other. He spoke first.

"I'm glad you told me before we saw that."

I had, and have now, no explanation for how or why I had

dreamt the ending of the cartoon ten minutes before we viewed it. I was, however, deeply impressed it had happened, partly because the cartoon was so mundane. It wasn't as if I had a vision saying, "The Titanic is about to sink, warn everyone." I just plugged in to an animated film that was about to be shown on television.

It wasn't the final time I had such a dream. One morning of a day on which I was going to make a risotto I dreamt I saw the ingredients of the dish listed as in a rebus. There was an onion, which would need to be chopped, a piece of parmesan cheese, which would have to be grated, and a box of Fino rice.

Fino rice? Arborio, perhaps, but Fino? What was that?

I woke up, surprised by the image of the strange box, and went to get the morning paper. There in *The Independent* was an article on an Italian grocer named Fino.

Oh. That explains the Fino rice. But why had I bothered to have such a monumentally trivial dream?.

After incidents like these, I concluded there was a mental level that we only occasionally tap in to. I never became the Radio 1 equivalent of Shirley MacLaine, but if someone I believed told me they had undergone an unusual spiritual experience, I gave them the benefit of the doubt.

One friend went through something akin to Telly Savalas' encounter with the deceased hitchhiker. My first philosophy tutorial partner at University College, Oxford had returned to education from Vietnam. He had been drafted from Yale and sent to the war. Needless to say, the experience changed his life. He calculated he had killed nearly twenty people in combat, and had found some comfort in Eastern religion.

One evening he was the house guest of a fellow veteran. Sleeping in a spare room, he was awakened to see one of his slain comrades standing at the foot of his bed. When he reached out to the man, the vision disappeared. The apparition was so lifelike my friend ran to his host's room to tell him of the visit. He only got as far as the hallway, where he ran into his host, who was rushing to tell him that he had just received a visit from the same soldier.

And so I believed. Why shouldn't I? If I could occasionally dream the future, and if my tutorial mate had been visited by a killed colleague, why shouldn't Telly Savalas have had a conversation with a spirit?

The morning came when Telly Savalas and I were in make-up together at TV-am. He was as engaging and personable as a man can be before sunrise. I felt I had to tell him.

"I saw you tell Michael Parkinson the story about the hitch-hiker," I told him. "I've never forgotten it."

His mood changed utterly.

"I never talk about that any more," he said solemnly. "It's too scary."

24

Smokey Robinson

In the mid-Eighties, director Rod Taylor and I did three series of a popular music programme for Channel 4 called *The Other Side Of The Tracks*. While we were roaming America interviewing subjects for the show we grabbed Motown artists wherever and whenever we could find them, holding the results for our eventual special *The Motown Story*. The linchpin of the programme, the man who appeared throughout as the Greek chorus of the tale, was Smokey Robinson. There could have been no one more appropriate except, perhaps, his media-shy friend Motown founder Berry Gordy himself.

The very first Tamla release, 'Way Over There' by The Miracles, was issued in 1960. Smokey was artist, writer, producer, and executive at Motown, accumulating a historic sequence of hits for The Miracles and later himself, while writing classic songs for a variety of artists. This interview has never previously appeared in print, but is the best source I know for Smokey stories – and there are a lot of them. Smokey's wife and former original Miracle Claudette sat in.

You started in the Fifties. I was wondering who the inspirations for your singing style might have been, and I thought of Clyde McPhatter. Was he a factor at all?

Of course. I grew up listening to Clyde McPhatter and Jackie Wilson, Frankie Lymon and people like that. They were definitely idols of mine as a teenager growing up. I had all their records.

That was how I recognised Berry Gordy by name when I first

met him. I first met him at this audition we'd gone to for Jackie Wilson's manager. Berry happened to be there delivering some new songs for Jackie, because he wrote all of Jackie Wilson's songs at that time. We had sung a bunch of songs that I had written while going to school at this audition, and this interested Berry. He wanted to find out where we had gotten the songs. He introduced himself, and when he told me he was Berry Gordy of course I knew who he was because I had all of Jackie Wilson's records.

Including 'Reet Petite', which had been a top ten record in Britain?

Oh, yes.

'Lonely Teardrops' was another big one Berry had written. Then he started producing and leasing records with Marv Johnson and yourself, is that correct?

Right.

He did your first two records for another label. Those were 'Got A Job' and 'Bad Girl'. Was 'Got A Job' intended to be an answer to The Silhouettes' 'Get A Job'?

Oh, of course. That's what inspired the song. 'Get A Job' was probably the number one record in the universe. It definitely inspired a young group to try to answer it.

You only achieved a minor chart placing with 'Bad Girl'. I suppose nonetheless that for youngsters it must have been a thrill?

It probably was. 'Bad Girl' was the very first song that got us national attention. Being a new group and hearing our song being played on television, on Dick Clark's show, was a big thrill, of course. We'd never had a record that had done that much for us.

You put that record out through Chess. Someone suggested to Berry Gordy that he might make more money if he put it out on his own label. Was it you that made that suggestion?

Not with that particular song. That was on a song called 'Way Over There'. 'Way Over There' was the record we made after 'Bad Girl'. Locally it was on the Tamla label. Up to that point we had not been set up to do national distribution because we only had local distributors and distributors around the Detroit area. We weren't being paid right on the records that were being leased to other companies. Berry wasn't being paid what was due on those records. So I just suggested that we go national with the 'Way Over There' record on The Miracles, because we really had nothing to lose. The companies that we were leasing the records to for national distribution weren't paying us properly anyway.

Was it true that Berry originally wanted to call the label 'Tammy'. I'm told he liked the movie with Debbie Reynolds.

That was the inspiration for the name Tamla. He didn't want to call the label Tammy, though. He just thought he would get something very close to that. And it wasn't because of the movie, it was because of the record. 'Tammy' by Debbie Reynolds was probably number one at the time. It was from the movie, but it was because of the record that he named the label Tamla.

Previously there'd been a record by Barrett Strong, 'Money', which Berry had co-written, that had been a hit. My copy was on the Anna label. Was that . . .

Do you have a copy of that on Anna? (Laughter)

That was named after Berry's sister. But it was short-lived. What was the story?

It was just a label she had started. Eventually I guess you would say she merged it into Motown, because she was not set up for national distribution. We were beginning to distribute nationally, so it was a good thing for her.

So 'Way Over There' was the first nationally distributed record. The first big one was 'Shop Around', released late 1960. It's Motown's first million-selling record. For a very small company this must have caused great excitement. What was the scene like as you reached number two in the charts?

It was probably like awe. I'm sure that everyone was in awe. We never had a record of that magnitude before and we were in our infancy. It was great for everyone involved to have a record receive that kind of attention around the world.

When 'Shop Around' started to really break big we would all get together, my wife and the guys in the group included, and we would package the record up and mail it out to different countries. In those days, everybody did everything. There was no "You do this" and "I do that", and "My speciality is so and so". Everybody did everything.

You had a big hit with that record. Claudette, those albums you had in the early Sixties which came after you started getting hits had hysterical album sleeves. Do you know what I'm referring to?

Claudette: Yes, I do. Basically they used the pictures I looked the worst on. (Laughter)

Smokey: No. You look pretty good on them.

Is it true that a lot of those early album covers had cartoon figures on the front. Or there's the case of you all holding up letters saying, "Hi, we're the Miracles". (Everyone laughs.) They're all kind of jokey sleeves, really. Was that because you wanted to go to the mass young audience?

Smokey: I think so, and I think at the time we thought they were great. (Laughter)

Claudette: That was a serious album, right?

Smokey: Especially *Hi, We're The Miracles*. Heck, that was our first album and we thought that was a great concept. Now here you come along and ruin that for us (laughter) in one evening, and all these years we've been clinging to that as a great album cover. Here you come along and just totally wash that out. (Laughter)

The same year as 'Shop Around', 1961, 'Please Mr. Postman' goes to number one. It's the first number one by the Motown companies. The Marvelettes are a strange case. Most people can name members of the various groups through the years, but they don't know The Marvelettes, or they may know Gladys Horton. Wasn't it true they changed members through the years?

The Marvelettes changed numbers, but only deductively. In other words, every time a girl left The Marvelettes no one replaced her. They started off with five girls and ended up being three, but these three were original girls. One girl left and then another girl left and then there were three of them. When the group disbanded, the original three girls were the group.

You said that everybody helped everybody out in those early days and did every job. Is that how you came to write and produce for other artists?

Not necessarily. Berry would take me in the studio with him and teach me different things about producing records. We had an earlier record of 'Shop Around' which was probably my very first production that ever hit the streets. It was slower and funkier than the one that became popular. It had been out for about two weeks, I guess, and Berry called one night, or one morning I should say, probably about three o'clock in the morning, and said he had not been able to sleep for the past couple of days because he was thinking about 'Shop Around'. He loved the song so much and he wanted to change the beat on the record. So call the group and come to the studio right now! It was three o'clock in the morning, you know. We did. We changed the beat on it, and that was the record that happened.

The very first artist I had a chance to produce and work with all on my own was Mary Wells. At that time we didn't have a bunch of artists like we eventually did have. It was fun. I enjoyed working with other people. The songs I wrote for the other artists I wrote specifically with those people who sang them in mind. It was always fun for me. I would always try to imagine the person who was going to sing the song from said group, or if I was working with a solo artist singing that song as I was writing it, I would put certain words in that I thought they said good and things like that.

Let's take Mary Wells' two biggest chart records. The first was 'Two Lovers', which you wrote. What unusual subject matter for the early Sixties, almost a bit risqué! 'Two Lovers' it sounds like all the way through the song, and then it turns out the poor fellow is a schizophrenic.

The idea for that particular song came from my wife. (Laughter) She's a Gemini and they're supposed to be like two people. I must admit she is very even-keeled, she is not a real drastic dual personality. But a lot of times when we were younger we'd be laughing and talking, and all of a sudden she'd just turn off. You know, something had made her sad and I'd say, "Baby, what happened? Why are you sad?", "I'm not sad", "Well, what happened?", "Nothing". This is like total day and night. So the thought of her inspired that particular song.

And then Mary Wells' giant around the world, 'My Guy'. Here is one again where you tailor wrote the piece. Was it difficult writing a love story about a guy from a woman's point of view?

No, because I think it's the same thing, man or woman. I don't think love categorises itself.

Perhaps we as men feel as though our idea of love is ours, because when it comes down to letting us know they're thinking the same thing women are basically very coy. They don't want us to know that they're thinking the same things that we're thinking, but they are. So that's why it doesn't bother me to write for a woman. In fact I enjoy very much writing for women, as much as I do for men.

It was easier for me to complete an idea for a girl in those days than if I was writing for a guy, because my personal self would get into the guy thing a bit. Whereas if I'm writing for a girl I feel totally free to say whatever I think she's thinking. When you're writing songs from a guy's point of view I don't think you're quite as open. He doesn't want to reveal all of the things that a guy might think.

Does that make sense? No? OK, scratch that.

No, it makes fine sense. I'm wondering if Mary Wells, when you gave her the piece, thought, "Yes, this is how it feels".

I don't know. I just enjoyed working so much with Mary.

Mary was very good for me. Her voice was so unique and it

just fit what I was trying to write about for her. I felt the same way about Wanda Rogers when I started to write for the Marvelettes. She had one of those little unique voices that I love to hear. It's easy for me to write for that sound.

Mary Wells so sadly left the company after scoring the number one with 'My Guy' and having a hit duet with Marvin Gaye. What enticed her away? It was such a shame.

Smokey: I thought Claudette told her she had to. (Laughter)

Claudette: No, I think it was her husband. Her husband at that time I believe thought she probably could become a bigger artist moving along. That was my impression at the time.

Smokey: I think probably that was accurate. He was her manager and at that time we were not totally established. We were still struggling to establish ourselves around the world as a label, and as always with our artists many people were after her at the time. Somebody just made them an offer they felt they couldn't refuse, like a Godfather offer. Maybe it was the Godfather.

Well, indeed she did go to Twentieth Century Records and never had that wonderful success again. You were struggling at the time, or the company was struggling, with another female act, The Supremes. Wasn't it true that before their first hit they had a series of non-starters?

Yes, they did. I think Claudette was working with them. (Laughter)

No, I was working with them because I'd known Diana forever. I first met her when she was ten or eleven, something like that. She lived down the street from me.

When we started to make records it was a big deal for everyone who knew us in Detroit. We weren't making any money, but the fact that we were making records made everyone think we were in the big time. So it was a very common thing for our friends to want to come to our rehearsals, and Diana did. She would sing, and her dream was that one day she would record.

When she started to go to high school, she and three other girls – there used to be four girls in the group – came by our rehearsal one night. We were rehearsing at Gordy's mother's house that night, in fact. They sang for me and I told them I would take them over and let Berry hear them because I liked them very much. I thought Diana had a hit sound to her voice. She was unique. No one sounded like her.

I took them over, and Berry told me that after they graduated from high school I would be able to record them, which I did. I recorded three or four records on them, and nothing happened. Then Holland-Dozier-Holland made a record on them called 'When The Lovelight Starts Shining In His Eyes'. This made a little noise and caused them to be on a Dick Clark tour. After the tour had been out for a while 'Where Did Our Love Go' came out, and the rest, for them, is history.

What was it that made them not have hits for a while and then have the wonderful streak of five number ones in a row?

I guess you'd have to say . . . no, I don't know. The record business is very strange. I don't know what makes that happen. An artist can be on a roll and have four or five hits in a row and then go quiet for a while. Then you have four or five hits more.

Some artists just continually have them, but I think most everybody has a dry spell. For myself, I think the dry spells are good for an artist because they bring back the reality of the record business and of life. It's good for you.

1963 was a good year for The Miracles, two top ten records beginning with 'You Really Got A Hold On Me'. This was of course covered by The Beatles, which created a lot of excitement. At least that's what it seemed from the outside. How was it from the inside?

It was exciting, of course. It was a beautiful phenomenon. There was a lot of excitement for anyone who had created whatever it was they touched.

And certainly bringing attention to the possibilities of covering your songs as a writer. Through the years this has happened a lot, but did you envision when you were started that other artists might be singing your songs?

I always hoped so. I still do today. Whenever I write a song, I always hope it's a song that other people will want to record and it's not just a personal thing for me.

Claudette, do you recall the making of that record? It was a good example of close harmony singing by the Miracles.

Claudette: Yes, I do recall that record because I actually didn't like it in the beginning. I thought it was a little too slow, a little too draggy. I kept saying, "I don't like you but I love you", and I thought, OK, and everyone's saying, "It's great, it's great." Of course, the more we sang it, you know it grows on you. But in the beginning I really didn't like that record.

But the public liked it . . .

Claudette: Which I was very happy about.

And later in the year they liked another one, too, 'Mickey's Monkey'. Unusually, this was not one of your songs. Holland-Dozier-Holland wrote it. How did it come about?

One day I walked into the studio and Lamont was sitting there at the piano. Lamont Dozier was the Dozier of the team. He was sitting at the piano and playing a little riff, a little musical riff, and he was singing [Smokey sings the hook]. He hadn't even started the song, hardly.

And I loved it. I asked him what he was doing and he said he was just writing a song. I said, "Hey, I really like that so will you record it on us?" He said, "Yes." In a day or two they had the song together and we recorded it and I'm really happy.

It was a top ten record and it appeared in the film Mean Streets *to marvellous effect with Robert de Niro bopping down the street to it. Did you ever see that?*

No, I didn't.

Claudette: Neither did I.

You might enjoy it. It's one of the best uses of a song in a film I have ever seen.

I'd love to see that.

It's marvellous. In those days, we're talking about 1963 and the mid-Sixties, the Motown acts would tour together. It wasn't like you would go on a tour separately. There were so many artists, was it chaos?

Sure, it was chaotic but it was chaotic fun. It was chaotic love and chaotic togetherness. Because we were like one big family there and everyone knew everyone. We were like the granddaddies. When I say that, I mean The Miracles.

Claudette was almost in charge of the other girls. The other girls came to her for everything, all kinds of road advice, what was happening with this, what was happening with that. A lot of times we went to townships where it was impossible for Claudette and I to stay together because of the lack of room or the lack of space or the lack of money to get rooms for everybody or else it was in the South where there were really no hotels for black people at that time. You had to stay in rooming houses, so a lot of the girls had to stay together and the guys had to stay together. We shared rooms.

I think she was like their leader at that time as being the first girl who was ever there. The guys always talked to the guys in The Miracles because we were the first group, the first ones who started to tour, and so on. It was a very good thing happening at that time. I regret the fact that those shows cannot take place any more.

For financial reasons?

Exactly.

Claudette, was it true that you once because of Smokey's illness sang lead for The Miracles?

Claudette: Yes, I did. That was one of the first Motown revues. Smokey was very ill with the Hong Kong flu, I think he probably had one of the first cases in the United States, so we had to go back to Detroit. The three guys – because Peter at that time was in the United States Army – so there was Bobby, Ronnie and myself and I sang lead. As we went down South, we had not appeared there before, so they all assumed I was Smokey.

175

So I was singing these songs, you know, because sometimes I can mimic quite well, and they said, "Oh sing, Smokey, sing." That was fun, it really was. It was a great experience for me.

You must have noticed when Smokey returned that he was attracting a female audience and becoming quite a sex symbol of the time.

Claudette: I suppose.

I recall reading a quote of someone, I think it was at the Apollo, who yelled out from the back, "Any time you want Smokey, you can come right up here." Now I'm not going to ask you if you actually went up there, but were you aware that you were a bit of a showman playing to the female fans at times?

I think women are freer with demonstrating their emotions than men are. I think basically men think they have to be cool. Either they are at the show with their lady, or they are trying to attract the ladies who are there, so they feel that even if they are inspired they should be cool with it. Whereas girls are different. They just express themselves. They feel a certain way and they are just going to express themselves.

I think they make shows happen more than guys do. Not to say they don't enjoy having guys there. It's a good balance and it makes me feel really good, being a male artist, that guys enjoy my music. But I think women make live shows happen. They do express themselves. I don't personalise it for myself because, heck, I go and see other guys and the girls are doing the same thing. It's just a part of this life.

Well, one guy for whom they also went wild was Marvin Gaye. Didn't he play the drums with you?

Yes, he did.

On the road?

Yes, he did. In the very beginning of his Motown career he was a drummer and played drums for us and several acts on records. But he played for us in person.

After his first couple of hits, you did work with him as a writer and producer and you gave him a couple of big ones. He was quoted as saying that you came to his aid when he was in a low period with 'I'll

Be Doggone' and 'Ain't That Peculiar'. What was the problem? He was so popular.

Like I said, everybody goes through it. At some time or another in the record business you are going to experience that and the people who are strong and really love what they are doing at least try to survive it. A lot of them do, a lot of them don't.

When you do survive and maintain for a number of years in this record business and in show business itself, it's a blessing, because it boils down to the fact that it can't really hinge upon talent or material or things like that because most of the time people who make a showing are talented. There's a lot of good material and for yours to edge through and be one of the top hundred or the top fifty or the top ten is really a blessing for you.

You did score with Marvin on 'Ain't That Peculiar' and 'I'll Be Doggone' and a couple of others. Records from this partnership were released for about a year. Were you sometimes bothered that these stints were short? Do you wish you could have kept working with Marvin?

Yes. I wish I could have probably kept working with all of the artists, but as the company grew, so did the artists. We became very separate as far as our time being at home. This is why the 25th anniversary special [*Motown 25*] is such a great piece of work. It brings all these people back home again for one more time for another Motown Revue for television. But the artists became too expensive to package together like that, so therefore it became harder and harder for us to work together.

You began working with The Temptations when they hadn't had success. Your song 'The Way You Do The Things You Do' was a smash and you had a series of hits. Here you really got a chance to bite your teeth into the marvellous dual lead singing capabilities of Eddie Kendricks and David Ruffin.

And Paul Williams, also.

That's right, he sang 'Don't Look Back'. When you started out with them did you have a plan in mind because, like The Supremes, they hadn't had hits the first time out.

Yes, I did. I had two other records out on them before 'The Way You Do The Things You Do', and I knew they were multi-talented. When I first started to work with them David Ruffin was not in the group. They had another singer who had to leave the group because of financial reasons. Like I said, at that time no one was really making any money so he really had to get a job because he had a family.

David Ruffin took his place in the group. They were so multi-talented already and then to receive another strong voice like that – it was really exciting for me to work with them because you had such a vast range of types of material and large scope of voice range you could record on them.

They had Paul Williams, who was a very soulful baritone-type tenor, and then you had David Ruffin who was like a little higher than Paul tenor-wise and he had the strong gruff growly sound, and then you had Eddie Kendricks who was very soft and high, so you had a wide range of areas to take them to. I really loved working with them. They were one of my favourite acts to work with.

Would you write the song and then think, that's right for such-and-such a vocal?

Usually I had the person in mind before I even started writing the song.

We come to their great classic written by you, 'My Girl'. Did you know straight away that would be David Ruffin?

Yes. No one had utilised his voice up to that point. I knew he had a great voice because before he was in The Temptations he was a solo artist and had been singing around Detroit for many years. I knew what his capabilities were and I knew no one was utilising them, not even me. And I knew that if he had the right song he would be great for it.

Did you write 'My Girl' because you had had a great success with 'My Guy'?

178

Not necessarily. 'My Girl' was one of those songs that was written maybe within a half hour or so, like 'Shop Around' was. Some songs are labour, and some ideas are labour. It's a good idea or a good phrase or a good group of words and you labour over them to finish them.

Some songs flow, it just happens. Before you have even finished this verse you have thought of what the next verse is. And 'My Girl' was one of those kind of songs.

I totally forgot, what was your question about the song?

I asked if you had been inspired to write it because you had had a big hit with 'My Guy'?

No. It was just that "my girl" was the perfect ending for what had been said up to that point. If I had said anything else it would have been too much.

Those lines that you had said before are almost a perfect example of one of the features of your writing, and that is comparisons, contrasts. "I've got sunshine on a cloudy day/When it's cold outside I've even got the month of May", along with analogies such as "Like push can turn to shove/Like can turn to love". I think this is almost a unique feature of your writing. Is this something you had worked on before you were a songwriter in some other kind of writing?

No. I think that one of the greatest things that ever happened to me as a songwriter was to meet Berry Gordy. When I met him I had a bunch of songs that I had written. I was always a good rhymer. I could rhyme words since I was a little kid. But my songs rambled and they didn't make sense verse by verse.

Everything would be rhymed great in the first verse. I could be talking about, "Boy, it is so great to be here with you and I really love being here with you like this holding you in my arms" and so on down the line. And then the second verse I would be saying, "Because I haven't seen you in so long, I just wish I could touch you." It would have nothing to do with the first verse.

He taught me that a song is a book and a song is a story. A

song should be a complete idea. Whether or not you complete it, it should be complete enough for the person to draw their own conclusions at the end of it if in fact you haven't concluded it for them.

I started thinking about that aspect of writing songs and listening to people like Lieber and Stoller who really wrote song songs. You know, they had a lot of words but their songs made so much sense. Burt Bacharach and Hal David and those people who wrote the kind of words the old people used to write, people like Sammy Cahn. Those songs were standards. They were played in my house all the time, and I always wanted to write like that, to write songs that had substance, that if they were recited without being heard as a melody would still make sense.

So Berry was a very good catalyst to show me what this meant, to be able to put a song down and make it mean something like that. Everything has been written about. There are no new subjects, no new melodies, no new notes, no new words, and every idea has been written about. So I try to write about it in a different manner, in a different way, so that it sounds different, so that a person hearing it will feel the familiarity of the old idea but also feel the newness of the new way to say it.

A perfect example of that comes in 1965 with 'Tracks Of My Tears', a beautifully written song which has been covered by many artists ranging from Linda Ronstadt to Bryan Ferry. That song originated with you hearing Marv Tarplin playing the guitar, didn't it?

Yes. Many songs have. He's a very musical man. He's been a great inspiration to me because he does play some beautiful melodies on that guitar. It's an extension of him. He always has it with him, he's always playing it and his sound is beautiful.

Is it still true that you've never played live on stage without him?

No, it isn't. November was the very first time I ever played a date that he wasn't there. We were playing in Lake Tahoe at Caesar's Palace and he was sick, he couldn't make the gig.

Every day we were talking on the phone, either he called me or I called him before we went on and he would say, "Well, I wish I was there." That is the only one he has ever missed.

'Tracks Of My Tears' has been such a favourite for so many people on so many different versions. You must have been inspired when you wrote it.

Yes. Marvin had done the music long before I could finish the song. We worked on that for many days and the chorus of the song "Take a good look at my face/You'll see my smile looks out of place/If you look closer it's easy to trace" was done probably a week before I figured out what to trace.

I do that with a lot of songs, you know. I figured that whatever it was you were tracing had to be something unique. I was still living in Detroit and Pete Moore, who was one of The Miracles, and Tarplin and myself were upstairs in my music room working on this particular song and playing it over and over again and all of a sudden I thought about crying and the fact that when you cry and you wipe your eyes, it's gone. Unless your eyes are red or something, no one would suspect it. 'The Tracks Of My Tears.' That was it. No one had ever said 'The Tracks Of My Tears' before.

That year 1965 you also had 'My Girl Has Gone' and 'Ooh Baby Baby'. What a great example of close harmony work and your falsetto that was. Did the group rehearse this close harmony at great length or did it just come naturally in the studio?

In the early days, we rehearsed all the time. The blending of Claudette's voice with the male voices was a unique sound. We always had a different sound than the other groups. To me we did, anyway.

We were the first group to come out with a girl in the group that utilised her fully. She was so finicky about it, it even got down to when we bought clothing. Rather than having a dress, when we would go buy suits she would buy a size 57 suit, right, so there would be a lot of material. She'd cut the suit up and make a dress to match exactly what we had on. She was very finicky.

We thought it was very bad for people who considered themselves to be professionals not to work on their sound or not to actually be able to sing outside the studio.

Claudette, seeing as you put so much effort into The Miracles, it must have been some kind of wrench for you to leave the group, which you did do in the late Sixties. Why did you decide to do that?

Claudette: After having about five miscarriages and losing about twenty pounds and becoming very anaemic, travelling on the road was really hard on me. Smokey and Berry Gordy decided that I should leave the group.

Smokey could now afford to take care of me. When Smokey and I got married, Motown paid him eight dollars a week. Well, at least we got it raised to eight dollars a week, it was originally five dollars a week, so it wasn't much more after that even when we were travelling on the road, for about the first two years at least. I did not want to leave the group, I wanted to stay on the road.

After all those miscarriages, I felt I probably would never have children, so it was so much fun being on the road and being with my husband all the time. I thought, "Why should I leave?" They said, "Well, we think you should go" and I was outvoted. We had like a club, and everyone had a vote. Of course the guys said, "Well, it's left up to Smokey" and they gave all their votes to Smokey.

Smokey: Tell you what, when the kids come home we'll ask them if they're glad.

The very names of the children show your love of the company. Your son . . .

Claudette: Is Berry William Borope, which is Bobby, Ronnie and Pete, the former Miracles.

And your daughter?

Claudette: Tamla Claudette.

You obviously knew your contract was going to be renewed.

We're in the Sixties and of course one of the great stars to emerge is Little Stevie Wonder, discovered by one of the Miracles.

Ronnie White brought Stevie over to the company to be heard when he was probably ten or eleven. He was a very musical kid. It was like he was never really a kid in his soul. He was one of those kids like Michael Jackson was, who sang and performed like someone who was much older than their years. Every now and then a kid comes along like that.

That's how Stevie was. He was very musical. He just picked up stuff and started playing it. He is a musical genius, he really is.
Can you explain that gift?

I explain it very simply. It is a gift from God. It was his calling. That was what he was meant to do and he does it well.

Creative people are all receiving creative forces through the Lord. It is in the air. It is there. You don't sit down and say, "I must think of a song today", it just happens. "I must think of an idea today", it just happens. "Gotta write this melody", it just happens.

Sometimes you'll have a deadline or you'll sit down and start from scratch at the piano. But the great majority of songs are instinctive. Therefore, I think they are a blessing.
You also had the ability to react to what was going around. Hence, in 1966, the hit 'Going To A Go-Go'. Discotheques were called go-gos at the time. That broke the string of ballads. Did you have a preference for the ballad or the uptempo material?

No. I enjoy singing everything, so I have no preference. They are all fun. Different emotions go with each song. It is very easy for me to feel those emotions over and over again. In playing and singing those songs, they never become routine.
It's a compliment for that song, 'Going To A Go-Go', that The Rolling Stones recently recorded it. The song has therefore outlived the expression.

Exactly. No question about it.
Here in 1966 you are working with The Marvelettes on a sequence of singles which have different kinds of sounds than the normal pop song. For example, 'My Baby Must Be A Magician' with that unusual spoken beginning and various effects. Did you have fun in the studio with that?

183

Oh yes. The spoken part was done by Melvin Franklin of The Temptations. He is the big heavy voice, you know. It was almost like a novelty record, but it wasn't. It had a story and substance to it.

As we turn the corner from the mid-Sixties to the late Sixties, Motown is having an almost unprecedented run for an independent label on the pop charts. There are top ten singles all the time by so many artists and indeed printed on the LPs is the expression 'The Sound of Young America'. Did you find it odd that here was a black company enjoying such success in white America where only a few years before you had been victims of segregation?

When you stopped to think about it you found it odd, but I very seldom did stop to think about it because it was like second nature by that time. In the late Fifties and early Sixties it was more apparent to those involved. We used to receive fan mail from young white kids. They had our records but their parents didn't know, so they were like underground records or something. They had to hide them in the house or whatever.

We got a lot of letters like that, so you could get the feeling. In the late Sixties we were so well-accepted everywhere and records were just records and whoever bought them was whoever bought them. And Motown has always been an integrated company business-wise, so therefore we didn't even look upon it like that by that time.

You were popular personally and with the release of 'The Love I Saw In You Was Just A Mirage' you get top billing on the records. It's not just limited to you, though you are the first. Martha Reeves gets top billing after being 'Martha and The Vandellas', Diana Ross gets top billing whereas it had just been 'The Supremes'. Was this a conscious decision to really give a focus to the lead singers?

Yes, it was a conscious decision, but not necessarily to give a focus to the lead singers. It had been proven by that time with, like, Little Anthony and The Imperials, Frankie Lymon and The Teenagers, Clyde McPhatter and The Drifters, and so on, that with a name out front, people identified with your group more. And it made more money. That was the reason we did it.

The first year of doing that you had a top five record with 'I Second That Emotion'. Do you remember writing that?

Oh, yeah. 'I Second That Emotion' was quite a slip of the tongue. Al Cleveland, who wrote the song with me, and I were Christmas shopping one year. We were at a department store and we were talking to one of the sales girls. She happened to say something to which Al replied, "I second that emotion" rather than "I second that motion" and we laughed about it. Then as we were shopping we said, "Hey, that's a great idea". We went home and wrote it.

It was a great hit and in Britain also a hit for The Supremes and Temptations in a duet. In the States they had a big one with 'I'm Gonna Make You Love Me', which was also a hit in Britain. Do you recall whose idea it was to mix those two groups?

Not directly, but I'm sure it was probably Berry. He was working very closely with The Supremes at that time and I'm sure it was probably him.

There were so many other acts in the charts at that time – Jr. Walker, Jimmy Ruffin, Gladys Knight and The Pips – was it chaos in the studio? Weren't all the sides done in the Hitsville Building in Michigan?

No. That's what's so funny about the theory of the Motown sound. They say, "Well, what is the Motown sound?" No one really knows whether to look upon it as an audible sound.

I think it is something very unique and spiritual. It's created by the people who sing it and play it and write it.

When we first started out, people were coming from every-where from all over the world to Detroit to record, because they thought they were going to get the Motown sound. If they came and recorded out on the streets they would get the Motown sound because it was in Detroit. It was in the air, so they came to Detroit to get it and they couldn't get it.

What they didn't realise was that all the time they were

migrating to Detroit to record, we were recording our acts on the road. We recorded them in Chicago, in New York, in Nashville, in Miami, in California, everywhere, and we still got the Motown sound. No one knew whether or not we recorded a record in Detroit or wherever.

Can you recall any particularly funny sessions in different cities?

In retrospect a lot of them are funny now, but at the time they were panics. If something is not going right at a recording session – especially in the early days for us, because a lot of the time when we recorded, everyone was there. There was no "you take this out and then you gotta mix it" or "you got so many tracks so you're going to re-do the guitar". It was mono, man, so when you came out of the studio that was it. Everybody who was going to sing on that record or play on that record was there. If they weren't, they missed that one.

So a lot of frantic things happened in the studio. Retrospectively they are probably funny, but they weren't then. A lot of things happened, like the tape breaking in the middle of a song or trying to run down one song and running out of time and everybody is panicking trying to get this one song done and you don't get it done.

Let's take one song, 'The Tears Of A Clown'. It first appears in 1967 as the last track on an album called Smokey Robinson And The Miracles Make It Happen. *It's not released as a single for three years. Did no one notice how commercial it was?*

Probably only Stevie Wonder [the composer of the music], Hank Cosby, who produced the track, and me. Because I always loved that music.

They gave me the music, and when they gave me the track it was just music, they didn't have a song. We used to do that a lot in the old days. One person would have music and the other person would have words, one person may have a melody or something.

They brought that track to me and it reminded me of the circus because of the calliope feeling. So I laboured over it to figure out what I could write about the circus that would mean something to people. What means something to people about the circus? Pagliacci – that means something. He is the clown, he's there and he's happy making everybody laugh. Then he goes to his dressing room and he's crying, because he's unhappy for real. His happiness is painted on. I thought that was a good idea and that's how it became 'The Tears Of A Clown'.

Three years later, released in Britain, it goes to number one. Was it then easy to convince Berry to put it out in the States?

No. Berry did the convincing on that because at that time I had two other records I was absolutely irate about. I just felt they were the greatest records in the world and I was getting ready to release one of them and Berry said, "No." He said, "If it's number one in Britain, it's got to be number one here, too," so he changed the release and he put out 'The Tears Of A Clown'.

Which did go to number one in the States. Which were the ones that you wanted?

There was a song called 'I Don't Blame You At All' which actually followed 'The Tears Of A Clown' eventually. And another song which I don't recall the name of.

'I Don't Blame You At All' did do well. It was actually the last really big record for Smokey Robinson and The Miracles. You decided to part just after Diana Ross and The Supremes had parted. Did you just get tired of being on the road or tired of being in a group?

I got tired. I didn't get tired of being in the group because I loved those guys right to today. In fact, being with them was the only thing that kept me going for the last two or three years. Because I absolutely hated everything else.

I hated the airplanes and the airports, and the train stations and the trains, and the buses and the cars and the hotels and the food and the restaurants – all that stuff. The only thing I really loved about it was being on the stage performing and the fact that I was with those guys that I loved. We were brothers. But other than that, I hated everything else about it.

I did want to be at home, my children were very small and, like my wife said, she had many miscarriages before our son was born. And so our children are probably extra precious to us, and I wanted to be there in their formative years. I wanted to know them as they were babies and growing up and learning to walk and talk. I was missing out on a lot of that because I was on the road.

I felt like my input was becoming very minimal because my heart and mind weren't there any more. I was doing them more of an injustice by staying than I would be by leaving.

You became the Vice President of Motown Records. Did you think the executive life was for you?

I actually became a Vice President in 1963. I think that most people probably think that was why I left The Miracles, to become the Vice President, but I had been all along since 1963.

There was no place for The Miracles to go. We had done everything a group could do. Like I said, the only joy I got out of it at the end was that I was with those guys. I do love them. And when we were on the stage performing. I loved that.

You wrote and performed a marvellous tribute to them called 'Sweet Harmony'. You obviously knew they would continue as they did for several years. Did you think you would have a very active solo career?

I wasn't planning on a solo career at all. I am serious. I thought I was going to be devoted to my job as Vice President, that I was going to be a manager or just produce some other act, or write for some other people. Do that and be at home and be happy. And I was very wrong.

It was not the thing for me. It was not what makes me happy. I enjoy my position as Vice President and I enjoy knowing what's going on intricately in the inner workings of the company. It's a good perspective from which to view everything. But my first love is being musical.

It was good for me that Claudette is musical and that she's

always supported me and been in my corner. She knew I was unhappy, just not doing this. On my very first album, she was still in Michigan. I had moved out here to California, because we were moving the home office of the operation here to Los Angeles. She was still in Michigan trying to sell our home, but after we discussed it and I told her I was going to record again, she came out and recorded my first album with me. She's been very supportive of me and my life. It makes it easier for me to function, and I'm so happy.

A lot of times when I look at a lot of changes some people have to go through with their spouses in this business, I'm so happy she grew up in it like I did. From a child, you know, we were just kids, and she grew up in this and she knows the ins and outs and ups and downs and what's happening and what makes it happen. That's good for me.

And indeed, Claudette, you feel that it's because you were there growing up in the same business that your marriage has been able to survive?

Claudette: Oh, I would agree to that, yes. It has been very helpful. At the beginning, because we were both new in the business, he didn't have any more knowledge than I had. To see exactly what went on, to see how other marriages were destroyed by gossip and a person's lack of knowledge in understanding their spouse, was very helpful.

Smokey, you cut a beautiful record on The Four Tops at the beginning of the Seventies, 'Still Water', 'Still Water' on both sides but 'Peace' on one and 'Love' on the other. Was this a rescue mission on the Tops? They had Holland-Dozier-Holland in the Sixties [but they had left the company].

The only thing I had to do with that record was to write the song. The track and the musical work was done by Frank Wilson, who was one of our producers at the time. He had a few big records on Eddie Kendricks. Frank had that music and the idea for that album, he was going to call it *Still Waters*. He brought it to me and said, "This is called *Still Waters*, write me a song to this music." And I did.

Was it actually written as one song and then divided up into an A and B side?

No. It was written as 'Still Water (Love)' and 'Still Water (Peace)'. He told me, "I want two different things, I want 'Still Water (Love)' here and I want like a recital for 'Still Water (Peace)' here." I worked on it and enjoyed it very much, because it is such a beautiful track and beautiful music. I am very happy to have been associated with that.

In 1974 you are back in the charts again on both sides of the Atlantic with different songs, in America with 'Baby Come Close' and in Britain with 'Just My Soul Responding'. Now do you recall making that record 'Just My Soul Responding'?

Oh, yeah.

You had as the guest vocalist a member of the group Exit.

Yes.

Quite a different sound.

Yes. That's also a song that was started by the music of Marv Tarplin. It's done in a very protesty political kind of lyric. At that time I think a lot of songs were in that vein and everybody wanted to say something about government or politics or racial barriers. That was my contribution to the protest song.

With 'Baby Come Close' a very slow and emotional ballad, and then 'Quiet Storm' . . .

Marv Tarplin's music once again, 'Baby Come Close'.

. . . And 'Quiet Storm' a more jazzy feel, you seem to be getting into new, almost adult musical fields, shall we say. Did you actually have musical goals in mind in the Seventies?

Yes, I did. When I came back to be a solo artist, I was no longer Smokey Robinson the boy. I wasn't Smokey Robinson the teenage singer, or whatever. I consciously did a lot of things, some very subtle, which a lot of people don't even realise today. But even the key that I sing in, I have dropped all my keys down probably two keys or two steps, because I felt as though I should sound more mature. I have a very high soprano voice and people used to say "Well, he sings falsetto", but the bulk of my singing is not falsetto. When I was in high school I sang soprano in the choir.

I knew that when I came back I wanted to play places like Tahoe and the bigger clubs. Not necessarily Vegas, because I think Vegas was my last resort of playing places like that. I knew my peers were older people and frequented these clubs now. I should go in a more adult direction with my music and with my sound. So that's what I attempted to do.

And to this day you include 'Quiet Storm' in your set, so that must have special meaning for you.

Yes.

As we enter the second half of the Seventies, both Motown and American radio seem to have changed. Motown, being in Los Angeles perhaps, seemed a bit more show-business oriented and seems to have fewer hits, but they are bigger in sales terms. For example, the Stevie Wonder albums, the Lady Sings The Blues *soundtrack, Diana Ross singles. Did you notice a change in the Seventies?*

More so than Motown making a drastic change, the competition became stiffer. There was a time when we had a corner on that particular market. We were the only ones doing what we were doing to any great effectiveness. We were the springboard for a lot of other companies and a lot of other artists of our same type.

Also the economy became a factor and still is in record sales and airplay. Everything is more scarce. It's like food, there are more people so there is less everything else. There are more records, so there's less of anything that makes records happen. We are very fortunate in as much as we do realise how to market records to the degree where we have been able to survive in a business like this.

As you've hinted before, people may assume that Motown will be there forever, but there is actually no reason why it has to be, is there?

None whatsoever. If we really get off our Ps and Qs then, as anyone else, we would probably go under.

You came up with several important talents, one of whom also was a

great love-song songwriter, Lionel Richie, who grew within The Com-
modores before going solo. Could you spot his talent early on?

Yes. I think we had spotted his talent before we ever signed
him. We don't sign anyone we don't feel has the talent to
eventually be a superstar.

He, of course, had many love ballads within the group, including
'Three Times A Lady', a number one on both sides of the Atlantic.

Right now he is number one in the world [with 'All Night
Long']. It's number one almost everywhere in the world. It's
terrific.

Who at the company, other than anyone directly involved with The
Commodores, thought that he should have gone solo?

I really don't know about that. I wasn't involved in what
happened, but I'm sure he thought it. Probably more so than
anyone.

You yourself were back in the top ten in 1979 with 'Cruisin''. Having
seen the film American Graffiti *and knowing The Beach Boys' car*
songs, I associate "cruisin'" with California automobile driving. Did
you at all when you wrote the song?

No. Sometimes I write to leave it open for the listener. If
that's what you want 'Cruisin'' to mean, then that's what it
means to you. It means cruisin' along the California coast in the
car with your lady, then that's what it means to you. If it means
making love, that's what it means to you. If it means taking an
airplane ride or a boat ride, that's what it means to you.

That record probably took the longest climb to get there of any of your
hits. It was into the twentieth week on the chart when it finally made
the top ten. Were you excited at the prospect of being there again?

Of course. Any artist, no matter how long they have been
doing this, loves to have a hit record. Mae West would love to
have a hit record, anybody, I don't care how long they have
been doing this. Frank Sinatra would love to have a hit record.
It's a fantastic feeling and a fantastic thing to have.

You had an even bigger one with 'Being With You', which went to
number one in Britain. The making of that record seemed to carry an

incredible coincidence. It was produced by George Tobin, who produced Kim Carnes on your old beautiful ballad 'More Love'. Didn't you speak to him about her and wind up recording 'Being With You'?

I had actually written 'Being With You' for her, or with her in mind. When I hear my songs being done by another artist, then I try to write some more songs and get them to them. Perhaps they'll record another one.

I had written three or four songs for Kim. I know being a record man that the best way to get a record to an artist is through their producer. I found out that George had produced a record on Kim of 'More Love' so I took the songs to him. And as I was sitting there playing them, I just played them on the piano and sang them, he said he loved me singing 'Being With You' and he wanted to record it with me.

We had a big argument about it, because I told him it was not for me and I didn't think I should record it, I wrote it for Kim. He convinced me to sing it. We went into a studio and recorded it. When I heard it back, I loved it.

One of your biggest records in sales, I'm sure. Recently, in the early Eighties, you've been in the charts a couple of times with duet records. This is something you hadn't done before. Marvin Gaye had always been the fellow who sang with the ladies, whether it be Mary Wells, Kim Weston, Tammi Terrell or Diana Ross. Are you just getting around to realising this is a good idea or is it something you had always wanted to do?

I had always wanted to do it. I think it's a good idea if you have the right song and the right ingredients and the right rapport. It's a very exciting thing. I enjoyed it very much. It was a new thing for me to do.

I had sung duet earlier on one of my albums with Claudette, she is actually singing lead and I just sang a little interlude part, but it was the closest thing I have ever done on a duet. That was on a song called 'Wine Women And Song', once again started by Marv Tarplin's music. And then the opportunity came through George to sing this song with Barbara

Mitchell from High Inergy and I was very excited about it. I enjoyed it.

That one did well, and at the moment you're in the charts with Rick James. Now there's a different artist for you. He came to Motown with his Punk Funk and sold several million copies of his Street Songs. *When did it ever occur to you that you might record with him?*

Never. It never occurred to me at all. I think it is a very, very strange marriage. I like Rick very much, Rick is cool with me, but musically we are at such different ends of the stick.

But I enjoyed that also. We had a great deal of fun in the studio doing it. Rick is a very ingenious producer. He is definitely great in the studio. The record's doing well. I'm happy about it.

You've also charted recently with a song 'I've Made Love To You A Thousand Times' in what I might call the classic Smokey Robinson groove. It is certainly one I hope you don't get tired of. And I wonder what you look forward to in the future for yourself?

Some hits, I hope. That's all I can say, I hope [for] some hits. Right now I am in the process of listening to many many songs by many many different writers and producers, because I am about to start my new album and am gathering material.

Does it excite you as much to do material by other writers as your own?

Yes, yes. I enjoy that because I don't think I can write everything. I also think that other writers and producers have a different perspective of me than I do. They may be on the right track, you know, you can never tell.

At the moment, Motown has a very hot young act called DeBarge. They have had three big ballads in a row and I don't think I'd be completely remiss if I say the lead singer sounds like he's been influenced by Smokey Robinson. Are you aware of a heritage that you've passed on to a new generation?

I don't really look at it like that. Imitation is a form of flattery, I know, and if in fact there are young guys out there who are influenced by me, it makes me happy, of course. I want to think that I have had some impact on somebody.

194

Incidentally, I'm really flattered that you say that about El [DeBarge]. He is a very good singer, a very good young singer and a nice person. They have a good group. I think they are going to go a long way.

You had a different kind of assignment in the middle of 1983 as a talent co-ordinator for the Motown 25th Anniversary TV special. It was a smash in the United States, winning an Emmy Award. How did you go about this? It sounds a Herculean task, getting everybody together again.

Everybody getting together again is strictly a Berry Gordy feat. I do not think that anyone connected with the 25th Anniversary special could have caused all those people to come together again for that night other than Berry Gordy. I mean other than anyone else in the world, because all the artists, no matter who they are, who have passed through the portals of Motown records have got to respect him. Those who know him personally have the utmost respect for him.

What is his magic effect on people? We have talked to Jr. Walker and he calls him Mr. Gordy. Everyone seems to be holding him in the highest esteem, almost as if he is not of this earth. What is special about Berry?

He is a very special person. Berry Gordy is a one in a trillion person. He is a very unique man. I know that he is the nucleus of the true success of Motown Records. He is first of all a musical man, which has made us survive. Usually Chairmen of the Board in any industry, including the record industry, are financial men. They are usually lawyers or accountants or somebody turned President of the record company.

Berry Gordy started out as being a musical man and that is his first love. Right now today he is in the studio recording somebody. Just because he wants to, because that's where he feels good and that's where his love is. So it has made us able to survive where others have failed.

He not only has that sense, but he is a business genius also. He was a young man who had the foresight to know that he didn't know it all and when we have got more money and made more money he would hire better people to take care of the finances, and so on and so on down the line. We're here today because of his foresight and his ingenuity and his street knowledge.

And you're confident of the future of Motown?

Yes I am, very.

Claudette, The Four Tops with The Temptations, Jackson Five, Supremes, was it a joyful reunion for you?

It was just wonderful. It was so exciting for me, because I had not actually been a part of the entertainment business on stage for what – 18 years? Just about 18 years. To get together again with all these people, especially with the Miracles, was just so exciting.

I cannot even describe to you the feelings I had that night. It was such joy. It was a wonderful, wonderful thing and I am very happy that I was able to be a part of it since I was, I will put this last quote in for myself, 'The First Lady of Motown'. I was actually the first lady that was signed to Motown Records, and I'm very happy to let everyone know that today.

Smokey, this feeling of family is one which you obviously have manifested through the years with The Miracles and Motown. As you look back over your career with the record company, could it have been better at all?

I don't know whether it could have been better or not. All I know is that I am very satisfied with what it has been. I think I have been very fortunate to live a life that I love, to be able to do something that I absolutely love and would do for free. I was blessed and fortunate enough to be able to do it, to earn a living doing it, and love it.

Thank you very much.

25

André Previn Caps My Career

One of the unexpected bonuses of working in media is free tickets. Note the plural. You might conceivably have as one of your crasser ambitions the desire to gain complimentary entry to the leading concerts and parties of your working life. It is doubtful, though, that you would enter the music business simply to arrange a lot of cheap dates. Yet this is a perk of the job.

Anyone who became a Radio 1 DJ in the Seventies had the opportunities for a sensational social life. The question became who to take to the events on offer. I used the chance to entertain a variety of friends, when possible matching evenings to the tastes of my guests.

One member of my Seventies social circle who remains etched in my memory is a woman I shall call Jane. She was a beautiful model, true, but since there was little chance for romance between us that was not the reason I continued to see her. Jane was fun, pure and simple. She seemed not to have a malicious thought in her head, and wherever we went she did something spontaneous to make the evening memorable.

Take, for example, our visit to the National Theatre production of *Equus*, which had transferred to a West End theatre on St. Martin's Lane. One of the cast members was an actress whose husband and son played in our Regent's Park Softball Club. In those days before I had walked into Jacqueline Onassis and had conversations with Princess Diana, I thought it was pretty impressive that I had kissed an actress who had kissed

Olivier, who had kissed Monroe. In the mid-Seventies, a mere three degrees of separation from Marilyn really impressed me.

At first I thought Jane was not going to make the show, but she rushed in as warning bells were ringing. Finding a parking space had been difficult. Indeed, the entire process of preparing for the show had been a rush for her. She had found just the amount of time needed to make herself look presentable – in anyone else's view, stunning – and she hadn't had time to eat. She was famished. Alright, we could get her something to eat after the show, and although we didn't have much time to talk before the curtain went up, we could always do that at the interval.

Or so I thought.

"I'll be back," Jane said, rushing off at the half with her coat. I presumed she was going to the women's room. Knowing the facilities for women in public places to be grossly less convenient than those for men, one of the last but most insulting reminders of sexual inequality, I wasn't overly surprised that it took her a good deal of time to return. When the three-minute warning for the second act rang, I did begin to worry. Had she fallen ill? Should I be looking for her? What if, for some bizarre reason, she had actually left the theatre and gone elsewhere?

I was in conflict. Should I leave my seat and search for Jane or wait for her to come to me? Just before the lights dimmed, she rushed in.

"I was hungry," she explained. As darkness filled the theatre, she took off her coat, revealing the take-away pizza she had purchased during the interval. She ate the pizza during the second half of the National Theatre production of *Equus*.

This was not the last of the evening's surprises. We returned to where my model friend had left her car at the last minute before the show. It was gone. She expressed surprise. I did not. She had parked on a triple yellow line. We found a policeman and asked where illegally parked cars were towed. Jane and I capped our night at the theatre with a visit to the Elephant and Castle car pound.

Not long afterward my beautiful companion joined me for an Elton John concert at Earl's Court. It was Elton's "Louder Than Concorde" tour. We were enjoying hospitality backstage before the show when Jane pointed out a corner of the cavernous hall.

"We did a shoot there recently," she related. "We found a box with kittens in it. Some of them were ill, and some were dead. I took one home.

"The next day it was poorly, so I took it to the vet.

" 'Madame,' " he said, " 'this cat is dead.' "

My heart was filled with affection for a woman who, surrounded by glamour, took an animal in need home to nurse. My mind, on the other hand, could not compute that anyone could fail to notice that a sick creature was, in sad fact, deceased. To take an analogy from Monty Python, Jane really did believe her dead parrot was pining for the fjords.

During the mid-Seventies Elton was involved promoting the career of his friend Kiki Dee. On one occasion, his label Rocket Records held a party for Kiki at a restaurant on the King's Road. Candles lit every table – candles for Kiki.

Jane, unusually clad in a monkey fur coat, was a hit with my friends. She was, as always, attractive, lively and unspoiled, a magic combination. She was the centre of attention. When hardened show business veterans encounter someone beautiful in both spirit and body who has yet to be corrupted, they react as if they were lepidopterists in whose midst a rare and beautiful butterfly has flown.

We were saying our goodbyes when we first noticed the pong of the place. How unusual, we commented, that we could have gone the entire evening without having registered this unpleasant smell. As soon as we mentioned it to our fellow guests, they noted it, too. Numerous pairs of eyes scanned the restaurant to see what could be causing the offensive odour.

I saw it first. Jane's coat was on fire. We were smelling burning monkey fur.

In saying goodbye to a couple, Jane had leaned over the table. A strand of fur had brushed against a candle. The coat had ignited. Using water and serviettes, and with the help of those seated at the table, we extinguished the blaze. This ended the threat to Jane's health, but did little for ours, for the smell of smouldering monkey fur was worse than that of the substance aflame. A moment ago we had chosen to leave the party. Now, for the sake of its continuation, we had to go.

When I had taken Jane to several events, she reciprocated by inviting me to her birthday party, to be held at her home in South London. Entertainment was provided by a fortune teller whom, I was told, had counselled Peter Sellers. I thought their conversation had probably not been very amusing. The only time I had encountered Sellers was when he had come across our softball game in Regents Park and engaged in conversation his old friend, the man who was the husband of the actress in *Equus*. When our squad, impressed by their teammate's acquaintance with the great Sellers, quizzed him on the subject of their talk, he simply replied, "Our heart surgeries." We asked no more questions.

I was never one for being told the future. I have a long life line on my palm, that's enough to know. But everybody at Jane's party was having a short session with the seer, so I submitted out of courtesy.

The woman, elderly and friendly, put me at ease with a few lines of pleasant chat and then began with statements scarcely more revealing than the "you were born to a mother and father" variety. I thought I had her figured out. She was just going to talk in generalities that could hardly be wrong. At the best, I would be impressed and think she had said something profound. At the worst, I would merely think she was a nice old woman.

Then she did something I have never seen a fortune teller

or astrologer do. She got specific. She put all her crystal balls in one basket.

"The highlight of your career," she told me solemnly, "will come when your work is conducted by André Previn."

I was shocked. It had never occurred to me that she would predict an actual event in a forecast that could, although probably not until the retirement of André Previn or myself, be proved to have been faulty. But the fact remained, I was not a composer. André Previn couldn't conduct my work even if he tried.

A few years later, in the 1980s, I was seated on an international flight directly behind André Previn. I agonised as to whether I should mention my experience to him. Discretion prevailed. I knew personally how little I liked having private moments interrupted by strangers. I also realised that, to him, I might seem a complete nutter. Even if he were engrossed by the episode, what could he do? He could only nod his head and say "that's strange" or commission me on the spot to compose something. The latter seemed unlikely, so I remained silent.

Then, in the 1990s, Deutsche Grammophon held a reception at the Savoy to honour their exclusive signing André Previn. I was invited as the presenter of the classical music programme with the highest listener reach in British radio, *The Classic Countdown* on Classic FM. I still hadn't composed anything, although I had written the lyrics to a musical called *The Ultimate Man*. I was not about to ask the maestro to spend our opening night in Vermont, where the show played, conducting the pianist, who was our one-man band. But I did accept an invitation from the DG press officer to sit with Previn.

In the course of the conversation I related the incident with the fortune teller, now two decades past. André nodded his head and said "that's strange". He did not commission me on the spot to compose something, but we did continue a perfectly pleasant and civilised conversation.

A thought occurred to me afterwards. Maybe the fortune teller had almost gotten it right, but her tea leaves were slightly twisted, her crystal ball too cloudy. Perhaps she had seen André Previn and the height of my career and assumed that the two were linked professionally, not socially. If she had been strictly accurate, she would have predicted that I would meet André Previn at the height of my career.

In that case, it was all downhill from the moment I left the Savoy. And I had better start believing in fortune tellers.

26

Barbra Teaches Me

Words of wisdom come from the strangest places. There is
never any telling who will say something that registers. I would
not for a moment wish to spend my leisure hours partying like
Dean Martin, but when he said he never worried about something that wasn't in his control, I recognised the words of
a sage. When Judy Collins, discussing her interpretation of
'Send In The Clowns', remarked that it was unwise to try to
maintain separate careers in more than one place, since stress
was an inevitable consequence, I accepted the advice of this
guidance counsellor and concentrated on my work in Britain.

But of all the celebrities whose offhand remarks might be
taken for wisdom, the sagest is Pete Townshend. The leader of
The Who made a great impact on me as well as many other
members of my generation with several of his observations.

Townshend wrote in *The Times* of London about the endur-
ing popularity of Mick Jagger. He speculated that one reason
Jagger had received an atypically good press through the years
was that he always treated reporters as his friends. Tickled at
the thought they were pals of a real Rolling Stone, they went
home and wrote glowing reviews. As I read the piece I recalled
that whenever we had met Mick had always called me "mate",
although he never once suggested we do anything matey. I've
had fish and chips with Elton John and oysters with Bryan
Ferry, but not even a sardine with Mick Jagger.

The lesson I took from Townshend's *Times* piece was not
that I wasn't really Mick's mate. I pretty much realised that
anyway. The point was that we reporters entered the lives of

celebrities at sudden moments and exited them just as quickly. There are a couple of exceptions, of course. We each make a few genuine friends in the business, and every artist does admire the work of a couple of media men and women. But in most cases, we exist for the stars for the length of time it takes to do the interview.

No one brought this home to me better than Barbra Streisand. I was flattered that, when she came to Britain in February 1992 to promote her film *Prince Of Tides,* I was one of the two television interviewers she saw. The other was Michael Aspel, who at that time hosted ITV's leading talk show. Michael was to go first, there was to be an hour break for Barbra to refresh herself, and then I was to speak to her for TV-am.

When she came into the suite to do our interview she immediately looked into the lens to check the camera shot. She then studied the lighting. Barbra Streisand was the first and only interview subject in my nineteen years of television to bother to see how she was going to be presented. Some might call her a control freak, but I considered this behaviour evidence of a perfectionist. It doesn't dent my ego in the slightest to acknowledge that Streisand knows more about the technical side of visual media than I, nor that she cared more than I about image.

I began to tell her about the programme for which we were doing the interview.

"You don't sound like you're from here," she observed. One New Yorker can always spot another.

"You're right," I replied, and explained how I had to come to England as a student and stayed on to work. "I found the television environment here suited me better." Choosing one London and one New York name she would know so I could make my point, I said, "I was always more a Michael Aspel than a Geraldo Rivera."

Her response startled me.

"Who's Michael Aspel?"

She had spoken to him only an hour before for a major prime time show, but one hour is as much in the past as one hundred years. Barbra, who had been attentive and professional in her interview with Michael, let him slip from her mind almost as soon as he walked out the door. Of course, unless we established an unusual rapport, I would suffer the same fate. I would remember Barbra Streisand; she would forget Paul Gambaccini. Knowing that, I proceeded, savouring my meeting with an extraordinary woman.

Two years later, by extraordinary coincidence, Michael Aspel and I were sitting on the breakfast television sofa at the same moment. By this time TV-am had been replaced by GMTV. I wanted to tell our Streisand story as an example of the transience of fame, and guessed, rightly, that Michael would be amused rather than upset. He was too mature to fantasise that an acquaintance of a star is automatically a friend of the star.

I enjoyed my interview with the director/actress/singer enormously. After the first couple of minutes she realised I knew the body of her work, and she began responding with detail and enthusiasm. I was particularly touched when I asked her why she made so few live concert performances.

"I don't like to sing in front of other people," she answered to the point. "Would you?"

She wasn't being impolite, she was being honest. By asking me, and through me the viewer, how we would feel vocalising in front of thousands of onlookers, she invited the audience to feel her embarrassment.

After our interview was concluded, Barbra drew me to the side of the room and quizzed me on my thoughts of her film's Oscar chances. I told her honestly that I thought Nick Nolte had a good chance to be named Best Actor, that the movie had a rough ride for Best Picture, and that she had been unfairly overlooked for a Best Director nomination. We both agreed that *Bugsy* had received more nominations than it deserved. Streisand then surprised me.

"Did you ever see *The Dresser*?" she asked me.

"Yes," I replied, not understanding at first why she was asking me about a years-old film. "Not as good as the play, which I saw here in the West End, but a good movie. Albert Finney and Tom Courtenay were excellent."

"Oh," Streisand responded cryptically. "I never saw it."

When I arrived home, I got a suspicion what that exchange might have been about. Barbra Streisand was a famous omission in the ranks of Best Director nominees, and had been earlier passed over for *Yentl*, a project that meant a great deal to her. One of the men nominated in her stead was Peter Yates, director of *The Dresser*.

A couple of years later I happened to be interviewing Yates for BBC Radio 4. I told him the tale.

"Oh, I'm so pleased you've told me that," he laughed with relief. "Now I understand. Barbra was wonderful when we worked together on *What's Up Doc?* After the time of *The Dresser*, she was polite to me, but not friendly. I never knew why. Now I see.

"It is sad, though."

I learned yet another lesson from my meeting with Barbra. While I was waiting, I noticed a member of her staff acting imperiously during preparations for her arrival. The aide nearly lost her cool when a buffet trolley arrived.

"There aren't any lobsters here, are there? Barbra is allergic to lobsters."

I knew shellfish is one of the three most common allergies since I suffer myself from one of the other top three, strawberries. But I found it hard to believe that a lobster could be easily concealed from view, and suspected that the assistant simply needed something to flap about.

Streisand had been professional in our interview and genuinely passionate in our subsequent discussion of films.

One difference between an artist and a member of her court crystallised in my mind. The artist never feels she has made it. No matter how many glorious accomplishments lie behind, her gaze is always on the challenge ahead. Had I seen *The Normal Heart*, the Larry Kramer play? Did I like it? (Streisand thought at this time she was going to make the movie version.)

A courtier, on the other hand, has made it. She is where she has always wanted to be, at the side of the star. There is nowhere else to ascend.

And so, ironically, the artist with the impressive achievements is less secure than the assistant. The latter has reached her final goal. For the artist, there is no final goal.

This was the last lesson I learned from my unknowing teacher, Barbra Streisand.

27

Hero Time Two

I would like to be able to say, "My grandmother taught me to read from Carl Barks comics" because it sounds so romantic, but I can't truly give either Gram or Carl the full credit. School did have something to do with it. But I can say truthfully that my grandmother helped fire my enthusiasm for reading by sharing with me the comic art of Carl Barks.

Comic book sales in the United States hit their all-time peak in the early Fifties, when Carl Barks was at his creative peak. It was during this time that he was producing a ten-page Donald Duck story every month for *Walt Disney's Comics And Stories* and an occasional *Donald Duck* book. In 1952 he began a separate title devoted to the globe-trotting adventures of the money-mad character he created, *Uncle Scrooge*.

Having been born in 1949, I was in the perfect position to have Barks as a formative force in my youth. Sales of *Walt Disney's Comics And Stories* were in seven figures every month, a circulation only dreamed of today in a dwindling comic market in which, to use an extreme example, that very Disney title now sells about seven thousand per month. *Comics And Stories* was ubiquitous. I thought of it and *Marge's Little Lulu* as "barber shop comics" – every barber, every doctor, every dentist had a few issues on hand to keep boys and girls happy.

We had no idea, of course, who actually wrote and drew the stories. Walt Disney and Marge (Buell) got the credit, even though Carl Barks and, in *Lulu's* case, John Stanley and Irving Tripp were doing the work. We just loved these books, passionately, with the combined zeal children nowadays apply to television cartoons and computer games.

I've just used the word "we". At the age of four or five, a child has no sense that there are millions of kids being amused in the same way he or she is. The discovery of verbal and visual entertainment is a personal one. It was only years later that I and other *Uncle Scrooge* and *Little Lulu* devotees learned there were others like us. By this time, the Sixties, through the same medium, fan magazines, we found out something else about our common love for Carl Barks. Thousands of us across the country had come to think of him in the same three words: "the good artist".

The reason for this was that the Disney comics featured the work of several illustrators, but none of the Donald Duck artists approached the standard of Barks. I, and all those other children across America, would go to the news-stand, open a Disney comic, and think either "the good artist" or "not the good artist". Imagine my excitement, even as a teenager, to discover that there were other readers, lots of them, who used precisely the same distinction in deciding whether to lay down a dime for a comic. Best of all, Don and Maggie Thompson's fanzine *Comic Art* informed us, there was now a name to go with our hero. "The good artist" was Carl Barks!

Barks is the most read creator in the history of comic books. His works, produced between 1942 and 1966, are being reprinted to this day around the world. The full-length Donald comic stories he produced, like the holiday tear-jerker "Christmas for Shacktown" and the incredibly imaginative "Lost in the Andes", and Uncle Scrooge epics like "Only a Poor Old Man" and "Back to the Klondike", are the English language equivalent of the Tin Tin books. I have seen them in airports and at supermarket check-outs in Norway, where sensationalist tabloid newspapers would be in the United States, another piece of evidence that, in some respects, the Scandinavian countries have an advanced civilisation.

Britain, curiously, is the odd nation out in resisting his genius, perhaps because it already had its own tradition of children's comic books before Barks started his four-colour career. But Uncle Carl's stories are enjoyed by adults as well as kids, perhaps because he was already over 40 when he started working on them. Born in 1901, he had headed the Disney Studio's "Duck Unit" before growing tired of cartoons produced for the war effort.

When he retired from the comics, Barks turned to painting, and in his Seventies turned out a memorable series of Donald and Scrooge images that have been reproduced as lithographs. His framed pieces line the hall of my home. They always draw compliments from visitors. I never dared to dream that one day Carl himself would be one of those visitors.

And yet that day did come in 1994. At the age of 93, Carl Barks came on a European tour to meet his fans. In several continental countries, his appearances created enthusiasm akin to that normally generated by pop stars. I knew his reception in London would be cooler, although polite, and I thought there might be an opportunity for me to work my way onto his itinerary. Sure enough, on 18 July, 1994, at 9:30 a.m., Carl Barks arrived at my house so I could interview him for GMTV.

The Duck Man sat on my sofa under one of his classic Uncle Scrooge lithographs. He was generous with recollections concerning both cartoons and comics. After the interview was over, I showed him my comic collection, which included all his *Donald Duck* and *Uncle Scrooge* books. I even showed him the one *Porky Pig* he had done as an emergency stand-in half a century ago.

"I've never seen this," he said nonchalantly, meaning that after he had handed in his artwork he had completely forgotten about the book, only revisiting the character for a purpose-drawn cover for an edition of *The Comic Book Price Guide*. In the

210

1997 version of that comic buyer's bible, a near mint copy of the *Porky Pig* one-shot was listed at $1000. Barks' first *Donald Duck* was priced at $7500.

I was humbled by his visit. After he and his helpers departed for his next appointment the GMTV camera crew could tell how moved I was. I felt, and still believe, that no one can spend their time on earth better than by adding to the quality of life of millions of people, both the few he meets and the many he does not.

I knew I would be meeting Carl again that evening in an interview at the national Comic Art Trust. Both to rest for that occasion, and because I was drained following the television interview, I retired for a nap as soon as the camera crew left.

I slept deeply and woke about an hour later. I looked out the front window of my bedroom and was startled. There was an unprecedented mid-day traffic jam on Hungerford Road, which is not a main road and usually only experiences traffic worth speaking of late Friday afternoons when cars are waiting to join backed-up roads leading to the A1 out of London. I then checked the view out my back window and was puzzled to see no cars at all. I went outside.

I was surrounded by concerned and distraught faces. Police officers stood in the road. I asked one what had happened. His reply spoke of a terrible tragedy.

"We've just had a helicopter rescue in the street. A speeding car hit a boy. He looked terrible."

The policeman successfully decoded my silent expression as a combination of disbelief and a request for his evaluation of the victim's chances.

"Of course we can hope," he said, "but I'll be surprised if he's OK."

A mix of strong feelings overwhelmed me. A child had suffered terrible injury and, if the officer was right, probable death right outside my house. I had slept through the accident. Even more incredibly, I had slept through a helicopter landing and taking off right outside my window. That showed how spent I was after my Carl Barks interview!

For about two seconds, I concentrated on how strange it was that I had missed this event. Then I realised how fortunate I was. If I had been the one who had heard the accident outside my house, if I had gone outside to see what had happened – the imagination does not wish to continue.

It had been with the same grandmother who had read to me from *Walt Disney's Comics And Stories* that I had first seen the aftermath of a traffic accident. When I still lived in the Bronx, when I was either four or five, we were on a bus on Kingsbridge Avenue. We saw on the side of a road a blood-covered leather-clad motorcyclist, moaning and writhing in pain, comforted by a policeman. At least that young man was still alive. In my juvenile extrapolation of the accident I envisioned him recovering fully in hospital. In 1994, as a grown-up, I did not wish to speculate about such things.

At 6:30 that evening I went to Camden Town and interviewed Carl Barks in front of a small but appreciative audience, sur-rounded by an exhibition of Barks lithographs, mostly mine, on loan for the occasion. I marvelled at how this 93-year-old gentleman was still firing on all cylinders, with no evidence of having taken a nap as deep as my own. Once again, he was very giving with his answers, which were recorded for posterity.

After this event, I was really shattered. I bade farewell to Carl and his team and went out into the night. I had so focused on meeting and interviewing my comic book hero that I had not planned anything afterwards. I was in such a blissful stupor leaving the hall that I walked almost on automatic pilot south into Soho, with no particular destination in mind.

I walked through Soho Square and into Frith Street when I saw him. He was tall and obese, wearing shorts and sandals, and he was lying on the street outside a restaurant. The eatery is in *The Good Food Guide*, but it would not wish me to name it here, for this man had turned grey. He was the first human being I ever saw who was ashen, and there was a reason he was grey. He was dead.

He had, I was informed by appalled onlookers, emerged from the restaurant with friends and simply collapsed. The friends were trying to resuscitate him. An ambulance arrived and began carrying out emergency procedures. I did not stay to see if the man regained consciousness.

Instead I had a most curious thought. As if the tragedy could somehow have anything to do with me, I reasoned, "Every time I interview Carl Barks, somebody dies. I must never interview him again."

Of course, I don't actually know if the two victims recovered or not, and I am not so ghoulish that I made further inquiries. There may have been no deaths, one, or two. So what? A pair of people suffered terribly because I can't interview Carl Barks without having somebody die, or come close to it.

I had my tapes. I had my memories. I had my comics. I didn't need to speak to Carl Barks again, and I never sought to.

28

Jonathan King Humbles Me

There are plenty of opportunities to stay humble in show business. As Shirley MacLaine wisely said, the public never knows about your failures. It only knows what it sees or hears. But every performer, no matter how successful, is aware of something in his or her career that didn't go quite as he or she had wished. Some programmes you would like to do never get commissioned or, if they are, are not renewed. Books you would like to write don't get contracted or, if they do, are quickly remaindered.

The people who really keep your feet on the ground are the very ones who give you your living: the public. If they don't like a certain radio show, they will vote with their ears, and not listen. A television programme not to their taste is dismissed with a single push of the remote button.

They also keep you on planet Earth in the shops, on the tubes, in the streets. This is done in a variety of ways. The first is direct confrontation. In 1997, Justine Frischmann of Elastica, Bob Geldof and I appeared on a Channel 4 special called *Music Of The Millenium*. Viewers, readers of *The Guardian* and customers at HMV had voted for the top 100 albums of all time. We were to react to the choices.

Bob and I had a charity evening together the following month. We found we had shared the same phenomenal experience: that seemingly all our friends and many of the strangers we met had seen *Music Of The Millenium* and felt compelled to give us their reactions, many of them of the "Stone Roses at number two!?!" variety. For weeks afterward, I knew that if the man sitting next to me on the underground, or the handsome fellow standing next to me in a pub, turned to speak, it was not going to be because he found me personally irresistible, but because he wanted to offer his verdict on the top 100.

The fact is, you never know why people are looking at you in public. In March 1998 I went to the Playhouse in London to see Liam Neeson as Oscar Wilde in David Hare's play *The Judas Kiss*. Seated one row in front and two seats to the left of me was Ringo Starr. I made the silent vow not to do the obvious thing and gape. Yet at the interval I happened to look to the left and saw Ringo's friend staring at me. What did this glance mean? Yes, I know you're a star too, even though one of a lower order of magnitude in a lesser constellation? Or, you're near Ringo's space, don't dare come any closer?

When you are recognised, it may not be because someone likes your work, it's just because they turned on the television and there you were. I was in the lift at Caledonian Road station once and an elegant black model said to me, "I know you. (Pause.) You're famous. (Another pause.) You're . . . Paul. (Longer pause.) Paul Gascoigne!"

Being mistaken for another celebrity with whom one has an extremely tenuous connection, like the first name of Paul, is an occupational hazard. It delighted as well as miffed Noel Edmonds when, on a Radio 1 reception on board the paddle steamer Waverly in the Clyde River, the boat from which he was to broadcast his breakfast show, someone asked him for his autograph, thinking he was John Peel.

I have been humbled over the last fifteen years by being mistaken once every six weeks or so for Jonathan King. In real life, there are certain key similarities. Jonathan is only five years older than I, we both went to Oxbridge, and his New York residence on 57th Street between 8th and 9th Avenues partially inspired me to buy a studio apartment on that block myself. We share certain private passions, including a great love for many of the same records and a near-evangelical desire to introduce our favourite discs to the public.

Yet in public life the notion of confusing me for Jonathan King seems daft. We are completely different people. Why should someone think I am he? The answer is that a little knowledge is, truly, a dangerous thing. In the Eighties we both had television series in which we spoke from the United States about popular music. A less-than-committed viewer of these two programmes might confuse the hosts. More importantly, yet utterly superficially, Jonathan's image is of a bespectacled man who often wears a baseball cap. In the winter, to keep my head warm, I wear a baseball cap, and walking in the streets, though not at home or on air, I wear glasses. A pedestrian making a quick judgement might think, TV, baseball cap, glasses, Jonathan King.

What has been most instructive about this misidentification is that when I am mistaken for Jonathan, I am treated as if I were him. If someone chooses to speak to "me" in these circumstances, it is not for something as impersonal as offering their comments on the top 100 albums of all time. Jonathan has cultivated the image of an outspoken figure. Merely to say that he speculated in print that Live Aid might be a bad idea is enough to convey the information that JK is by choice a controversial soul. People who approach me thinking I am Jonathan King often do so to harangue me.

"How dare you say what you did about Janet Jackson?" a black teenager accosted me in Piccadilly Circus.

"I didn't say anything about Janet Jackson," I stated accurately, not realising what was happening.

"Yes, you did," the girl's female friend claimed. "I read it in the newspaper."

Uh oh, I thought, Jonathan's column . . .

"Wait a minute," I stopped play. "Who do you think I am?"

"You're Jonathan King," the original accuser identified me. "You insulted Janet Jackson . . ."

"I'm not Jonathan King," I told the two.

"You're not?" they chorused.

"And I like Janet Jackson," I said, which was true of many of her records. I was certainly not going to offer my critical analysis of her then-recent Wembley concert to these partisans.

"Oh." Rage and spirit left their faces. "Sorry." They slinked away, mortified to have accosted a middle-aged man in Piccadilly Circus.

Being mistaken for Jonathan King is not only humbling when it happens. It is a constant reminder never to be flattered by public recognition, because the faulty sighting could occur at any time. The person waving to me at this moment might think he is waving to JK. The newsagent calling out, "How's it going, Jonathan?" is not interested in Paul's purchase of the *International Herald-Tribune*. In a balancing act that would interest the blindfolded woman holding the scales of justice, the 99% of the time I am recognised for myself is countered by the one in a hundred occasions I am taken for King.

But once I was grateful to be mistaken for Jonathan. It may only have been once, but the circumstances were so important it compensated for all the others.

In the early Nineties, I briefly had a female lodger living in the house. She was a delightful person I loved dearly. One weekend her brother came to visit, and she showed him the sights of London.

I returned from my radio programme to hear a sequence of messages from her mother on the answerphone. They were of increasing distress, asking, then pleading for her to phone. It did not take genius to understand that tragedy had struck her family, and a taped mention of my friend's father suggested the nature of the news. I knew I would have to be not only considerate but tactful in telling her of her messages.

When the brother and sister pair returned, literally laughing and smiling about their adventures, we retired to the kitchen for beverages. I told them that mother wished them to call. Brother went to the phone. Sister stood alongside to wait her turn. I positioned myself next to her, to be able to support her in case she collapsed.

Brother made the call. The conversation lasted about ten seconds before his face took on a dreadful countenance. A further five seconds later, he turned to sister.

"Dad's dead," he moaned.

It was a good thing I was standing where I was. My physical support proved useful. Sister and I tearfully embraced as brother got the unhappy details. At a moment like this, it was inconceivable that either would laugh again soon.

After both children had spoken to their mother, we agreed they should leave to be with her as soon as possible. We got the train time from Paddington and I called a cab. They quickly packed. We waited in the foyer for the cab.

The driver rang the doorbell. I opened the door.

"Taxi for Paddington," the driver recited by rote. Then he looked at me.

"You're Jonathan King," he said.

And the bereaved siblings laughed. They laughed to release the tension that had built up over the last quarter of an hour, they laughed so as not to cry, they laughed because they had just heard something so ludicrous to them it was hilarious.

Now as we embraced the tears were mixed with smiles. Recovery, however tentative, had already begun. As they and the cab driver walked toward the gate, I had reason to think that maybe being mistaken for Jonathan King every once in a while was worth it after all.

29

Stevie Wonder Comes Back

When I think of an artist expressing affection for another artist, I think of Ray Charles, telling me backstage at Leverone Field House at Dartmouth College in the late Sixties, "I love Aretha", in a drawn-out way, making "love" sound like a three-syllable word, purring like a contented cat. When I think of an artist expressing concern for another artist, I think of Pete Townshend asking me, "Have you seen Billy lately?", referring to Billy Idol when the young Englishman was attempting to find himself, and a solo career, in New York City.

There is no artist in my time who has inspired the amount of love and, at the time of his serious injury in 1973, the concern that Stevie Wonder has. His trilogy *Talking Book* (1972), *Innervisions* (1973) and *Fulfillingness' First Finale* (1974) left all his peers worshipping at his altar. Not for nothing did Paul Simon, accepting the 1975 Best Album Grammy for *Still Crazy After All These Years*, "thank Stevie Wonder for not releasing an album this year." Steve had scooped the category the two preceding years, and the only reason he hadn't made it three in a row was that *Talking Book* and *Innervisions* were eligible in the same October-to-October Grammy year. It wasn't that *Talking Book* went unrepresented when *Innervisions* won the 1973 prize. Its standout tracks 'Superstition' and 'You Are The Sunshine Of My Life' both won separate trophies at the same ceremony.

Wonder told me he agreed with the Academy's evaluation of the relative merit of his two LPs.

"Between the last two albums, I prefer *Innervisions* as a total statement. As far as tunes, I like several from *Talking Book*: 'Looking For Another Pure Love', 'Superstition', 'You've Got It Bad, Girl' and 'Sunshine Of My Life'."

This three-part statement of musical maturity capped the most astonishing childhood in pop history. Before he was 21, Stevie had scored 25 hit singles in the United States, including the one that started it all, 'Fingertips (Pt. 2)', which hit number one when he was thirteen. 'Uptight (Everything's Alright)', 'I Was Made To Love Her' and 'For Once In My Life' were just three of his classic singles. Upon reaching adulthood, he embarked on his self-contained career, forsaking the customary Motown songwriting and production support to make his own recordings.

After the above-mentioned trilogy came his personal peak and one of the highest summits in popular music, the 1976 double album *Songs In The Key Of Life*. This gem contained among its golden grooves two number ones ('I Wish' and 'Sir Duke'), a song that would become for another artist the world's number one of 1995 ('Pastime Paradise' recorded by Coolio as 'Gangsta's Paradise'), and a track that would have been a number one had Wonder agreed to its edit for single release. This cut, 'Isn't She Lovely', contained the birth cries of his daughter, and Stevie declined to edit out the sounds of the child who inspired it.

It wasn't just that Wonder made great music that won the respect of his peers. He seemed to be a conduit for it. It flowed from him as if from some higher source. This sounds like, but is not, pretentious pap. There are always a couple of young artists at any time who seem to have a divine gift. There does not appear to be any rational explanation for the beauty of their art. In the mid-1990s, the dancer Savion Glover, the pianist Evgeny Kissin, and the violinist Maxim Vengerov made me feel this way. I could not imagine how their perfection could be improved; I could not conceive how they had achieved such purity of performance. Of course, relentless practice is essential, but one feels something else, something indefinable, is at work. When Vengerov taped a *Kaleidoscope* appearance with me in Broadcasting House in 1996, I sat alone with him as he played in the studio. I realised it was quite possible that the most beautiful music being made in the world at that moment was being made in my solitary presence.

Stevie Wonder inspired such feelings in the mid-Seventies, and he did so with a touchingly uncorrupted love for humanity as well as music. Mere mortals were spooked at how Stevie seemed to radiate as well as inspire love. Whatever nasty experiences had qualified our affection for our fellow man seemed to have passed him by. Like Ray Charles, he refused to curse his blindness. Indeed, he commented that almost every-one has some kind of handicap, and he was glad his was not bigotry.

It was no wonder, then, that when Stevie Wonder made his first appearance after his 16 August, 1973 automobile acci-dent, the current royalty of rock turned out. The venue for this January, 1974 event was the Rainbow Theatre in Finsbury Park, London. Stevie performed not one show, but two.

"I want to play," he told me the next day. "I haven't played onstage in a long time. It's almost like when you have a woman you love very much and you haven't seen her for a long time, you want to just get to it right away." Among the pilgrims to the comeback concerts were David Bowie, Eric Clapton, Paul and Linda McCartney, The Staple Singers, and Ringo Starr.

The first show was a tentative return.

"I was feeling the people, getting warm," Wonder explained. "I was feeling their presence, but we had a lot of sound problems that went unresolved."

The second show was a smash. Stevie received two stand-ing ovations and performed two encores. He and Wonder-love performed material from *Talking Book* and *Innervisions,* 'Uptight' and 'Signed Sealed Delivered I'm Yours' "from two thousand years ago", and three new songs, 'Bumblebee Of Love', 'Sky Blue Afternoon', and 'Contusion'. He ended the show with 'Superstition', although "ended" is strictly inaccurate. He turned on a synthesized howl that continued as he left the stage.

"To me, 'Superstition' is such an exciting tune that I can't just end it", he explained. " 'Superstition' brings back thousands of outasight memories, so I just put the synthesizer on and split."

He also discussed some of his other recent compositions.

" 'Sunshine Of My Life' is a favourite in that it deals with the earth. There is an intimate relation, and it also applies to people generally. 'Visions' is the tune where I try to say what I think is the most important message today, one which some people are not even paying attention to: that we must come closer together and love each other.

"With *Innervisions*, I was going through a lot of changes. Although I didn't know we were going to have an accident, I knew I was undergoing changes. 'Higher Ground' is the only time I've ever done a whole track in one hour, and the words just came out. That's the only time, and that's very heavy."

Stevie revealed he had unreleased material from the *Talking Book* and *Innervisions* sessions, which he was considering releasing, "but while I'm being undecided, I'm cutting new stuff!"

And so it went for twenty years. When I reminded him, two decades later, that I was still waiting for the release of 'Bumblebee Of Love', which had always sounded like a potential hit, he said he still had it and was still thinking about it. On one thing he was sure: he had stayed with Motown Records for over thirty years as a salute to Berry Gordy, Jr., to what he had meant to his life, and what Motown had meant to black America. At several points of his career Stevie could have commanded his own terms with almost any label. I respected his decision to stay with Motown, and his reasons for it, almost as much as I respected his music.

30

Diana Dies

On the end table next to my bed I keep a lamp, an alarm clock, a telephone, a glass of water and a portable radio. With the exception of the glass of water, which I refill every night, these items are constants. They have spent a greater percentage of my life next to my head than any person or other object. Although I walk around the apartment with the radio on during the day and listen to several stations, I always set it on Radio 4 before going to bed and place it back on the end table.

At 6:54 a.m. on the morning of the 31st of August, 1997, I woke up and turned on Radio 4, expecting to hear the weather forecast at 6:55. Instead I heard the identifiable voice of Henry Kissinger talking about Diana, Princess of Wales, in the past tense.

"Oh, no," I thought in disbelief, "and why did I have to hear it from him?"

One minute later, the Teutonic foghorn of Kissinger was succeeded by the Scots brogue of James Naughtie. This was a very bad omen. The weekday host of the *Today* programme would never be brought in on a Sunday unless there was a grave lead story. My sad suspicions were confirmed as Naughtie announced the news, "for those of you who are just waking up," that Diana, Princess of Wales, had been killed in a car crash in Paris.

I had been awakened one morning in June, 1968 by my clock radio. The unusually solemn voice of my WDCR radio colleague David Graves yanked me from sleep to consciousness with the

223

news that, "The senator was shot shortly after accepting victory in the California primary." I had to gird myself for one of four possibilities. Either Robert Kennedy had been injured or killed, or Eugene McCarthy had been hurt or slain. Within thirty seconds my uncertainty had been cleared with the fatal news of Senator Kennedy's assassination.

Ever since I had learned to wake up very quickly and be prepared to believe the unthinkable. On 9 December, 1980, my brother Peter rang from New York at 5:30 a.m., London time, saying, "I know your phone will start ringing soon with requests from the media, and I thought you might want to hear from me rather than a stranger that John Lennon has been murdered." The second shock Pete had to give me was that the shooting had occurred within four city blocks of his own New York City front door. It was extremely considerate for Peter to call as he did. I hate getting horrible news from people I don't know.

So hearing of sudden death first thing in the morning was not a new experience. But, I came to realise, I was only accustomed to gun killings. The most famous person in the world, dead in a car crash? In Paris?

How did she get there? The last thing I knew, she was sunning herself in some holiday resort with Dodi. I didn't know exactly where because I deliberately ignored the tabloid newspapers and tabloid-style television programmes that force-fed the public its daily diet of Di doings. I had passed a newsagent and seen some papers with colour photos of her in a bathing suit, so I figured she was on vacation. But I had about the same interest in knowing exactly where she was in the world as I had in knowing the name of her latest boyfriend.

Which was about none. I had only recently interviewed Sandra Bullock and Jason Patric on the occasion of the British release of their movie *Speed 2*. When I informed Jason that Diana had liked his film *Rush* but thought it a bit strong, he said he had heard that and wondered how I knew. I answered that she had told me so at a private screening. (A check of my correspondence shows that she expressed a similar view in a letter dated 9 June, 1992.) Jason asked if I could arrange an introduction.

"What's the latest on her and Dodi?" Sandra interrupted, now the fan rather than the idol. So that's his name, I thought. I had been under the impression it was Dee Dee.

Dee Dee, Dodi, Dido, it's their business, I felt. I had long ago been disgusted by the way the British press treated the Princess. I had defended her against its intrusions on breakfast television and, feeling that I had done my bit publicly, felt I had to do it privately too, not seeking to know anything she or her brother would not wish to tell me themselves.

I had first met Charles Spencer, whom I knew as Charlie Althorp, when he was a schoolboy. He was familiar with my Radio 1 work and loved talking about broadcasters. Not much later he asked me if I could give an interview to the Eton newspaper when I was passing through on the harrowing Radio 1 "Three Men In a Boat" trip from Kingston to Oxford, during which Noel Edmonds, Mike Read and I were doing the breakfast show every day from a cruiser on the Thames. Charlie and a friend met me at the river. At this point, it was any excuse for a bit of dry land, but I was always touched by his combination of enthusiasm and politeness.

Being an American, I never had too much of a grip on when a titled or landed person was supposed to be known by their family surname or by the name of their property. I thought it rather cute that someone could have two names without having an actual alter ego, as if Bruce Wayne could call himself Batman without having to save anybody. Charlie Althorp, or whoever he was, was one of my favourite young Englishmen, and I was delighted that he seemed to be doing well on life's course.

In the early Eighties Charlie flirted with the idea of becoming a restaurateur. As part of the reconnaissance process we lunched at Mirabelle's, an establishment in Curzon Street that was at that time considered the ultimate in fine London dining. In reality it was a spectacularly well-appointed place in which to have a better-than-average meal. I recall being particularly disappointed in the chocolate mousse. Charlie was buoyed in his thinking that with the right team he could launch a better restaurant.

Family responsibilities inevitably interfered with his pet project. Upon the death of his father, he became Earl Spencer and assumed the demanding task of managing Althorp, the family estate in Northamptonshire. Ten years after we had eaten at Mirabelle, I was Charlie's guest for Sunday lunch in even grander surroundings at his home.

He had retained his excitement about food. The vegetables to be served were home-grown, and there was a further treat in store. "Wait until later," he whispered into my ear during the first course. "We've got an illegal cheese!"

By this he meant that an unpasteurised French cheese was going to be served after the main dish. Through some arcane legislation, such deteriorating dairy products were not supposed to be imported into Britain.

Charlie's enthusiasm was matched by my horror. I had in my middle age become allergic to active dairy products. I relished parmesan cheese and ice cream, but experienced breathing difficulties after downing Stilton or sour cream. My predicament had become so extreme that I grew nauseous whenever passing the formerly enticing duty free cheese counter at Charles de Gaulle airport.

I told my host of my allergy and pardoned myself in advance for any eccentric behaviour in the presence of an illegal cheese. I feared the service of a mouldy dairy product might cause me a quarter hour of discomfort, but the arrival of the beast was even more upsetting. I literally could not bear to be in the presence of the foul white oval, and had to leave the room before swooning. With Charlie's understanding, I spent fifteen minutes taking refuge in one of Althorp's bathrooms. At least, in keeping with the house, it was visually interesting.

My greatest embarrassment concerning the meal did not occur until the following day. It had been a delightful visit seeing Charlie again, meeting his wife and friends, sharing good food and watching wind-blown snow showers occasionally cover the grounds in a thin coat of white. I was in a good mood until the next morning, when I rose and urinated a red liquid.

This had never happened to me before. All my life I had avoided any symptoms of venereal disease. Now it appeared I was passing blood.

What had happened? I could not think of any private behaviour that could have led to such an outcome, but I made sure I was checked immediately. Within two hours I was in my doctor's surgery, providing him with another tinted sample.

After I had proclaimed my sexual innocence, he asked me what I had eaten the previous day. I told him I had been a guest for lunch and went through the menu, including the dessert and the vegetables.

"What precisely were the vegetables?" he queried.

I named a couple of the Althorp-grown beauties, finishing with beets.

"It's the beets," he said simply.

Case closed. I had feared I might have developed some sort of terrible social disease all because I had eaten my vegetables.

What a schmuck! I considered sharing my embarrassment with Diana, but thought twice about telling the Princess of Wales any anecdote that involved passing water. Her brother, though, had to hear. He replied that the Beetroot Syndrome had struck him in the past as well, except that his variety of hypochondria had convinced him he had developed kidney problems.

I first met Charlie's sister Diana at his twenty-first birthday party, at which pop trivia fans should note the cabaret was provided by satellite from the United States by Phyllis Nelson. In her spoken greeting to the birthday boy and his guests, the singer of "Move Closer" fame was visibly abashed. She was addressing an audience she believed included the recent newlyweds the Prince and Princess of Wales. Nancy Reagan debated whether or not to curtsy before the Queen, but at least she could see Her Majesty when the moment of introduction came. Phyllis Nelson was performing to a camera uncertain as to whether Charles and Diana were actually watching at the time. (Indeed, I am not sure the couple were still in the building.)

In what must be a refreshing departure in recent literature, I will not claim to be a special friend of the late Princess of Wales. We met on several occasions, at the type of show business and charity functions at which performers and royalty meet, and our conversations were always pleasant and personal, in contrast to the rather formal remarks I've heard from some elder members of the Royal Family ("America lost its way when it abandoned John Wayne values," Prince Philip told me in a conversation opening and stopping remark; "We didn't like being on early television, it gave us big snouts," Princess Margaret said in a comment-defying report).

Diana would have met scores, perhaps hundreds, of persons in a working day, every one of whom would remember her regardless of whether or not they had made an impression on her. Indeed, as I noted the week after her death how many persons turned up in print and broadcast media identified as her "friend", I speculated that it would probably be possible to do one of those mathematical calculations, multiplying number of persons met in a day by number of days on the job, that yields a result that Diana had more "friends" than there are human beings in the world.

When on a couple of occasions Diana sought me out at a public function, it was for the solace of friendly conversation in an impersonal environment. Of all the pulped trees felled to satisfy the public demand for Dianaiana in the fortnight following her demise, the only ones that seemed to me not to have died in vain were those that printed Clive James' article in *The New Yorker*. In analysing his own, more numerous, meetings with the late Princess, James put his finger on what was for me the most appealing part of her personality. If she liked a celebrity, she would be disarmingly frank in her talk. The universe would be reduced to two conspiring individuals. If the other person were to reproduce her remarks in public, there would be uproar, but none did, at least not in her lifetime, and there had to be more of us than Clive James and myself. Diana sensed she could trust certain individuals with the kind of feelings every person has to express to someone.

Of course, I had an advantage in that I knew her brother, and she loved her brother. It was, and always will be, that simple. She loved her brother.

A real oddity, however, was that I had met her stepmother before she did. Raine had been the wife of Lord Dartmouth when this titled gentleman visited Dartmouth College in Hanover, New Hampshire in 1969, on the occasion of its bicentenary. I was one of the model students chosen to meet the couple. He was bemused he had been invited to northern New England because an Ivy League school had been named after one of his ancestors, and I was charmed by his lack of pretension. But I was quite dumbstruck by his wife. For the first time in my young life, an impression was made on me that I came to associate with the expression "henpecked husband". Imagine my surprise over a decade later to find this same woman now the stepmother of young Charlie Althorp. Based on what he and his sister told me, I now came to associate her with the expression "feathering one's nest".

In a break with the tendency of those who have rushed to retrospectively touch the hem of Diana's garment, I claim no unfinished business between us, although I do acknowledge one unfulfilled promise on my part. I had told her that, on her enthusiastic recommendation, I would go to the opera in Verona to see the gigantic forces marshalled in production. "Twelve hundred gentlemen of Verona?" I quipped weakly in response to her report of an ensemble of 1200, not realising that almost certainly at least a quarter of the participants would be women. How unsatisfactory that my only unfulfilled pledge to the Princess of Wales should have involved a major mathematical error.

After Henry Kissinger and James Naughtie had informed me of her horrible death, I switched on BBC1 to see if television had anything to offer radio had not. It took less than a quarter of an hour to determine that none of the channels had anything important to offer. I decided to go to the gym in the basement of my building and exercise in solitude for an hour or so. This is a response of which I am sure Diana would have approved, and indeed sought, because if one thing is certain it is that she did not find privacy in her gym.

I knew that, in time, this event would become history, and it would make some sort of rational, though not emotional, sense. Car crashes take the lives of young people all the time. I know, and this sounds obscene but I must say it, I have probably been an unknowing voyeur at the scene of some persons' last moments. As Kid Jensen once reminded me, many people who have lost their lives in automobile accidents were listening to the radio at the time, and the programmes continued to transmit through and after their final agonies.

I was spooked. It wasn't just that it was a young woman, a mother of two, who had died. It wasn't even that this person was a woman of whom I was fond and was the sister of a man I liked.

It was that in the space of time in which young Charlie Althorp had become Earl Spencer, Diana had travelled her entire fantastic journey, from teacher to princess to most-loved person in the world to car crash victim, and the time I had known Charlie seemed to have gone by in the snap of two fingers. If a person could go that enormous distance in a relative instant, all our lives will be measured in a mere few fingersnaps.

I am mortal, and have known this for some time, but that Sunday morning I felt more so than ever before.

I could reconcile my knowledge of Diana's own humanity with the already growing image of her as some sort of super-being, albeit one dressed in designer clothes rather than a cape and tights. She was a person who made the most of the unique opportunities someone in her position is given, and she often, though not always, did so publicly. She consequently registered singular achievements. Any member of the royal family could have embraced an AIDS patient, for example, but she did so, and struck an important blow against prejudice and ignorance.

The morning Diana's death was announced I walked the short journey from my County Hall flat to Buckingham Palace. I had the feeling that many members of the public, unable to express their grief in any prescribed way, would merely gravitate to places associated with the Princess. This had been the case in the death of John Lennon, when, my brother reported, a large crowd gathered at the Dakota building to light candles and sing Beatles songs, not because it was particularly useful but because it was a way of sharing sadness with like-minded others.

It was still around 11 a.m., but already a substantial group of mourners was gathering. I will never forget the individual vignettes of grief I saw that morning. A woman who appeared to be in her thirties stood with her hand frozen inches from her mouth, as if she was preparing to stifle a sob. A young man inscribed his floral tribute and then stood on the pavement, waiting for traffic to stop so he could cross the road to lay his bouquet on the already growing fragrant pile.

I checked in again several times during the course of the week. My home was so close to the palace it would have required a deliberate effort to steer clear. The Mall and environs became a Woodstock of grief, with thousands of people milling around looking lost. They had lost an anchor, and were drifting.

Where the minority of mostly male commentators who dismissed the distraught public reaction to the Princess's passing were completely wrong was in analysing it as if it could be analysed. It simply existed, in pure and elemental form, and if you didn't understand that thousands of people here on the Mall and millions more around the world felt a personal loss at Diana's death, you were not merely cruel and heartless, you were irrelevant. A useful question might be why the legions did feel a personal identification with the Princess, one which many didn't even know they had until she was gone.

For the first time in my life I understood firsthand how revolutions could occur. I had been on protest marches against the Vietnam War and apartheid, but had not seriously thought that my action those days would lead directly to my desired result. With the crowds in London that week, I speculated that if this number of people had been as angry as they were bereft, no armed forces could hold them down.

As I approached the palace one evening I heard a group of young people singing 'Yesterday'. This Paul McCartney song had been written before they were even born, yet they had taken it to heart. More frequently heard was Elton John's 'Candle In The Wind'. Like a mist rising off the morning dew, the demand to hear this song grew from grief and coalesced into its assumption as the anthem of the event. I was not really surprised when I heard that Elton would be playing an updated version at the Westminster Abbey funeral.

This was the cue for the media to ring me. In popular music circles in Britain I am the Voice of Doom, the man radio and television stations phone when they want a tribute to a deceased pop star. As my brother Peter had predicted, the day after John Lennon's death was one of the busiest of my career, as I shunted from studio to studio from morning to night trying to think of some tribute I hadn't offered two or three studios previously. Elton at the Abbey was a twist, but one with even greater media interest. I could tell because this time the networks were willing to come to my apartment.

The following week, when Elton's by now well-received 'Candle In The Wind 1997' was about to be released as a single, international television interest was even keener. The camera crews came flocking to my humble abode. ABC and CBS, BBC and ITV, as long as they weren't in my living room at the same time, they were welcome. I offered each outfit whatever camera perspective they wanted, but each one wanted a variation of yours truly in front of the CD shelves.

I knew they would. There is a sense in presenters for what shot the media will want, not because we're brilliant, but because it doesn't take long to learn. I recall one charity photo call where a variety of celebrities posed to promote the cause. When two young female pop stars embraced, Kid Jensen said, "That's it. There's no point in doing any more. That's what they're all going to run." He was right.

I was also aware that, in this era of sound bites, that none of the networks would run my potted history of 'Candle in the Wind'. It's fascinating as a study of how songs take on lives of their own, but it had no direct bearing on the public reaction to Diana's demise, so it would wind up on editing floors on two continents. When the song originally appeared on the double album *Goodbye Yellow Brick Road* in 1973, lyricist Bernie Taupin explained to me that he had heard the expression "candle in the wind" in a conversation he had with Clive Davis, then the head of Columbia Records. The two men were talking about one of Clive's artists, Janis Joplin, whom they had both admired. "She was a candle in the wind," Davis sighed sadly about his deceased star, and left the subject. Taupin remembered the line and used it in his own tribute to Marilyn Monroe.

Years later, I reminded Clive that his Janis remark had inspired the title of Elton's tribute to Marilyn. By this time he had forgotten that he had ever made it. I couldn't believe it, but I believed it. On one hand, the man had coined a phrase that had become popular the world over. On the other, everybody says hundreds of things every day they forget within minutes of uttering them.

The image was so powerful it would not go away. It had applied to Janis, then Marilyn, and now Diana. Bernie Taupin had found in words, and Elton John in music, the way the world wanted to remember its icon. It was obvious an historic sale was about to occur, but no pop pundit predicted the scale of the success. I told all the networks who wore down the carpet in County Hall that 'Candle In The Wind 1997' would become Britain's all-time best-selling single, topping four million and thus passing Band Aid's 'Do They Know It's Christmas', and would reach fifteen million in world sales. However, I pointed out, 'White Christmas' by Bing Crosby had over half a century to accumulate more than thirty million in sales, and beating that would require a stretch.

The first morning the disc was available in London I visited Tower Records in Piccadilly Circus to buy the Sunday *New York Times*. I was astonished to see that three entire racks of Elton singles had been cleared out in about two hours. My sales clerk was still shaking.

"I can't believe it," he trembled. "Someone said they were buying forty copies to take back to Kuala Lumpur."

Two days later the scene was even more hysterical. There are four sales tills near the front entrance of Tower Records. The last one in the sequence had a sign that read, "Express Till for customers not buying the Elton John single".

I had observed for television news that the sale of 'Candle In The Wind 1997' would be a barometer of the public's continuing grief, just as the record-breaking purchase of flowers had been during the week of the tragedy. The historic scale of the general upset was reflected in the record-breaking sales of Elton's song. Almost before you could say "1997", 'Candle In The Wind' had streaked past my predicted fifteen million. Within a month it had done better than double that, and easily eclipsed Bing Crosby's holiday hit.

Elton, of course, received no financial benefit, his proceeds going entirely to the Diana, Princess of Wales Memorial Fund. True, sales of his back catalogue, particularly albums including the original 'Candle In The Wind', temporarily soared, but this may have been at the momentary expense of his new album *The Big Picture,* which had been scheduled for release in September. Gradually what had always been planned as the first single from that album, 'Something About The Way You Look Tonight', which remained one of the two other tracks on the single CD, began to receive delayed airplay. Weeks after the funeral, radio programmers around the world began to consider airing the still-selling song a morbid exercise, and broadcast the alternative. The double-A side wound up being at fourteen weeks the longest-running American number one by a British artist.

The morning of Diana's funeral in Westminster Abbey, Saturday, the sixth of September, my friend Andy came over to the apartment at eight. He joined me for my customary breakfast of orange juice and a muffin. It was a cloudless start to the day, and we realised we would be the ultimate in blasé couch potatoes if we viewed the ceremony on television when we could see it in person by merely crossing Westminster Bridge.

At 8:30, we left my County Hall apartment. Small clusters of people, in twos, threes and fours, were doing the same thing. The bridge was closed to vehicular traffic. When we reached the north bank of the Thames police diverted us along the Embankment. Parliament Square was already filled with mourners.

This closure was fine by me. I had a favourite pedestrian

cut-through alongside the Ministry of Defence, which connected the Embankment with Whitehall. Andy and I took this route to Whitehall, where many people had arrived hours earlier to jockey for standing space on a low wall protecting the Ministry's lawn. But no one was occupying the standing room on the pavement against the wall, and by staying there, leaving room in front of us for pedestrian traffic approximately one person wide, we were able to have as clear a view as if we had arrived hours earlier.

I felt it was appropriate for me to be in the street to express my respects to Diana not as someone who had met her or her family, but as a member of the public, for it was in that capacity that I had attended the fireworks in Hyde Park on the eve of her wedding and stood on the Mall as the happy procession passed the next day. In some horrible but apt way, it was right that I should be with the people as they both welcomed and said goodbye to their princess.

Standing on Whitehall opposite Downing Street, just north of the Cenotaph, Andy and I settled in amongst a truly motley crew. In my immediate three-foot radius were whites, blacks and Asians, men and women, adults and children. One woman who had brought a radio assumed the role of play-by-play commentator.

"They're leaving Kensington Palace!" she would exclaim. "They've reached Hyde Park Corner!" "They're on the Mall!"

As soon as the procession had reached Horse Guards Parade, the entire crowd went quiet. It had been noted during the week of mourning that central London had not been so silent in living memory. This was the capper. No one made a sound, except for the occasional squeal of grief.

When four horses and their riders came into sight I thought, here's the start of it, we're in for the bands and the armies now. I was in for a shock. The drawn casket came next. No bands, no armies, just Diana. The impact was devastating. Whatever genius had thought this up had cut out the fat and gone straight to the elemental heart of the event.

Within seconds she was gone. Again there was no padding. Four princes and Earl Spencer on foot were next. Her brother, her children, their father and grandfather walked solemnly past. This arrangement may have been last minute, but the effect was numbing. Then came the charity workers, representatives of the causes with which the deceased had become identified. It was the antithesis of what anyone lining Whitehall could have expected, and it was perfect. A life had been distilled to its essentials. Millions of trees could have given their lives for the copy written about her, and workers around the world might have lost even more millions of hours of productivity watching commentators yap on television, yet here was evidence that the life of Diana, Princess of Wales, could be summarised, without words, in a simple procession lasting slightly more than one minute.

Having thought we had experienced the emotional peak of the day, Andy and I retired to my flat to watch the funeral on television, only to reach a new high when Elton sang his tribute with an exquisite sense of occasion. Alright, we thought when the applause outside the Abbey died down, we can calm down now. No. Earl Spencer delivered his historic address, so perfectly, so powerfully, he probably could have won any snap election to any post in any country had there been one held that day. As it is, his words will probably be studied as an example of effective oratory for years to come.

When the service ended, Andy and I thought that the unexpectedly emotional jolts had been exhausted. We were wrong again. As the hearse left on its journey northward it was pelted by floral tributes all the way to the motorway. No one could have warned the driver he would have to cope with this unique form of precipitation.

I had been with the thousands as they had mourned on the Mall and at the Palace during the week. They, at least, knew that they were joining their fellows in lighting candles, queuing to sign the condolence book, or singing sad pop songs. But these citizens who had lined the streets to throw flowers at an automobile had each made the same private decision. They could not have known legions of others were going to do the same thing. There would have been no time to see someone on television toss a bouquet at the car, rush out to the florist to buy a tribute, and get back to throw the thing at the hearse. This unforeseen and unplanned group gesture matched in eloquence the planned procession to Westminster, perfectly bookending the most moving public occasion I have ever experienced.

There is a photographer somewhere in London who has a photo of me talking to Diana at Charlie Althorp's 21st birthday party. I know there is because at a later event he told me he had it and would send it to me. Of course, he didn't. But I don't mind. After all, there must be many thousands of pictures of the Princess in conversation with someone. There are people she loved, people she didn't care about, people she knew well, people she only saw once.

One thing I do know. That photo of Diana and I, if it had survived until 1997, will certainly not now be destroyed. None of those many thousands will. What may be the most well-documented life of the last twenty years of the twentieth century will continue to be recorded, and none of the original research materials will be thrown away. I would not be surprised if the only photograph of me to be published years after I am gone is one of Diana, Princess of Wales, speaking to an unidentified guest at a private party.

CODA

Ten Most Memorable Remarks

There are some things a person can never be prepared to hear. Outside of my personal life, where I always expected to hear odd things, I thought I was always going to hear only carefully considered examples of reason and wisdom. I could not have been more wrong. Here are the ten remarks I least expected to hear.

I

"I can't believe it. We're all going to be so rich!"

As the Seventies drew to a close Tim and Jane Rice held a lunch at their home in Great Milton, Oxfordshire. I always enjoyed visiting them there, and for several reasons.

Tim was a great friend, and I had the utmost respect and affection for Jane. I felt she was the prime catch for any heterosexual Englishman of my generation, having both brains and beauty, and that in marrying her Tim had been the winner of one of life's sweepstakes.

The house, Romeyns Court, was wonderful. It was large without being vast, luxurious without being ostentatious. It's difficult to find a big home that feels more like home than big.

Third, Raymond Blanc established his award-winning, trend-setting Manoir aux Quat' Saisons literally across the street. You can't go wrong inviting guests to your local when it's one of the top ten restaurants in the country.

Finally, Great Milton's smaller neighbour, Little Milton, was the only village in England that shared the name of an

239

American bluesman. I had always loved the 1965 soul smash "We're Gonna Make It" by Little Milton.

For the lunch in question, my fellow guests were Bob Geldof, Paula Yates and Joanna Lumley. We discussed our individual aspirations for the coming decade. All of us were optimistic, a few bullish. Joanna got excited.

"I can't believe it," she enthused. "We're all going to be so rich!" She emphasised the last word.

Bob has an expression that simultaneously conveys and feigns shock, as if he doesn't know which is more stunning, the content of someone's statement or their audacity in making it. He widens his eyes, drops his jaw and shakes his head vertically. At the Rice table, he courteously omitted the last two, but as our eyes met I could see he was as bowled over as I was by Joanna's prediction.

The funny thing was, of course, she was right. Everyone at that table did well in the Eighties, a couple spectacularly so. The irony was that a decade further on, in the Nineties, Joanna would have her peak of popularity as Patsy, a television character who would have sounded so natural saying, "I can't believe it, we're all going to be so rich" that Bob wouldn't even have widened his eyes.

II

"Fuck my children!"

There are some things you don't report. This is an axiom I followed during my years in music journalism during the Seventies. Nowadays any throwaway remark, no matter how ill-considered, is fair game, but I felt I had a duty to report on what my interview subjects thought, not just what they said. Like anyone, a celebrity is likely to occasionally ad-lib something that doesn't communicate the intended effect. When I realised a star did not literally mean something they had said, and there might be drastic consequences for themselves or others if the remark was taken at face value, I chose not to report what I had heard.

John Lennon said, "Fuck my children!" Printed like that, the words read horribly. So, although I knew that John Lennon had made the remark, I didn't report it.

Here is the context. I was talking to Lee Eastman, Linda's lawyer father, who had advised Paul McCartney during the last days of the Beatles. After I had first interviewed Paul for *Rolling Stone*, Lee took a shine to me. My being an Oxford and Dartmouth graduate impressed him greatly, and he believed I would make a great friend for his son-in-law. I seriously doubted that Paul was looking for a new mate with whom to see a film or go bowling, but I was touched by Lee's sentiment. He shared with me some of the strange tales of the negotiations during the difficult period.

On one occasion, standing outside his office in Manhattan, he told me how he had pleaded with John Lennon not to give up his resistance to selling the Lennon-McCartney song copyrights, correctly assuming they would be worth many millions in the years to come.

"If not for yourself," Eastman recalled his own words, "then for the sake of your children."

"Fuck my children!" Lennon replied.

Of course, John was rather rattled at the time and didn't mean his words literally or even figuratively. He was devoted to Julian, even if in absentia, and he would in the future be a good father to Sean. But, in the context of a business negotiation, he did blurt out those words.

I knew that if I told this story in print it would read sensationally. I chose not to upset any of the parties involved, and a good thing, too. I later came to know and like both Julian and his mother, John's first wife Cynthia. I would have been humiliated to have caused them distress.

Still, the remark makes this all-time top ten. Whoever expects to hear anyone say, "Fuck my children!"?

III

"When I was dead . . ."

During my years on Radio 1, I was frequently sent demonstration tapes from hopeful young musicians, looking for airtime, a record contract, or merely encouragement. I spoke to one of these aspirants and was startled to hear him preface a sentence with the clause, "When I was dead". It transpired he had been declared clinically dead after taking bad drugs but returned to life after having an out-of-body experience he hated. He's the only person I've ever spoken to who reported an unpleasant afterlife or supernatural event; several others have been highly positive. In describing his dark and despair-inducing moments after having been presumed lost, he accurately began the account with the words, "When I was dead." I do not expect to hear that expression again.

IV

"I thought I'd come over and sing a song."

I had the privilege of introducing Cat Stevens at his final performance, a benefit for a children's charity at Wembley Arena. He had already changed his name to Yuseef Islam, and was giving up popular music for a religious life.

There was almost another performance, however. When I was at my broadcasting post backstage at Wembley during the Live Aid concert, I was approached by a bearded man in what the average Westerner would call Middle Eastern costume, whether it actually was or not.

"How's it going?" the stranger asked engagingly.

"Fine," I blurted, wondering why he was talking to me. "Bob says he just got a million pound pledge."

"I was watching at home on television," the interloper continued. "I thought I'd come over and sing a song." He waved goodbye.

I thought I'd come over and sing a song? I couldn't believe it. Who was this nut, who thought he'd wander over to Wembley

in the course of the world's most-watched concert and inter-
rupt a carefully constructed running order?

Then I realised who he was. Good Lord, I thought, it's Cat
Stevens. Of course, he would have been welcome on the bill
when it was being assembled, and Bob Geldof was grateful
he'd come by, but the organisers could not alter the tight
schedule while the event was in progress.

I deeply regretted Yuseef Islam's support for the fatwa
against Salman Rushdie. I had reason to be personally grateful
to the novelist. Before the release of *The Satanic Verses*, he had
participated in an AIDS benefit I hosted at the Shaw Theatre
in London in which leading writers read from their works.
Rushdie read from his book *Shame*. All the authors, from Terry
Jones to Iris Murdoch, donated their services. It was an early
and inspiring example of artists assembling to fight the
disease.

During the controversy over Yuseef's call against the writer, I
was able to remark that I was in the unique position of having
introduced to live audiences both Salman Rushdie and Cat
Stevens, though not on the same occasion. Indeed, bizarrely, I
have seen Rushdie at pop music events more recently than
Stevens. He appeared publicly on the stage of Wembley
Stadium, when Bono phoned him during a U2 concert and he
emerged from the wings in a brilliant *coup de théâtre*.

I watched Salman groove as he sat at my feet in the living
room of a best-selling author who was hosting an acoustic
performance by Sixties stars in his North London home.
Entering the room too late to get one of the chairs, Salman sat
on the floor and removed his shoes. As a female vocalist grew
soulful, he started doing Sixties dancing while seated, as if the
kids on *Hullabaloo* could no longer be bothered to get to their
feet but still wanted to do the monkey, shimmy, and swim. Let
me tell you, Rushdie can rock. I leaned over to George Martin
and asked, "Would it cause an international incident if we
threw his shoes out the window?"

Cat Stevens was always sincere and often quirky. The two were not mutually exclusive. His closing comment at the end of his March, 1974 Theatre Royal performance summed him up.

"Well, that's all for another year," he said with a trace of relief. "You've been nice, but cool . . . but then, I was cool, wasn't I?"

V

"I don't know whether to break her opera or pop first."

Andrew Lloyd Webber took me to lunch to enthuse about his new protégée, Sarah Brightman. He said of her prodigious vocal talent, "I don't know whether to break her opera or pop first."

You could have knocked me over with a soufflé. It was almost impossible in the music business for anyone to have the power to "break", that is make a star of, another artist. History was full of examples of the great floundering in their attempts to popularise the merely good by releasing work on their own custom labels: of The Beatles launching Jackie Lomax on Apple, Elton John promoting Blue on Rocket, and so forth. Here was Andrew assuming that he could lead Sarah to success at will, and not just in one form of music, but two.

The only artist who had ever really succeeded in both opera and pop had been Enrico Caruso, the first star of the gramophone, who had enjoyed American number ones with both 'Vesti La Giubba' from *I Pagliacci* and 'Over There', George M. Cohan's patriotic First World War anthem. For Andrew to assume that he could lead any artist to such historic success was audacious. Furthermore, the subject of his enthusiasm had yet to show great promise in either opera or pop. Miss Brightman's chart career to date was her top ten hit, a 1978 novelty with Hot Gossip, 'I Lost My Heart To A Starship Trooper'. The follow-up, 'The Adventures Of The Love Crusader' by Sarah Brightman and The Starship

Troopers, had fallen short of the top forty.

What Lloyd Webber could not possibly have known was that Sarah and I had already shared a mutual moment of our artistic lives. In 1973, a singer/songwriter piano player named Richard Graves had been the first signing to Elton John's Rocket Records. Everyone at the label thought that Dick Graves was a bit too close to Dig Graves for comfort, so the young man needed a name change. Elton asked him what his astrological sign was. Dick said Pisces, so Elton informed him that henceforth he would be known as Frankie Fish. When I rode with Elton to his home in Virginia Water after having met Frankie in the Rocket office in Wardour Street, we speculated as to what material Fish could record, including 'Salmon Chanted Evening' and 'Cod Only Knows'.

Of course, the company did not need another singing songwriting pianist, they already had one, so Frankie never actually did get recorded on Rocket. But he did ask me to write him some lyrics, and I obliged. One was a song called 'Tonight I Met A Man'. I received an invitation one day in the mid-Seventies to attend a demonstration recording of this song. Since Frankie did not wish to voice a tune with this title, a female session singer was engaged. It was Sarah Brightman. Heaven knows what she thought of our flop song, which is not worth reviving on an album of anybody's outtakes, but Frankie and I both thought, to be brutally honest, that Sarah was caterwauling.

And this was the woman my luncheon host was telling me he could break either opera or pop! Of course, it was precisely the failure of her performance on the demo that contained the key to her subsequent success: she was giving our modest pop song a nearly operatic treatment. Once she learned that different types of material required varied approaches, she could sing in a wide range.

I had known Andrew long enough to suspect that he could pull off basically anything he put his mind to. After all, successfully staging a musical in which the lead characters were train carriages has to rank as one of the West End's most unlikely achievements. If Lloyd Webber really thought he could do it, he could, and would.

Within three years, he had. Sarah was the female voice on his number one classical album *Requiem* and its top three single 'Pie Jesu'. In 1986 she enjoyed two top ten hits in the UK with material from Andrew's *Phantom Of The Opera,* the title song with Steve Harley and 'All I Ask Of You' with Cliff Richard.

Her success in this show was the cue for another meal with Andrew, this time a dinner. My composer friend was extremely upset that Sarah had not been nominated for an Olivier Award in the category Best Actress In A Musical. I was a judge that year; what had gone wrong?

I had to tell Andrew that the answer was simple, and was not an insult to her performance. Every member of the panel saw every show submitted to the committee, which in the mid-Eighties averaged about eighty-five a year. If, on the morning of a planned visit, a judge learned that a leading artist could not appear due to illness, he or she would have to reschedule attendance. However, if the artist simply did not go on without prior notice, the panellist would obviously show up at the theatre for his or her planned viewing.

Sarah had not appeared, and no warning had been given, on two occasions when a total of three committee members came to the Haymarket Theatre to see *Phantom Of The Opera.* Consequently, three out of the eleven judges could not vote for her even if they had wished to. I told Andrew quite honestly that if the ballot had been limited to the eight who had seen Sarah, she would have been in the final four nominees, but getting no points from three judges had doomed her chances.

Andrew was quite civil with me about this, although he was not quite as happy with the Society of West End Theatre, which administered the awards. His disappointment was understandable, considering that Sarah had provided him with inspiration to write the piece.

Of course, Lloyd Webber had the last laugh on the matter. *Phantom* will probably continue to run into the twenty-first century in both London and New York, Sarah enjoyed one of America's biggest tours singing selections of Andrew's music, and she and Andrea Bocelli had one of Europe's top hits of 1997, 'Time to Say Goodbye'. Andrew had succeeded after all in breaking her classical and pop and, in the case of 'Amigos Para Siempre' with Jose Carreras, the 1992 Barcelona Games. Even Enrico Caruso never made it at the Olympics.

VI

"Why Peter, the last time we met we were discussing the length of men's penises."

While still a student at Oxford in 1973 I interviewed one of the world's major rock stars for *Rolling Stone*. During the course of our conversation he related his shock at his first meeting with one of the British princesses.

"I was having lunch with Peter Cook in a restaurant," he related. "She came over and without any introduction said, 'Why Peter, the last time we met we were discussing the length of men's penises.' "

I thought this surely must be wishful thinking on the part of my celebrity friend. How could a princess walk up to a table of diners in a public place and greet the party with, "Why Peter, the last time we met we were discussing the length of men's penises"?

If I ever met Peter Cook, I had to ask him if this anecdote were true. I got my chance when we were both drafted to help Kevin Godley and Lol Creme on their first post-10 c.c. album, *Consequences*. Peter was to write and perform a comic playlet that would punctuate the songs of Godley and Creme and I was to keep a journal of the recording process that would be released with the LP in a boxed set.

When we were introduced, I waited a few minutes before jumping in with the big question. Could he authenticate the quotation?

"Absolutely," he confirmed. "We were at Ken Tynan's watching blue films and she said, 'What is that?' 'That, Your Holiness, is a man's penis,' I replied. 'It's a bit small, isn't it?' she asked. I said, 'Yours would be, too, after the fifth take'."

"Excuse me," I interrupted, "but you called her Your Holiness to her face?"

"Oh yes," Peter said. "She doesn't reply well if you are conventionally deferential. You have to be either completely sycophantic or utterly irreverent. She loves it."

I subsequently met the princess in question. I can't remember how we marked time until she was introduced to someone she found more interesting. But I cannot forget Peter.

When he first presented his work for Godley and Creme he effectively killed the *Consequences* project, not because it wasn't any good, but because his patrons worshipped him. They thought his material was so funny that they let him go on and on, beyond the confines of the planned double album onto a third disc.

"Peter Cook has scripted the comic playlet for the second album of the set," I wrote in the published journal entry for 22 April 1977. "It is sad that few people will ever hear his one-take tour de force voicing all male characters in a non-stop run-through." By 17 June, I had changed my printed tune. "The collaboration with Peter Cook was the surprising artistic development of the album," I reported, "since neither Godley nor Creme had foreseen it in 1976. They finally did ask him to do all the voices, rather than try to assemble a super-group of comedians."

But still few people heard his achievement, because in expanding the work to accommodate their hero the musical twosome doomed the commercial prospects of their début as a duo. What had been intended to be a major recording event, the introduction of the instrument the gizmo, a work with the revolutionary impact of *Tubular Bells*, turned out to be an expensive boxed white elephant.

We had a great time working on it, though. My most vivid memory was a Sunday morning spent alone with Peter walking the streets of Amsterdam. The whole team had been flown over to the city to do a Eurolaunch of the album at Phonogram's expense. The promotional event was done on a Saturday evening, leaving us a few hours in Amsterdam on Sunday morning before our flight back to London.

Peter had begun to fall prey to the appetite for drink that would ultimately shorten his life. He had to find the Dutch equivalent of a pub before customary opening hours. We roamed the roads of the city searching for an open bar. Along the way we passed vending machines dispensing sausages. I was treated to an extremely rude and very funny ad lib routine that would not have been out of place on a Derek and Clive album. Not being a drinker myself, however, I was keenly aware of the way in which alcohol was taking control of this comic genius before me. It occurred to me that maybe my temperance and his overindulgence could be averaged into two conventional appetites.

This is not to say that Peter Cook could not be sober when he wanted or had to be. On one occasion a few years later *Private Eye*, his magazine, seriously wronged a friend of mine from Oxford. I couldn't be sure of the accuracy of the particular untypical incident reported, but the character of the man described was so far from that of the person I knew that I believed the story as well must be false. When my friend wrote me in distress, asking me if I had any contact that might rectify the wrong, I called Peter.

He received me in his Hampstead home, one-on-one, heard me tell him that the staff had got it wrong this time, and passed on my friend's request for a retraction in the precise position of the original insult, which happened to be the lead paragraph of the issue. A complete gentleman, Peter promised he would arrange it, and did. My friend was vindicated by a complete apology in the first item of the next issue.

I was deeply impressed. Peter had not excused the magazine on any grounds of freedom of the press or bad sources. He recognised a hurtful error had been made and corrected it.

When Peter died, nearly twenty years after we began work on *Consequences,* I reflected on those two moments alone with him, listening to him deliver his monologue on Dutch sausages and watching him carefully consider the need to make restitution for *Private Eye*'s mistake. They were examples of two very different sides of his personality. More than that, they were two moments in the history of the world that had been shared by only two people, and now only one was left. As we age, we get more and more intimations of mortality, and the passing of Peter Cook, the loss of my opportunity to recall with another person those times in my life, was a distinct reminder to me that my time is not unlimited.

VII

"I kept seeing posters about that dead Chinese guy – what's his name, Mao Tse-Tung?"

On Monday, the 20th of September, 1976, I was one of a small group of London-based journalists flown to Paris to interview Ringo Starr at the George V Hotel. The occasion was the launch of his new album *Ringo's Rotogravure.* This event was obscured in the press by the death of Mao Tse-Tung, chairman of the Chinese Communist Party. I saw news hoardings with headlines of the like of "Morte du Mao" all over the Champs Élysées.

I don't remember anything about meeting Ringo other than that I met Ringo. Talk about *Meet The Beatles.* This was *Meet And Then Forget The Beatles.*

It wasn't that Ringo wasn't charming. He was. But something more memorable than any Fab quote occurred right after my one-on-one. I went to the restaurant where the journalists, unofficially led by the much-respected Ray Coleman, were gathered for lunch. I was seated next to Philip Norman, then the anonymous columnist Atticus in the *Sunday Times*, and began devouring a delicious lobster starter that I calculated to cost approximately £17. At this moment a latecomer arrived.

It was Tony Prince, the Royal Ruler of Radio Luxembourg. He offered his apologies in unique fashion.

"Hi everybody," he effused. "Sorry I'm late. I kept seeing posters about that dead Chinese guy – what's his name, Mao Tse-Tung?"

Philip Norman's face lit up like a child at Christmas. I knew this was going to wind up in the *Sunday Times*. It did. It's here, too. I've heard many things said about Chairman Mao before and since, but never "what's his name?" and I've certainly never heard him referred to as "that dead Chinese guy."

Tony Prince entertained millions of listeners for years. He thrilled a table of journalists at lunch, once, in Paris. Ringo should've been there.

VIII

"Them niggers ain't fit to shine my shoes."

In the year that I first listened to pop radio, 1957, Jerry Lee Lewis issued one of the great breakthrough singles of all time, "Whole Lotta Shakin' Going On". His performances on *The Steve Allen Show* and *The Dick Clark Show* remain in memory, particularly the frantic Allen broadcast in which objects including a rubber chicken sailed through the air over the head of the singing pianist.

It was with great trepidation that sixteen years later, as a reporter for *Rolling Stone*, I encountered this legend of my boyhood. He had come to London to record an album with several giants of British rock. It was intended that this LP should mark Lewis's comeback, as the freak success of the international number one hit single 'My Ding-a-Ling' had rejuvenated the fortunes of Chuck Berry the previous year.

I journeyed to the studio and was granted an audience with Jerry Lee. I only remember one exchange from our brief interview.

"During the rock'n'roll years of the late Fifties, did you socialise with your fellow stars, such as Chuck Berry and Fats Domino?" I asked naïvely.

"Them niggers ain't fit to shine my shoes," he replied.

So ended my interest in the career of Jerry Lee Lewis. I noticed his son, 19-year-old Jerry Lee Jr., drumming in the studio, and wondered what it was like for him having a racist father. Later that year, I read of Jerry Lee Jr.'s death. The vehicle he was driving hit a bridge in Mississippi. Lewis's only other son had drowned in 1962. I wondered if I had ever met a man with as much pain in and around him as Jerry Lee Lewis.

IX

"How did you get the tickets?"

"I fucked him."

In the late Seventies, in the era before AIDS awareness, the bisexual boyfriend of a female acquaintance of mine went from Los Angeles to San Francisco for a weekend. My friend asked him to see if he could acquire a pair of tickets to the forthcoming dance performance by the world's foremost ballet star, Rudolf Nureyev. They were the hottest tickets in town, and she thought the possibility of getting one, let alone two, was remote.

The boyfriend phoned her towards the end of his trip.

"I got us two seats for Nureyev," he told his girl excitedly.

"How did you get the tickets?" she asked.

"I fucked him."

Sure enough, he had gone to a club in San Francisco and encountered the star, who propositioned him. The American then entertained the Russian.

A few years later I saw Nureyev dance at Covent Garden. I

bought my tickets. I still recall his leaping entrance in *AFTER-NOON OF THE FAUN.* It was as if he had been suspended in air indefinitely. This is how I remember this great artist: flying across the stage, legs almost at a 180 degree angle. One day he will touch ground, but it hasn't happened yet.

X

"Be prepared to take the wheel in the event of the death of the driver."

In 1977 I was flown by Paul McCartney's office to the Virgin Islands to witness recording sessions for the *London Town* album. I was to write the press kit for the LP.

Several aspects of the trip made deep impressions on me. The first was the unusual arrangement in which the members of Wings were accommodated. Paul and Linda McCartney and family lived on one boat, other players in Wings on another. Joe English, Denny Laine and Jimmy McCulloch were aware of the inequity of the situation – they were not allowed to bring their own wives or girl friends – but fully understood that it reflected the power structure within the band. Wings was Paul's group, and he lived as he wished. He wished to be with his beloved wife and children at all times. Although I can think of a few couples who matched them, I have not known any pair of people more devoted to each other than the McCartneys.

I was deeply affected, more than I might have anticipated, by Linda's premature death. I recalled at once how she had been kind and encouraging to me when, as an Oxford student, I conducted Paul's first post-Beatle major interview for *Rolling Stone.* Linda introduced me to her family: I came to know her father Lee and would see him at times when I visited New York, and the one-year-old Stella wore my watch on her ankle, giving an early indication of her fashion sense. Linda was the first person in England to call me "Gambo", a nickname which stuck. In the Nineties she would greet me upon every meeting with the words, "Are you veggie yet?". I had ceased eating red meat in 1983, but she kept telling me that I wasn't doing the full job and should also give up chicken and fish. Her friend Chrissie Hynde reminded me a couple of times that prawns and other shellfish contained large amounts of dirt and filth. If only to meet Linda's challenge, I finally banned fish and fowl from my home. The last time I saw her, at one of Paul's annual Buddy Holly Week lunches, she asked, "Are you veggie yet?" and I was able to say, "Yes." All the above constitutes a remarkable legacy from someone who was not family.

Upon hearing the news of her death from the BBC World Service, which hoped I would go on air to discuss the story, I made the decision not to make any such appearances. I knew that, since I had developed an unsought reputation as Mr. Rock Obituary, the phone would ring all night requesting interviews, and so it did. But I felt that, since Linda left no recorded legacy in the sense that pop stars do, I was not professionally engaged and that my reactions were personal. I made one exception and spoke to ABC Radio, fearing that if I did not they might resort to someone in the United States who knew her hardly at all and might speak from an insensitive perspective.

Not every member of Wings was as personally happy as Paul and Linda. I remember one evening when Jimmy McCulloch, the brilliant young guitarist, became impossibly intoxicated. He was not just out of it, he was somewhere else. As he bellowed to me in obvious emotional pain, his voice came from a place deep inside to which we on the outside had no access. It was haunting to see the contradiction between a beautiful physical appearance, with which Jimmy was blessed, and a troubled internal existence. I was extremely sad, but not surprised, to hear of his early death the following year.

I will never forget the boat trip I had to take between Virgin Islands to reach the McCartney entourage. I had not been warned that I would be travelling in a "water taxi", a small open craft in which I was the only passenger. The driver was wearing a T-shirt calling for the legalisation of marijuana. He was not personally waiting for a change in the law before smoking, and was in fact stoned as we made the 45-minute journey. At one point we reached the turbulent area where the Atlantic met the Caribbean, and our taxi stood up nearly on end. It sounds like a circumstance under which someone could quite understandably go mad, but I managed to survive by assuming a "ride 'em cowboy" mentality.

But the strongest and daftest memory I have of this McCartney outing is of the sign that greeted me when I climbed into the passenger seat of a taxi cab at the Virgin Islands airport. "Passengers in this seat should be prepared to take the wheel in the event of the death of the driver," it read. I looked at the young man entering the cab to start the car. He looks perfectly healthy, I thought. How many of these guys have dropped dead?